Jakarta EE Application Development

Build enterprise applications with Jakarta CDI, RESTful
web services, JSON Binding, persistence, and security

David R. Heffelfinger

Jakarta EE Application Development

Group Product Manager: Kunal Sawant
Publishing Product Manager: Akash Sharma
Book Project Manager: Prajakta Naik
Senior Editor: Esha Banerjee
Technical Editor: Vidhisha Patidar
Copy Editor: Safis Editing
Indexer: Hemangini Bari
Production Designer: Shankar Kalbhor
DevRel Marketing Coordinator: Samriddhi Murarka

First published: December 2017
Second edition: February 2024
Production reference: 1160224

Published by
Packt Publishing Ltd.
Grosvenor House
11 St Paul's Square
Birmingham
B3 1RB, UK

ISBN 978-1-83508-526-4

www.packtpub.com

Contributors

About the author

David R. Heffelfinger is an independent consultant based in the Washington D.C. area. He is a Java Champion and Apache Netbeans Project Management Committee.

He has written several books on Java EE, application servers, NetBeans, and JasperReports. His previous titles include *Java EE 8 Application Development*, *Java EE 7 Development with NetBeans 8*, *Java EE 7 with GlassFish 4 Application Server*, *JasperReports 3.5 For Java Developers*, among others.

David has spoken at various software conferences, including JavaOne and Oracle Code One, multiple times. He has also presented at NetBeans Day in both San Francisco and Montreal.

About the reviewers

Amol Gote is a seasoned technology professional adept at building scalable, resilient microservices in both Java and .NET. He excels in deploying and managing microservices in AWS and Azure environments, boasting technical proficiency across multiple applications and tools. His expertise spans full-stack capabilities, from designing to constructing end-to-end solutions that include databases (SQL/NoSQL), back-end services, messaging services, and modern interactive web applications using web sockets.

Currently serving as a Solutions Architect at a Fintech startup, Amol has built the underwriting platform from scratch, along with multiple horizontal and vertical business domain-specific microservices. Previously, he has engaged in consulting roles with major clients like Bank of America, Morgan Stanley, and the Associated Press, and has worked with Microsoft for seven years.

With over 18 years of experience, Amol is passionate about writing blogs and technical articles for online platforms like DZone, Baeldung, and InfoQ. He has also served as a judge and mentor at various Hackathon events. Amol's commitment to excellence is evident in his multiple certifications, including AWS Certified Solutions Architect and various Microsoft certifications.

Edwin Derks is a Java Champion from The Netherlands who loves solving complex and strategic IT challenges. He is passionate about gathering and sharing knowledge about anything related to the Java ecosystem, composable architectures, and cloud-driven development in general. He contributes to MicroProfile and Jakarta EE and often speaks at conferences, passionately sharing his knowledge and experience.

In his spare time, he is a loving husband and a father of three. He can often be found in the gym or having a good time at dance parties or heavy metal concerts.

Table of Contents

7

8

9

Preface

Jakarta EE provides functionality that eases the development of cloud applications, as well as more traditional web applications, including server-side enterprise applications. This book includes coverage for the latest version of the most popular Jakarta EE specifications, including coverage of Jakarta Faces, Jakarta Persistence, Jakarta Enterprise JavaBeans, Contexts and Dependency Injection (CDI), the Jakarta JSON Processing, Jakarta JSON Binding, Jakarta WebSocket, Jakarta Messaging, Jakarta Enterprise Web Services, Jakarta REST, as well as coverage for securing Jakarta EE applications via Jakarta EE Security.

Who this book is for

This book is designed for readers who are already familiar with the Java language. Its target audience includes existing Java developers wishing to learn Jakarta EE, and existing Java EE developers wishing to update their skills to Jakarta EE.

What this book covers

Chapter 1, Introduction to Jakarta EE, provides a brief introduction to Jakarta EE, covering how it is developed as a community effort, it also clears some common misconceptions about Jakarta EE.

Chapter 2, Contexts and Dependency Injection, includes coverage of CDI named beans, dependency injection using CDI and CDI qualifiers, as well as CDI event functionality.

Chapter 3, Jakarta RESTful Web Services, discusses how to develop RESTful web services using Jakarta REST, as well as how to develop RESTful web service clients via the Jakarta REST client API. The chapter also covers how to send automatic updates to a RESTful web service client via Server-sent events.

Chapter 4, JSON Processing and JSON Binding, covers how to generate and parse JavaScript Object Notation (JSON) data using Jakarta JSON Processing and Jakarta JSON Binding.

Chapter 5, Microservices Development with Jakarta EE, explains how to leverage Jakarta EE functionality to develop microservices-based architectures.

Chapter 6, Jakarta Faces, covers development of web applications using Jakarta Faces.

Chapter 7, Additional Jakarta Faces Features, covers additional Jakarta Faces functionality, such as HTML5 friendly markup, WebSocket support and Faces Flows

Chapter 8, Object Relational Mapping with Jakarta Persistence, discusses how to develop code that interacts with a Relational Database Management System (RDBMS) such as Oracle or MySQL through Jakarta Persistence.

Chapter 9, WebSockets, explains how to develop web based applications featuring full duplex communication between the browser and the server.

Chapter 10, Securing Jakarta EE Applications, covers how to secure Jakarta EE applications using Jakarta Security.

Chapter 11, Servlet Development and Deployment, explains how to develop server-side functionality in Java EE applications using Jakarta Servlet.

Chapter 12, Jakarta Enterprise Beans, explains how to develop applications using Session and Message Driven beans. Enterprise Bean features such as transaction management, the timer service and security are covered. *Chapter 13, Jakarta Messaging*, discusses how to develop messaging applications using Jakarta Messaging.

Chapter 14, Web Services with Jakarta XML Web Services, explains how to develop SOAP-based web services using Jakarta Enterprise Web Services.

Chapter 15, Putting it All Together, explains how to develop applications integrating several Jakarta EE APIs.

To get the most out of this book

In order to compile and execute the examples in this book, a number of required and recommended tools are needed.

Required or Recommended Software	Operating system requirements
Java 17 or newer required	Windows, macOS, or Linux
Apache Maven 3.6 or newer required	Windows, macOS, or Linux
Java IDE such as Eclipse IDE, IntelliJ IDEA or NetBeans recommended	Windows, macOS, or Linux
A Jakarta EE 10 compliant implementation such as GlassFish, WildFly, or Apache TomEE required	Windows, macOS, or Linux

Technical requirements

To compile and build the examples in this book, the following tools are required:

- A recent Java Development Kit, examples in this book were built using OpenJDK 17.
- Apache Maven 3.6 or newer

- A Java Integrated Development Environment (IDE) such as Apache NetBeans, Eclipse IDE or IntelliJ IDEA is recommended but not required (Apache NetBeans was used to develop the examples in the book, but readers are encouraged to use their preferred Java IDE)

- A Jakarta EE 10 compliant runtime (Eclipse GlassFish was used to deploy the examples on the book, but any Jakarta EE 10 compliant runtime will work)

If you are using the digital version of this book, we advise you to type the code yourself or access the code from the book's GitHub repository (a link is available in the next section). Doing so will help you avoid any potential errors related to the copying and pasting of code.

Download the example code files

You can download the example code files for this book from GitHub at `https://github.com/ PacktPublishing/Jakarta-EE-Application-Development`. If there's an update to the code, it will be updated in the GitHub repository.

We also have other code bundles from our rich catalog of books and videos available at `https:// github.com/PacktPublishing/`. Check them out!

Conventions used

There are a number of text conventions used throughout this book.

`Code in text`: Indicates code words in text, database table names, folder names, filenames, file extensions, pathnames, dummy URLs, user input, and Twitter handles. Here is an example: "As can be seen in the example, we generate an instance of `JsonObject` by invoking the `add()` method on an instance of `JsonObjectBuilder`."

A block of code is set as follows:

```
<!DOCTYPE html>
<html>
  <head>
    <meta http-equiv="Content-Type" content="text/html;
      charset=UTF-8">
    <title>Login Error</title>
  </head>
  <body>
    There was an error logging in.
    <br />
    <a href="login.html">Try again</a>
  </body>
</html>
```

When we wish to draw your attention to a particular part of a code block, the relevant lines or items are set in bold:

```
package com.ensode.jakartaeebook.security.basicauthexample;
//imports omitted for brevity
@BasicAuthenticationMechanismDefinition
@WebServlet(name = "SecuredServlet", urlPatterns = {"/
securedServlet"})
@ServletSecurity(
        @HttpConstraint(rolesAllowed = "admin"))
public class SecuredServlet extends HttpServlet {
  @Override
  protected void doGet(HttpServletRequest request,
    HttpServletResponse response) throws ServletException, IOException
{
    response.getOutputStream().print(
      "Congratulations, login successful.");
  }
}
```

Any command-line input or output is written as follows:

```
appclient -client simplesessionbeanclient.jar
```

Bold: Indicates a new term, an important word, or words that you see onscreen. For instance, words in menus or dialog boxes appear in **bold**. Here is an example: "Now that we have created a customer, our **Customer List** page displays a data table listing the customer we just created."

> **Tips or important notes**
> Appear like this.

Get in touch

Feedback from our readers is always welcome.

General feedback: If you have questions about any aspect of this book, email us at customercare@ packtpub.com and mention the book title in the subject of your message.

Errata: Although we have taken every care to ensure the accuracy of our content, mistakes do happen. If you have found a mistake in this book, we would be grateful if you would report this to us. Please visit www.packtpub.com/support/errata and fill in the form.

Piracy: If you come across any illegal copies of our works in any form on the internet, we would be grateful if you would provide us with the location address or website name. Please contact us at copyright@packtpub.com with a link to the material.

If you are interested in becoming an author: If there is a topic that you have expertise in and you are interested in either writing or contributing to a book, please visit authors.packtpub.com

Share Your Thoughts

Once you've read *Jakarta EE Application Development*, we'd love to hear your thoughts! Scan the QR code below to go straight to the Amazon review page for this book and share your feedback.

https://packt.link/r/1835085261

Your review is important to us and the tech community and will help us make sure we're delivering excellent quality content.

Download a free PDF copy of this book

Thanks for purchasing this book!

Do you like to read on the go but are unable to carry your print books everywhere?

Is your eBook purchase not compatible with the device of your choice?

Don't worry, now with every Packt book you get a DRM-free PDF version of that book at no cost.

Read anywhere, any place, on any device. Search, copy, and paste code from your favorite technical books directly into your application.

The perks don't stop there, you can get exclusive access to discounts, newsletters, and great free content in your inbox daily

Follow these simple steps to get the benefits:

1.   Scan the QR code or visit the link below

https://packt.link/free-ebook/978-1-83508-526-4

2.   Submit your proof of purchase

3.   That's it! We'll send your free PDF and other benefits to your email directly

1

Introduction to Jakarta EE

Jakarta EE consists of a set of **Application Programming Interface** (**API**) specifications used to develop server-side enterprise Java applications. Most chapters in this book will cover a single Jakarta EE specification, such as **Contexts and Dependency Injection** (**CDI**), which is used to integrate different parts of an application, or Jakarta RESTful Web Services, which is used to develop RESTful web services. We also cover Jakarta EE APIs for processing data in JSON format, as well as Jakarta Faces, which is used to develop web-based user interfaces. We also delve into how to interact with relational databases, implementing two-way communication between clients and servers in web applications, security, and messaging.

In this chapter, we will cover the following topics:

- Introduction to Jakarta EE
- Jakarta EE, Java EE, J2EE, and the Spring Framework

Introduction to Jakarta EE

Jakarta EE is a collection of API specifications designed to work together when developing server-side enterprise Java applications. Jakarta EE is a standard for which there are multiple implementations. This fact prevents vendor lock-in since code developed against the Jakarta EE specification can be deployed in any Jakarta EE-compliant implementation.

Jakarta EE is an **Eclipse Software Foundation** project. Since the Jakarta EE specification is open source, any organization or individual wishing to contribute is free to do so.

Contributing to Jakarta EE

There are many ways of contributing, including participating in discussions and providing suggestions for future versions of Jakarta EE. To do so, one simply needs to subscribe to the appropriate mailing list, which can be done by visiting `https://jakarta.ee/connect/mailing-lists/`.

In order to subscribe to the mailing list, you need to create a free Eclipse.org account at `https://accounts.eclipse.org/user/register`.

To go beyond participating in discussions and actually contribute code or documentation, the Eclipse Contributor Agreement must be signed. The Eclipse Contributor Agreement can be found at `https://www.eclipse.org/legal/ECA.php`.

Jakarta EE APIs

As previously mentioned, Jakarta EE is a collection of API specifications designed to work together when developing server-side enterprise Java applications.

In addition to the full Jakarta EE platform, there are two Jakarta EE profiles that contain a subset of the specifications and APIs included in the full platform. The **Jakarta EE Web Profile** contains a subset of specifications and APIs suitable for developing web applications. The **Jakarta EE Core Profile** contains an even smaller subset of specifications and APIs more suitable for developing microservices.

The Jakarta EE core profile APIs include the following:

- Jakarta Context and Dependency Injection Lite (CDI Lite)
- Jakarta RESTful Web Services
- Jakarta JSON Processing
- Jakarta JSON Binding

The version of Contexts and Dependency Injection API included in the core profile is a subset of the full specification. The Jakarta EE Web Profile APIs include the full CDI specification instead of CDI Lite, plus all other specifications and APIs in the core profile, along with some additional ones:

- Jakarta Context and Dependency Injection
- Jakarta Faces
- Jakarta Persistence
- Jakarta WebSocket
- Jakarta Security
- Jakarta Servlet
- Jakarta Enterprise Beans Lite

The version of Jakarta Enterprise Beans included in the Web Profile is a subset of the full enterprise beans specification.

The full Jakarta EE Platform includes the full Jakarta Enterprise Beans spec, plus all other specifications and APIs included in the Web Profile, along with some additional ones:

- Jakarta Enterprise Beans
- Jakarta Messaging
- Jakarta Enterprise Web Services

> **Full list of Jakarta EE APIs**
>
> The preceding list is not exhaustive, and only lists some of the most popular Jakarta EE APIs. For an exhaustive list of Jakarta EE APIs, please refer to `https://jakarta.ee/specifications/`.

Application server vendors or the open-source community need to provide compatible implementations for each Jakarta EE API specification in the preceding list.

One standard, multiple implementations

At its core, Jakarta EE is a specification, a piece of paper, if you will. Implementations of Jakarta EE specifications need to be developed so that application developers can actually develop server-side enterprise Java applications against the Jakarta EE standard.

Each Jakarta EE API can have multiple implementations. The popular Hibernate Object-Relational Mapping tool, for example, is an implementation of Jakarta Persistence, but it is by no means the only one. Other Jakarta Persistence implementations include EclipseLink and Open JPA. Similarly, there are multiple implementations of every single Jakarta EE specification.

Jakarta EE applications are typically deployed to an application server. Some popular application servers include JBoss, Websphere, Weblogic, and GlassFish. Each application server is considered to be a Jakarta EE implementation. Application server vendors either develop their own implementations of the several Jakarta EE specifications or choose to include an existing implementation.

Application developers benefit from the Jakarta EE standard by not being tied to a specific Jakarta EE implementation. As long as an application is developed against the standard Jakarta EE APIs, it should be very portable across application server vendors.

Application server vendors then bundle a set of Jakarta EE API implementations together as part of their application server offerings. Since each implementation is compliant with the corresponding Jakarta EE specification, code developed against one implementation can run unmodified against any other implementation, avoiding a vendor lock-in.

The following table lists some popular Jakarta EE implementations:

Jakarta EE Implementation	Vendor	License	URL
Apache Tomee	Tomitribe	Apache License, Version 2.0	`https://tomee.apache.org/`
Eclipse GlassFish	Eclipse Foundation	Eclipse Public License - v 2.0	`https://glassfish.org/`
IBM Websphere Liberty	IBM	Commercial	`https://www.ibm.com/ products/websphere- liberty`
JBoss Enterprise Application Platform	Red Hat	Commercial	`https://www.redhat.com/ en/technologies/jboss- middleware/application- platform`
Open Liberty	IBM	Eclipse Public License 2.0	`https://openliberty.io/`
Payara Server Community	Payara Services Ltd	Dual licensed :CDDL 1.1 / GPL v2 + Classpath Exception	`https://www.payara.fish/ products/payara-platform- community/`
Payara Server Enterprise	Payara Services Ltd	Commercial	`https://www.payara.fish/ products/payara-platform- community/`
Wildfly	Red Hat	LGPL v2.1	`https://www.wildfly.org/`

Table 1.1 – Popular Jakarta EE Implementations

> **Note**
>
> For the full list of Jakarta EE-compatible implementations, please refer to `https://jakarta.ee/compatibility/`.

For most examples in this book, we will be using **GlassFish** as our Jakarta EE runtime. This is because it is a high-quality, up-to-date, open-source implementation not tied to any particular vendor; all examples should be deployable to any Jakarta EE-compliant implementation.

Jakarta EE, Java EE, J2EE, and the Spring Framework

In 2017, Oracle donated **Java EE** to the Eclipse Foundation and as part of the process, Java EE was renamed Jakarta EE. The donation to the Eclipse Foundation meant that the Jakarta EE specification became truly vendor-neutral, with no single vendor having control over the specifications.

Java EE, in turn, was introduced back in 2006 by Sun Microsystems. The first version of Java EE was Java EE 5. Java EE replaced **J2EE**; the last version of J2EE was J2EE 1.4, released back in 2003. Even though J2EE can be considered obsolete technology, having been superseded by Java EE several years ago and then renamed Jakarta EE, the term *J2EE* refuses to die. Many individuals to this day still refer to Jakarta EE as J2EE and many companies advertise on their websites and job boards that they are looking for "J2EE developers", seemingly unaware that they are referring to a technology that has been obsolete for several years. The current correct term for the technology is Jakarta EE.

Additionally, the term J2EE has become a "catch-all" term for any server-side Java technology; frequently Spring applications are referred to as J2EE applications. **Spring** is not and never has been J2EE. As a matter of fact, Spring was created by Rod Johnson as an alternative to J2EE back in 2002. Just as with Jakarta EE, Spring applications are frequently erroneously referred to as J2EE applications.

Summary

In this chapter, we provided an introduction to Jakarta EE, outlining a list of several technologies and APIs included with Jakarta EE:

- We covered how Jakarta EE is openly developed both by software vendors and the Java community at large via the Eclipse Software Foundation

- We explained how there are multiple implementations of Jakarta EE, a fact that avoids vendor lock-in and allows us to easily migrate our Jakarta EE applications from one implementation to another

- We cleared up the confusion between Jakarta EE, Java EE, J2EE, and Spring, explaining how Jakarta EE and Spring applications are frequently referred to as J2EE applications, even though J2EE has been obsolete for several years

Now that we've had a general overview of Jakarta EE, we are ready to start learning how to use Jakarta EE to develop our applications.

2

Contexts and
Dependency Injection

Contexts and Dependency Injection (**CDI**) is a powerful dependency injection framework that allows us to easily integrate different parts of our Jakarta EE applications. CDI beans can have different scopes, allowing their life cycle to be managed automatically by the Jakarta EE runtime. They can be easily injected as dependencies by using a simple annotation. CDI also includes an event mechanism to allow decoupled communication between different parts of our application.

In this chapter, we will cover the following topics:

- Named beans

- Dependency injection

- Qualifiers

- CDI bean scopes

- CDI events

- CDI Lite

> **Note**
>
> Code samples for this chapter can be found on GitHub at `https://github.com/PacktPublishing/Jakarta-EE-Application-Development/tree/main/ch02_src`.

Named beans

CDI provides us with the ability to name our beans via the @Named annotation. Named beans allow us to easily inject our beans into other classes that depend on them (see the next section) and to easily refer to them from Jakarta Faces via the unified expression language.

> **Note**
>
> Jakarta Faces is covered in detail in *Chapters 6* and *7*.

The following example shows the @Named annotation in action:

```
package com.ensode.jakartaeebook.cdidependencyinjection.beans;

import jakarta.enterprise.context.RequestScoped;
import jakarta.inject.Named;
@Named
@RequestScoped
public class Customer {

  private String firstName;
  private String lastName;

  public String getFirstName() {
    return firstName;
  }

  public void setFirstName(String firstName) {
    this.firstName = firstName;
  }

  public String getLastName() {
    return lastName;
  }

  public void setLastName(String lastName) {
    this.lastName = lastName;
  }
}
```

As we can see, all we need to do to name our class is to decorate it with the @Named annotation. By default, the name of the bean will be the class name with its first letter switched to lowercase. In our example, the name of the bean would be customer. If we wish to use a different name, we can do so by setting the `value` attribute of the `@Named` annotation. For example, if we wanted to use the name `customerBean` for our bean, we could have done so by modifying the `@Named` annotation as follows:

```
@Named(value="customerBean")
```

Or, we could simply use the following:

```
@Named("customerBean")
```

Since the `value` attribute name does not need to be specified, if we don't use an attribute name, then `value` is implied.

This name can be used to access our bean from Jakarta Faces pages using the unified expression language:

```
<?xml version='1.0' encoding='UTF-8' ?>
<!DOCTYPE html PUBLIC "-//W3C//DTD XHTML 1.0 Transitional//EN"
"http://www.w3.org/TR/xhtml1/DTD/xhtml1-transitional.dtd">
<html xmlns="http://www.w3.org/1999/xhtml"
      xmlns:h="jakarta.faces.html">
  <h:head>
    <title>Enter Customer Information</title>
  </h:head>
  <h:body>
    <h:form>
      <h:panelGrid columns="2">
        <h:outputLabel for="firstName" value="First Name"/>
        <h:inputText id="firstName"
          value="#{customer.firstName}"/>
        <h:outputLabel for="lastName" value="Last Name"/>
        <h:inputText id="lastName"
          value="#{customer.lastName}"/>
        <h:panelGroup/>
        <h:commandButton value="Submit"
          action="#{customerController.saveCustomer}"/>
      </h:panelGrid>
    </h:form>
  </h:body>
</html>
```

In our example, the `firstName` and `lastName` properties or our `Customer` named bean are bound to two text input fields in our Jakarta Faces page.

When deployed and executed, our simple application looks like this:

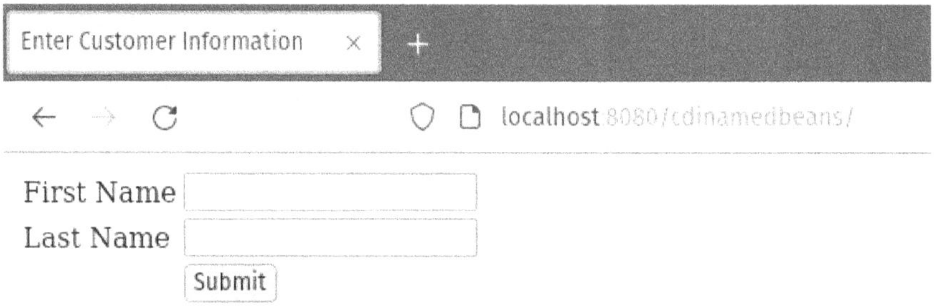

Figure 2.1 – CDI named beans in action

Now that we've seen how we can name our CDI beans, we will focus our attention on the dependency injection capabilities of CDI.

Dependency injection

Dependency injection is a technique for supplying external dependencies to a Java class. CDI includes the @Inject annotation, which can be used to inject instances of CDI beans into any dependent objects.

Jakarta Faces applications typically follow the **Model-View-Controller** (**MVC**) design pattern. As such, frequently some Jakarta Faces managed beans take the role of controllers in the pattern, while others take the role of the model. This approach typically requires the controller-managed bean to have access to one or more of the model-managed beans. CDI's dependency injection capabilities make injecting beans into one another very simple, as illustrated in the following example:

```
package com.ensode.jakartaeebook.cdinamedbeans.beans;
//imports omitted for brevity
@Named
@RequestScoped
public class CustomerController {

  private static final Logger logger = Logger.getLogger(
      CustomerController.class.getName());
  @Inject
  private Customer customer;

  public String saveCustomer() {

    logger.info("Saving the following information \n" +
      customer.toString());

    //If this was a real application,
```

```
        //we would have code to save customer data to the
        //database here.

        return "confirmation";
    }
}
```

Notice that all we had to do to initialize our `Customer` instance was to annotate it with the `@Inject` annotation. When the bean is constructed by the application server, an instance of the `Customer` bean is automatically injected into this field. Notice that the injected bean is used in the `saveCustomer()` method.

As we have seen in this section, CDI dependency injection is very simple. We simply need to annotate the instance variable of the class we wish to inject with the `@Inject` annotation.

Qualifiers

In some instances, the type of bean we wish to inject into our code may be an interface or a Java superclass. However, we may be interested in injecting a specific subclass or a class implementing the interface. For cases like this, CDI provides qualifiers we can use to indicate the specific type we wish to inject into our code.

A CDI qualifier is an annotation that must be decorated with the `@Qualifier` annotation. This annotation can then be used to decorate the specific subclass or interface implementation we wish to qualify. Additionally, the injected field in the client code needs to be decorated with the qualifier as well.

Suppose our application could have a special kind of customer; for example, frequent customers could be given the status of premium customers. To handle these premium customers, we could extend our `Customer` named bean and decorate it with the following qualifier:

```
package package com.ensode.jakartaeebook.qualifiers;

import jakarta.inject.Qualifier;
import static java.lang.annotation.ElementType.TYPE;
import static java.lang.annotation.ElementType.FIELD;
import static java.lang.annotation.ElementType.PARAMETER;
import static java.lang.annotation.ElementType.METHOD;
import static java.lang.annotation.RetentionPolicy.RUNTIME;
import java.lang.annotation.Retention;
import java.lang.annotation.Target;

@Qualifier
@Retention(RUNTIME)
@Target({METHOD, FIELD, PARAMETER, TYPE})
public @interface Premium {
}
```

As we mentioned before, qualifiers are standard annotations. They typically have retention of runtime and can target methods, fields, parameters, or types, as illustrated in the preceding example. The only difference between a qualifier and a standard annotation however is that qualifiers are decorated with the @Qualifier annotation.

Once we have our qualifier in place, we need to use it to decorate the specific subclass or interface implementation, as illustrated in the following example:

```
package com.ensode.jakartaeebook.cdidependencyinjection.beans;

import com.ensode.jakartaeebook.qualifiers.Premium;
import jakarta.enterprise.context.RequestScoped;
import jakarta.inject.Named;

@Named
@RequestScoped
@Premium
public class PremiumCustomer extends Customer {

  private Integer discountCode;

  public Integer getDiscountCode() {
    return discountCode;
  }

  public void setDiscountCode(Integer discountCode) {
    this.discountCode = discountCode;
  }
}
```

Once we have decorated the specific instance, we need to qualify it. We can use our qualifiers in the controller to specify the exact type of dependency we need:

```
package com.ensode.jakartaeebook.cdidependencyinjection.beans;

import java.util.logging.Logger;
import com.ensode.jakartaeebook.qualifiers.Premium;
import jakarta.enterprise.context.RequestScoped;
import jakarta.inject.Inject;
import jakarta.inject.Named;

@Named
@RequestScoped
public class CustomerController {
```

```
private static final Logger logger = Logger.getLogger(
    CustomerController.class.getName());
@Inject
@Premium
private Customer customer;

public String saveCustomer() {

  PremiumCustomer premiumCustomer =
    (PremiumCustomer) customer;
  logger.info("Saving the following information \n"
      + premiumCustomer.getFirstName() + " "
      + premiumCustomer.getLastName()
      + ", discount code = "
      + premiumCustomer.getDiscountCode());

  //If this was a real application, we would have code
  // to save customer data to the database here.

  return "confirmation";
  }
}
```

Since we used our @Premium qualifier to annotate the customer field, an instance of PremiumCustomer is injected into that field, since this class is also decorated with the @Premium qualifier.

As far as our Jakarta Faces pages go, we simply access our named bean as usual using its name, as shown in the following example:

```
<?xml version='1.0' encoding='UTF-8' ?>
<!DOCTYPE html PUBLIC "-//W3C//DTD XHTML 1.0 Transitional//EN"
"http://www.w3.org/TR/xhtml1/DTD/xhtml1-transitional.dtd">
<html xmlns="http://www.w3.org/1999/xhtml"
    xmlns:h="jakarta.faces.html">
  <h:head>
      <title>Enter Customer Information</title>
  </h:head>
  <h:body>
      <h:form>
          <h:panelGrid columns="2">
              <h:outputLabel for="firstName" value="First Name"/>
              <h:inputText id="firstName"
```

```
                value="#{premiumCustomer.firstName}"/>
            <h:outputLabel for="lastName"
              value="Last Name"/>
            <h:inputText id="lastName"
               value="#{premiumCustomer.lastName}"/>
            <h:outputLabel for="discountCode"
              value="Discount Code"/>
            <h:inputText id="discountCode"
               value="#{premiumCustomer.discountCode}"/>
            <h:panelGroup/>
            <h:commandButton value="Submit" action=
              "#{customerController.saveCustomer}"/>
          </h:panelGrid>
        </h:form>
      </h:body>
  </html>
```

In this example, we are using the default name for our bean, which is the class name with the first letter switched to lowercase.

Our simple application renders and acts just like a "plain" Jakarta Faces application, as far as the user is concerned. See *Figure 2.2*.

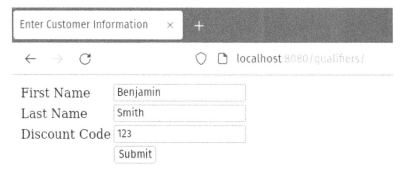

Figure 2.2 – Premium customer data displayed in the browser

Now that we've seen how to use CDI qualifiers to inject different implementations of the same type, we'll focus our attention on CDI scopes.

CDI bean scopes

CDI stands for "Contexts and Dependency Injection," CDI Beans have a scope which defines their lifecycle, their scope determines when the Jakarta EE runtime creates and destroys CDI beans. "Contexts" in "Contexts and Dependency Injection" refers to CDI scopes. When a CDI bean is needed, either because of injection or because it is referred to from a Jakarta Faces page, CDI looks for an instance of the bean in the scope it belongs to and injects it into the dependent code. If no instance is found, one is created and stored in the appropriate scope for future use. The different scopes are the context in which the bean exists.

The following table lists the different valid CDI scopes:

Scope	Annotation	Description
Request	`@RequestScoped`	Request-scoped beans are shared through the duration of a single request. A single request could refer to an HTTP request, an invocation to a method in an EJB, a web service invocation, or sending a JMS message to a message-driven bean.
Conversation	`@ConversationScoped`	The conversation scope can span multiple requests, but is typically shorter than the session scope.
Session	`@SessionScoped`	Session-scoped beans are shared across all requests in an HTTP session. Each user of an application gets their own instance of a session-scoped bean.
Application	`@ApplicationScoped`	Application-scoped beans live through the whole application lifetime. Beans in this scope are shared across user sessions.
Dependent	`@Dependent`	Dependent-scoped beans are not shared. Any time a dependent scoped bean is injected, a new instance is created.

Table 2.1 – CDI scopes

CDI's **request scope** does not necessarily refer to an HTTP request; it could simply be an invocation on an EJB method, a web service invocation, or sending a JMS message to a message-driven bean.

The **conversation scope** is longer than the request scope but shorter than the session scope. It typically spans three or more pages. Classes wishing to access a conversation-scoped bean must have an instance of `jakarta.enterprise.context.Conversation` injected. At the point, where we want to start the conversation, the `begin()` method must be invoked on this object. At the point where we want to end the conversation, its `end()` method must be invoked on it.

CDI's **session scope** ties the life cycle of a CDI bean to an HTTP session. Session-scoped CDI beans are created when they are first injected, and stick around until the HTTP session is destroyed, usually when a user logs out of a web application or closes the browser.

CDI's **application scope** ties the life cycle of a CDI bean to the life of an application. A single instance of each application-scoped bean exists per application, which means that the same instance is accessible to all HTTP sessions.

CDI's **dependent scope** is the default scope if none is explicitly specified. A new instance of a dependent-scoped bean is instantiated every time it is needed, usually when it is injected into a class that depends on it.

For most of CDI's scopes, simply annotating our CDI bean with the desired scope annotation is all we need to do. The Jakarta EE runtime then manages the bean's life cycle behind the scenes. The conversation scope requires a bit more work on our part, namely we need to indicate when a conversation starts and ends. For this reason, we will use the conversation scope to illustrate the usage of CDI scopes.

Suppose we wanted to have a user enter some data that would be stored in a single named bean; however, this bean has several fields. Therefore, we would like to split the data entry into several pages. For cases like this, CDI's conversation scope is a good solution. The following example illustrates how to use CDI's conversation scope:

```
package com.ensode.jakartaeebook.conversationscope.model;

import jakarta.enterprise.context.ConversationScoped;
import jakarta.inject.Named;
import java.io.Serializable;

@Named
@ConversationScoped
public class Customer implements Serializable {

  private String firstName;
  private String middleName;
  private String lastName;
  private String addrLine1;
  private String addrLine2;
  private String addrCity;
  private String state;
  private String zip;
  private String phoneHome;
  private String phoneWork;
  private String phoneMobile;

  //getters and setters omitted for brevity
  @Override
  public String toString() {
    StringBuilder sb = new StringBuilder();
    sb.append("Customer{");
    sb.append("firstName=").append(firstName);
    sb.append(", middleName=").append(middleName);
    sb.append(", lastName=").append(lastName);
```

```
        sb.append(", addrLine1=").append(addrLine1);
        sb.append(", addrLine2=").append(addrLine2);
        sb.append(", addrCity=").append(addrCity);
        sb.append(", state=").append(state);
        sb.append(", zip=").append(zip);
        sb.append(", phoneHome=").append(phoneHome);
        sb.append(", phoneWork=").append(phoneWork);
        sb.append(", phoneMobile=").append(phoneMobile);
        sb.append('}');
        return sb.toString();
    }
}
```

We declare that our bean is conversation scoped by decorating it with the @ConversationScoped annotation. Conversation-scoped beans also need to implement java.io.Serializable. Other than these two requirements, there is nothing special about our code; it is a simple Java class with private properties and corresponding getter and setter methods.

In addition to having our conversation-scoped bean injected, our client code must also have an instance of jakarta.enterprise.context.Conversation injected, as illustrated in the following example:

```
package com.ensode.jakartaeebook.conversationscope.controller;

import jakarta.enterprise.context.Conversation;
import jakarta.enterprise.context.RequestScoped;
import jakarta.inject.Inject;
import jakarta.inject.Named;
import java.io.Serializable;
import com.ensode.jakartaeebook.conversationscope.model.Customer;

@Named
@RequestScoped
public class CustomerInfoController implements Serializable {

    @Inject
    private Conversation conversation;
    @Inject
    private Customer customer;

    public String customerInfoEntry() {
        conversation.begin();
        System.out.println(customer);
        return "page1";
```

```
    }

    public String navigateToPage1() {
        System.out.println(customer);
        return "page1";
    }

    public String navigateToPage2() {
        System.out.println(customer);
        return "page2";
    }

    public String navigateToPage3() {
        System.out.println(customer);
        return "page3";
    }

    public String navigateToConfirmationPage() {
        System.out.println(customer);
        conversation.end();
        return "confirmation";
    }
}
```

Conversations can be either **long-running** or **transient**. Transient conversations end at the end of a request. Long-running conversations span multiple requests. In most cases, we will use long-running conversations to hold a reference to a conversation-scoped bean across multiple HTTP requests in a web application.

A long-running conversation starts when the `begin()` method is invoked in the injected `Conversation` instance, and it ends when we invoke the `end()` method on this same object.

Jakarta Faces pages simply access our CDI beans as usual:

```
<?xml version='1.0' encoding='UTF-8' ?>
<!DOCTYPE html PUBLIC "-//W3C//DTD XHTML 1.0 Transitional//EN"
"http://www.w3.org/TR/xhtml1/DTD/xhtml1-transitional.dtd">
<html xmlns="http://www.w3.org/1999/xhtml"
      xmlns:h="jakarta.faces.html">
    <h:head>
        <title>Customer Information</title>
    </h:head>
    <h:body>
        <h3>Enter Customer Information (Page 1 of 3)</h3>
        <h:form>
```

```
<h:panelGrid columns="2">
    <h:outputLabel for="firstName"
      value="First Name"/>
    <h:inputText  id="firstName"
      value="#{customer.firstName}"/>
    <h:outputLabel for="middleName"
      value="Middle Name"/>
    <h:inputText id="middleName"
      value="#{customer.middleName}"/>
    <h:outputLabel for="lastName"
      value="Last Name"/>
    <h:inputText  id="lastName"
      value="#{customer.lastName}"/>
    <h:panelGroup/>
    <h:commandButton value="Next"
      action=
    "#{customerInfoController.navigateToPage2}"/>
  </h:panelGrid>
    </h:form>
  </h:body>
</html>
```

As we navigate from one page to the next, we keep the same instance of our conversation-scoped bean; therefore, all user-entered data remains. When the end() method is called on our Conversation bean, the conversation ends and our conversation-scoped bean is destroyed.

Keeping our bean in the conversation scope simplifies the task of implementing "wizard-style" user interfaces, where data can be entered across several pages. See *Figure 2.3*.

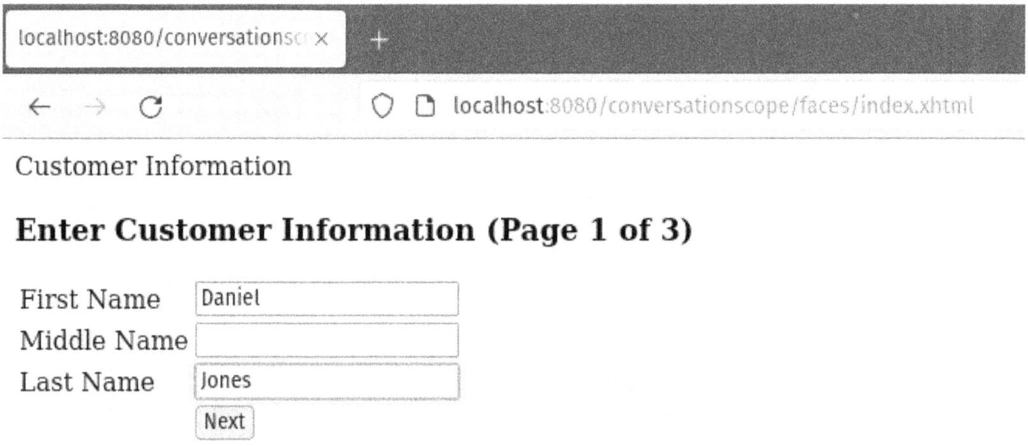

Figure 2.3 – Page 1 of CDI Conversation Scope Example

In our example, after clicking the **Next** button on the first page, we can see our partially populated bean in the application server log.

```
[2023-05-28T08:33:35.113817-04:00] [GF 7.0.4] [INFO] [] [jakarta.
enterprise.logging.stdout] [tid: _ThreadID=35 _ThreadName=http-
listener-1(2)] [levelValue: 800] [[
    Customer{firstName=Daniel, middleName=, lastName=Jones,
addrLine1=null, addrLine2=null, addrCity=null, state=null, zip=null,
phoneHome=null, phoneWork=null, phoneMobile=null}]]
```

At this point, the second page in our simple wizard is displayed, as shown in *Figure 2.4*.

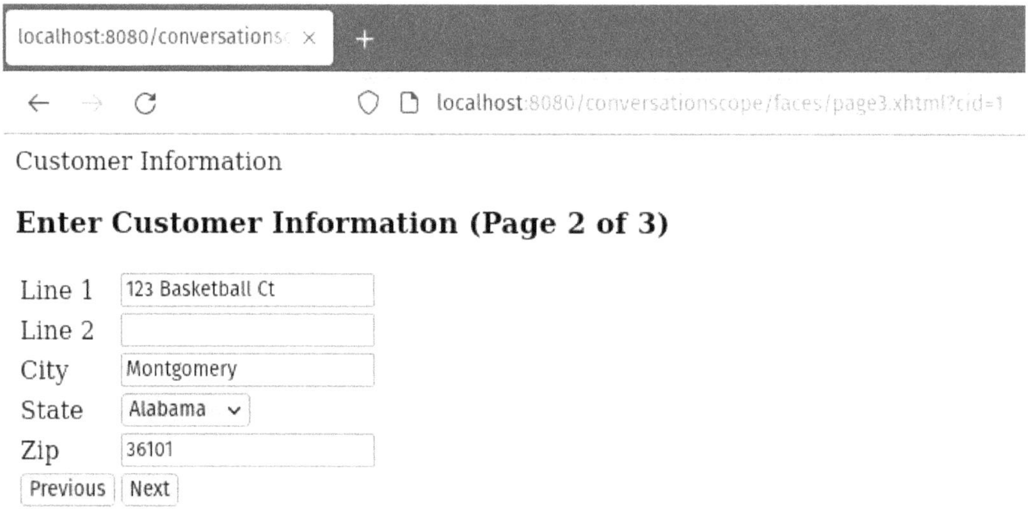

Figure 2.4 – Page 2 of CDI Conversation Scope Example

When clicking **Next**, we can see that additional fields are populated in our conversation-scoped bean.

```
[2023-05-28T08:44:23.434029-04:00] [GF 7.0.4] [INFO] [] [jakarta.
enterprise.logging.stdout] [tid: _ThreadID=36 _ThreadName=http-
listener-1(3)] [levelValue: 800] [[
    Customer{firstName=Daniel, middleName=, lastName=Jones,
addrLine1=123 Basketball Ct, addrLine2=, addrCity=Montgomery,
state=AL, zip=36101, phoneHome=, phoneWork=, phoneMobile=}]]
```

When we submit the third page in our wizard (not shown), additional bean properties corresponding to the fields on that page are populated.

When we are at the point where we don't need to keep the customer information in memory anymore, we need to call the end() method on the Conversation bean that was injected into our code. This is exactly what we do in our code before displaying the confirmation page:

```
public String navigateToConfirmationPage() {
        System.out.println(customer);
```

```
        conversation.end();
        return "confirmation";
    }
```

After the request to show the confirmation page is completed, our conversation-scoped bean is destroyed, since we invoked the end() method in our injected Conversation class.

Now that we've seen all scopes supported by CDI, we will turn our attention to how we can implement loosely coupled communication via CDI events.

CDI events

CDI provides event-handling facilities. Events allow loosely coupled communication between different CDI beans. A CDI bean can fire an event, then one or more event listeners handle the event.

Firing CDI events

The following example is a new version of the CustomerInfoController class we discussed in the previous section. The class has been modified to fire an event every time the user navigates to a new page:

```
package com.ensode.jakartaeebook.cdievents.controller;

import jakarta.enterprise.context.Conversation;
import jakarta.enterprise.context.RequestScoped;
import jakarta.inject.Inject;
import jakarta.inject.Named;
import java.io.Serializable;
import com.ensode.jakartaeebook.cdievents.event.NavigationInfo;
import com.ensode.jakartaeebook.cdievents.model.Customer;
import jakarta.enterprise.event.Event;

@Named
@RequestScoped
public class CustomerInfoController implements Serializable {

    @Inject
    private Conversation conversation;
    @Inject
    private Customer customer;
    @Inject
    private Event<NavigationInfo> navigationInfoEvent;

    public String customerInfoEntry() {
```

```
        conversation.begin();
        NavigationInfo navigationInfo =
          new NavigationInfo();
        navigationInfo.setPage("1");
        navigationInfo.setCustomer(customer);

        navigationInfoEvent.fire(navigationInfo);
        return "page1";
    }

    public String navigateToPage1() {
        NavigationInfo navigationInfo =
          new NavigationInfo();
        navigationInfo.setPage("1");
        navigationInfo.setCustomer(customer);

        navigationInfoEvent.fire(navigationInfo);

        return "page1";
    }

    public String navigateToPage2() {
        NavigationInfo navigationInfo =
          new NavigationInfo();
        navigationInfo.setPage("2");
        navigationInfo.setCustomer(customer);

        navigationInfoEvent.fire(navigationInfo);
        return "page2";
    }

    public String navigateToPage3() {
        NavigationInfo navigationInfo =
          new NavigationInfo();
        navigationInfo.setPage("3");
        navigationInfo.setCustomer(customer);

        navigationInfoEvent.fire(navigationInfo);
        return "page3";
    }

    public String navigateToConfirmationPage() {
        NavigationInfo navigationInfo =
```

```
        new NavigationInfo();
    navigationInfo.setPage("confirmation");
    navigationInfo.setCustomer(customer);

    navigationInfoEvent.fire(navigationInfo);
    conversation.end();
    return "confirmation";
    }
}
```

As we can see, to create an event, we inject an instance of jakarta.enterprise.event.
Event. This class uses generics; therefore, we need to specify its type. The type of the Event class
can be any class implementing java.io.Serializable. In our case, we are passing an instance
of a simple POJO we wrote as the type parameter, our POJO is called NavigationInfo and has
two properties, one of type Customer and a String containing the page the user is navigating to.
Recall from the previous sections that each of the methods on our CustomerInfoController
class triggers navigation from one page in the application to another. In this version of the controller,
a CDI event is fired every time we navigate to a new page. In each case, we create a new instance of
NavigationInfo, populate it, then fire the event by invoking the fire() method on our instance
of jakarta.enterprise.event.Event.

Handling CDI events

To handle CDI events, the CDI bean handling the event needs to implement an **observer method**.
Observer methods accept a parameter of the type that was used to fire the event, that is, the generic
type used to create the event that was fired. In our example, the generic type of our event is an instance
of a class named NavigationInfo, as can be seen in the declaration of our event in the preceding
section. To handle the event, the observer method needs to annotate the corresponding parameter
with the @Observes annotation, as illustrated in the following example:

```
package com.ensode.jakartaeebook.cdievents.eventlistener;

import jakarta.enterprise.context.SessionScoped;
import jakarta.enterprise.event.Observes;
import java.io.Serializable;
import com.ensode.jakartaeebook.cdievents.event.NavigationInfo;
import java.util.logging.Level;
import java.util.logging.Logger;

@SessionScoped
public class NavigationEventListener implements Serializable {
    private static final Logger LOG =
        Logger.getLogger(
```

```
                    NavigationEventListener.class.getName());

         public void handleNavigationEvent(
           @Observes NavigationInfo navigationInfo) {
             LOG.info("Navigation event fired");
             LOG.log(Level.INFO, "Page: {0}",
               navigationInfo.getPage());
             LOG.log(Level.INFO, "Customer: {0}",
               navigationInfo.getCustomer());
         }
    }
```

In this example event handler, the `handleNavigationEvent()` method takes an instance of `NavigationInfo` as a parameter. Notice that this parameter is annotated with @Observes. This causes the method to be invoked automatically by CDI every time an event of type `NavigationInfo` is fired. Notice that we never explicitly call this method; the Jakarta EE runtime invokes it automatically whenever a navigation event is fired.

CDI events allow us to implement loosely coupled communication between CDI beans. In our example, notice that our `CustomerController` CDI bean has no direct reference to `NavigationEventListener`. In general, the CDI bean firing the event does not need to know any details about the listeners; it just fires the event and CDI takes over the details.

> **Note**
>
> In our example, we have only one event listener, but in practice, we can have as many event listeners as we need.

Asynchronous events

CDI has the ability to fire events asynchronously. Firing events asynchronously can help with performance, since various observer methods can be invoked concurrently. Firing an event asynchronously is very similar to firing an event synchronously. The only syntactical difference is that instead of invoking the `fire()` method in our `Event` instance, we invoke its `fireAsync()` method. The following example illustrates how to do this:

```
public class EventSource{
  @Inject Event<MyEvent> myEvent;
  public void fireEvent(){
    myEvent.fireAsync(myEvent);
  }
}
```

Observer methods to handle asynchronous events are identical to their synchronous counterparts.

Event ordering

Another new feature introduced in CDI 2.0 is the ability to specify in what order our observer methods handle CDI events. This can be accomplished via the @Priority annotation, as illustrated in the following example:

```
import jakarta.enterprise.context.SessionScoped;
import jakarta.enterprise.event.Observes;
import jakarta.annotation.Priority;
import jakarta.interceptor.Interceptor;

@SessionScoped
public class EventHandler{
    void handleIt (
      @Observes @Priority(
        Interceptor.Priority.APPLICATION) MyEvent me){
      //handle the event
    }
}
```

The @Priority annotation takes an argument of type int. This argument specifies the priority for the observer method. The highest priority is defined by the APPLICATION constant defined in the Interceptor.Priority class. This is the priority we gave to the observer method in our example. Lower-priority values take precedence and the default priority is Interceptor. Priority.APPLICATION + 100.

As mentioned in *Chapter 1*, in addition to the full Jakarta EE specification, there are two Jakarta EE profiles we can use if we are developing simpler applications that don't need the full power of Jakarta EE. There's the Web Profile, suitable for web applications, and the Core Profile, suitable for microservices. The Core Profile includes CDI support but does not support all of CDI's features. This lightweight version of CDI included in the Jakarta EE Core Profile is called CDI Lite.

CDI Lite

The Jakarta EE Core Profile contains a subset of the full CDI specification, named, appropriately enough, CDI Lite. Most of the changes of CDI Lite are at the implementation level; namely, some functionality that the full CDI implementation performs at runtime is moved to build time, allowing applications utilizing CDI Lite to initialize faster.

CDI Lite is primarily meant to be used in microservices applications, implementing functionality as RESTful web services. Since REST applications are typically stateless, not all CDI scopes are applicable when working on this type of application. For this reason, the session and conversation scopes are not available when using CDI Lite. This is the primary limitation of CDI Lite when compared to the full CDI specification.

We only need to be concerned with CDI Lite limitations when deploying our code to a Jakarta EE Core Profile implementation. The Jakarta EE Web Profile and the full Jakarta EE platform contain full CDI functionality.

Summary

In this chapter, we provided an introduction to CDI, an integral part of the Jakarta EE specification. We looked into the following:

- We covered how Jakarta Faces pages can access CDI-named beans via the unified expression language.

- We also covered how CDI makes it easy to inject dependencies into our code via the `@Inject` annotation.

- Additionally, we explained how we can use qualifiers to determine what specific implementation of a dependency to inject into our code.

- We also discussed all the scopes that a CDI bean can be placed into, allowing us to delegate the life cycle of CDI beans to the Jakarta EE runtime.

- We discussed how to implement loosely coupled communication between CDI beans via CDI's event handling.

- Lastly, we discussed CDI Lite, a lightweight version of CDI suitable for microservices development.

CDI is an integral part of Jakarta EE, as it is used to integrate different layers of our Jakarta EE applications.

3

Jakarta RESTful Web Services

Representational State Transfer (**REST**) is an architectural style in which web services are viewed as resources and can be identified by **Uniform Resource Identifiers** (**URIs**).

Web services developed using the REST styles are known as RESTful web services. We can develop RESTful web services in Jakarta EE via the **Jakarta RESTful Web Services API**, commonly known as **Jakarta REST**. In this chapter, we will cover how to develop RESTful web services using Jakarta REST.

The following topics will be covered in this chapter:

- Introduction to RESTful web services
- Developing a simple RESTful web service
- Developing a RESTful web service client
- Seamlessly converting between Java and JSON
- Query and path parameters
- Server-sent events

> **Note**
>
> Code samples for this chapter can be found at `https://github.com/PacktPublishing/Jakarta-EE-Application-Development/tree/main/ch03_src`.

Introduction to RESTful web services

RESTful web services are very flexible. RESTful web services can consume several types of different MIME types, although they are typically written to consume and/or produce data in **JavaScript Object Notation** (**JSON**) format.

> **MIME types**
>
> MIME stands for Multipurpose Internet Mail Extensions; it is used to indicate the data type that is consumed or produced by RESTful web services.

Web services must support one or more of the following six HTTP methods:

- **GET** – By convention, a GET request is used to retrieve an existing resource
- **POST** – By convention, a POST request is used to update an existing resource
- **PUT** – By convention, a PUT request is used to create or replace a new resource
- **DELETE** – By convention, a DELETE request is used to delete an existing resource
- **HEAD** – By convention, a HEAD request returns an HTTP header with no body
- **PATCH** – By convention, a PATCH request is used for partial resource modification

We develop a RESTful web service with Jakarta REST by creating a class with annotated methods that are invoked when our web service receives one of the preceding HTTP request methods. Once we have developed and deployed our RESTful web service, we need to develop a client that will send requests to our service. Frontend web technologies are frequently used to develop RESTful web service clients. However, Jakarta REST includes a standard client-side API that we can use to develop RESTful web service clients in Java.

Developing a simple RESTful web service

In this section, we will develop a simple web service to illustrate how we can make methods in our service respond to the different HTTP request methods.

Developing a RESTful web service using Jakarta REST is simple and straightforward. Each of our RESTful web services needs to be invoked via its **Unique Resource Identifier** (**URI**). Our RESTful web service URI is specified by the @Path annotation, which we need to use to decorate our RESTful web service resource class.

When developing RESTful web services, we need to develop methods that will be invoked when our web service receives an HTTP request. We need to implement methods to handle one or more of the six types of requests that RESTful web services handle – GET, POST, PUT, DELETE, HEAD and/or PATCH.

> **Note**
>
> We will only cover the most frequently used HTTP request types as implementing all HTTP request types is very similar.

Jakarta REST provides annotations that we can use to decorate methods in our web service. For example, @GET, @POST, @PUT, and @DELETE are used to implement the corresponding HTTP methods. Decorating a method in our web service with one of these annotations will make it respond to the corresponding HTTP method request.

Additionally, each method in our service must produce and/or consume a specific MIME type. The MIME type to be produced needs to be specified with the @Produces annotation. Similarly, the MIME type to be consumed must be specified with the @Consumes annotation.

The following example illustrates the concepts we have just explained:

```java
package com.ensode.jakartaeebook.jakartarestintro.service;
//imports omitted for brevity
@Path("customer")
public class CustomerResource {
  private static final Logger LOG =
      Logger.getLogger(CustomerResource.class.getName());
  @GET
  @Produces(MediaType.APPLICATION_JSON)
  public String getCustomer() {
    LOG.log(Level.INFO, "{0}.getCustomer() invoked",
        this.getClass().getCanonicalName());

    return """
              {
                "customer": {
                  "id": 123,
                  "firstName": "Joseph",
                  "middleName": "William",
                  "lastName": "Graystone"
                }
              }
              """;
  }

  @PUT
  @Consumes(MediaType.APPLICATION_JSON)
  public void createCustomer(String customerJson) {
    LOG.log(Level.INFO, "{0}.createCustomer() invoked",
        this.getClass().getCanonicalName());

    LOG.log(Level.INFO, "customerJson = {0}", customerJson);
  }
```

```
@POST
@Consumes(MediaType.APPLICATION_JSON)
public void updateCustomer(String customerJson) {
  LOG.log(Level.INFO, "{0}.updateCustomer() invoked",
    this.getClass().getCanonicalName());

  LOG.log(Level.INFO, "customerJson = {0}", customerJson);
  }
}
```

> **Note**
>
> Please note that this example does not *really* do anything. The purpose of the example is to illustrate how to make different methods in our RESTful web service resource class respond to the different HTTP methods.

Notice that this class is annotated with the @Path annotation. This annotation designates the URI for our RESTful web service. The complete URI for our service will include the protocol, server name, port, context root, the REST resources path (see the next sub-section), and the value passed to this annotation.

Assuming our web service was deployed to a server called example.com, using the HTTP protocol on port 8080, and has a context root of jakartarestintro and a REST resources path of resources, then the complete URI for our service would be the following:

```
http://example.com:8080/jakartarestintro/resources/customer
```

> **Note**
>
> Since web browsers generate a GET request when pointed to a URL, we can test the GET method of our service simply by pointing the browser to our service's URI.

Notice that each of the methods in our class is annotated with one of the @GET, @POST, or @PUT annotations. These annotations make our methods respond to the corresponding HTTP method.

> **Note**
>
> HTTP DELETE requests typically require a parameter. We will cover them in the *Path and query parameters* section later in the chapter.

Additionally, if our method returns data to the client, we declare the MIME type of the data to be returned in the @Produces annotation. In our example, only the getCustomer() method returns data to the client. We wish to return data in JSON format; therefore, we set the value of the

@Produces annotation to the Jakarta REST-provided MediaType.APPLICATION_JSON constant, which has a value of "application/json". Similarly, if our method needs to consume data from the client, we need to specify the MIME type of the data to be consumed; this is done via the @Consumes annotation. All methods except getCustomer() in our service consume data. In all cases, we expect the data to be in JSON format; therefore, we again specify MediaType. APPLICATION_JSON as the MIME type to be consumed.

Before moving on, it is worth mentioning that the @Path annotation can be used both at the class level and at the method level. Using the @Path annotation at the method level allows us to write multiple methods that handle the same HTTP request type in a single RESTful web service. For example, if we needed a second method in our example RESTful web service, we would simply add the @Path annotation to it:

```
@GET
@Produces(MediaType.TEXT_PLAIN)
@Path("customername")
public String getCustomerName() {
   return "Joseph Graystone";
}
```

The URI of this particular endpoint would be the value we used in our method-level @Path annotation, appended to the URI of our RESTful web service.

In our example, the URI of our RESTful web service would be something like http://localhost:8080/jakartarestintro/resources/customer/, assuming we deployed to our local workstation and the server is listening on port 8080.

The URI for the endpoint with the method-level annotation would then be curl http://localhost:8080/jakartarestintro/resources/customer/customername. Notice that the value of the method-level @Path annotation was appended to the "root" URI of our RESTful web service.

Configuring the REST resources path for our application

As briefly mentioned in the previous section, before successfully deploying a RESTful web service developed using Jakarta REST, we need to configure the REST resources path for our application. We can do this by developing a class that extends jakarta.ws.rs.core.Application and decorating it with the @ApplicationPath annotation.

Configuring via the @ApplicationPath annotation

To configure our REST resources path, all we need to do is write a class that extends jakarta.ws.rs.core.Application, and decorate it with the @ApplicationPath annotation; the value passed to this annotation is the REST resources path for our services.

The following code sample illustrates this process:

```
package com.ensode.jakartaeebook.jakartarestintro.service.config;

//imports omitted for brevity

@ApplicationPath("resources")
public class JakartaRestConfig extends Application {
}
```

Notice that the class does not have to implement any methods. It simply needs to extend `jakarta.ws.rs.Application` and be annotated with the `@ApplicationPath` annotation. The class must be public, may have any name, and may be placed in any package.

Testing our web service

As we mentioned earlier, web browsers send a GET request to any URLs we point them to. Therefore, the easiest way to test GET requests to our service is to simply point the browser to our service's URI, as illustrated in *Figure 3.1*.

Figure 3.1 – HTTP GET request from a web browser

> **Note**
> Firefox includes a JSON viewer that by default parses the JSON data and displays it in a user-friendly manner. To view the actual JSON string sent by our service in Firefox, we need to click on the **Raw Data** tab.

Web browsers only support HTTP GET and POST requests. To test a POST request through the browser, we would have to write a web application containing an HTML form that has an action attribute value of our service's URI. Although trivial for a single service, it can become cumbersome to do this for every RESTful web service we develop.

Thankfully, there is a popular open source command-line utility called `curl` that we can use to test our web services. `curl` is included with most Linux distributions, and can be easily downloaded for Windows, macOS, and several other platforms. `curl` can be downloaded at `http://curl.haxx.se/`.

`curl` can send all HTTP request method types (GET, POST, PUT, DELETE, etc.) to our service. Our server's response will simply be displayed on the command-line console. `curl` takes an `-X` command-line option, which allows us to specify what request method to send. To send a GET request, we simply need to type the following into the command line:

```
curl -XGET http://localhost:8080/jakartarestintro/resources/customer
```

Doing so results in the following output:

```
{
   "customer": {
      "id": 123,
      "firstName": "Joseph",
      "middleName": "William",
      "lastName": "Graystone"
   }
}
```

This, unsurprisingly, is the same output we saw when we pointed our browser to the service's URI.

The default request method for `curl` is GET; therefore, the `-X` parameter in our preceding example is redundant. We could have achieved the same result by invoking the following command from the command line:

```
curl http://localhost:8080/jakartarestintro/resources/customer
```

After submitting any of the two preceding commands and examining the application server log, we should see the output of the logging statements we added to the `getCustomer()` method:

```
com.ensode.jakartaeebook.jakartarestintro.service.CustomerResource.
getCustomer() invoked|#]
```

> **Note**
>
> The exact location of the application server log depends on the Jakarta EE implementation we are using. For GlassFish, when using the default domain, it can be found at [`glassfish installation directory`]`/glassfish/domains/domain1/logs/server.log`.

For all other request method types, we need to send some data to our service. This can be accomplished by the `--data` command-line argument to `curl`:

```
curl -XPUT -HContent-type:application/json --data "{
  "customer": {
    "id": 321,
    "firstName": "Amanda",
    "middleName": "Zoe",
    "lastName": "Adams"
  }
}" http://localhost:8080/jakartarestintro/resources/customer
```

We need to specify the MIME type via `curl`'s `-H` command-line argument using the format seen in the preceding example.

We can verify that the preceding command worked as expected by inspecting the application server log:

```
com.ensode.jakartaeebook.jakartarestintro.service.CustomerResource.
createCustomer() invoked|#]
  customerJson = {
  customer: {
    id: 321,
    firstName: Amanda,
    middleName: Zoe,
    lastName: Adams
  }
}|#]
```

We can test other request method types just as easily:

```
curl -XPOST -HContent-type:application/json --data "{
  "customer": {
    "id": 321,
    "firstName": "Amanda",
    "middleName": "Tamara",
    "lastName": "Adams"
  }
}" http://localhost:8080/jakartarestintro/resources/customer
```

This results in the following output in the application server log:

```
com.ensode.jakartaeebook.jakartarestintro.service.CustomerResource.
updateCustomer() invoked|#]
    customerJson = {
    customer: {
        id: 321,
        firstName: Amanda,
        middleName: Tamara,
        lastName: Adams
    }
}|#]
```

`curl` allows us to quickly test our RESTful web services. However, in a real application, we need to develop RESTful web service clients to invoke our RESTful web services and retrieve data from them. Jakarta REST provides a client API we can use for this purpose.

Developing a RESTful web service client

Although `curl` allows us to quickly test our RESTful web services and is a developer-friendly tool, we need a way for our Java applications to invoke the RESTful web services we develop. Jakarta REST includes a client-side API we can use to develop RESTful web service clients.

The following example illustrates how to use the Jakarta REST client API:

```
package com.ensode.jakartaeebook.jakartarestintroclient;

//imports omitted for brevity
public class App {

    public static void main(String[] args) {
        App app = new App();
        app.insertCustomer();
    }

    public void insertCustomer() {
        String customerJson = """
                    {
                        "customer": {
                            "id": 234,
                            "firstName": "Tamara",
                            "middleName": "Adeline",
                            "lastName": "Graystone"
                        }
                    }
```

```
                    """;
        Client client = ClientBuilder.newClient();
        client.target(
          "http://localhost:8080/" +
          "jakartarestintro/resources/customer").
          request().put(
            Entity.entity(customerJson,
              MediaType.APPLICATION_JSON),
              String.class);
    }
  }
```

The first thing we need to do is create an instance of `jakarta.ws.rs.client.Client` by invoking the static `newClient()` method on the `jakarta.ws.rs.client.ClientBuilder` class.

We then invoke the `target()` method on our `Client` instance, passing the URI of our RESTful web service as a parameter. The `target()` method returns an instance of a class implementing the `jakarta.ws.rs.client.WebTarget` interface.

At this point, we invoke the `request()` method on our `WebTarget` instance. This method returns an implementation of the `jakarta.ws.rs.client.Invocation.Builder` interface.

In this particular example, we are sending an HTTP PUT request to our RESTful web service; therefore, at this point, we invoke the `put()` method of our `Invocation.Builder` implementation.

The first parameter of the `put()` method is a `jakarta.ws.rs.client.Entity` instance; we can create one on the fly by invoking the static `entity()` method on the `Entity` class. The first parameter for this method is the object we wish to pass to our RESTful web service, and the second parameter is the string representation of the MIME type of the data we will be passing to the RESTful web service. In our example, we are using the `MediaType.APPLICATION_JSON` constant, which resolves to `"application/json"`. The second parameter of the `put()` method is the type of response the client expects from the service. In our case we expect a `String`; therefore, we used `String.class` for this parameter. After we invoke the `put()` method, an HTTP PUT request is sent to our RESTful web service and the method we decorated with the @Put annotation (`createCustomer()` in our example) is invoked. There are similar `get()`, `post()`, and `delete()` methods we can invoke to send the corresponding HTTP requests to our RESTful web service.

Now that we've seen how to develop both RESTful web services and clients, we'll take a look at how Jakarta EE can seamlessly convert between Java and JSON.

Seamlessly converting between Java and JSON

RESTful web services transfer data in plain text, typically, but this is not limited to JSON-formatted data. In our examples so far, we have been sending and receiving JSON strings between our RESTful services and their clients.

Frequently, we would like to populate Java objects from the JSON data we receive, manipulate the data somehow, and then build a JSON string to send as a response. The population of Java objects from JSON, and the generation of JSON data from Java objects, is so common that the Jakarta REST implementation provides a way to do it seamlessly and automatically.

In previous examples in this chapter, we have been sending and receiving raw JSON data as strings. Our sample data contains customer information such as first name, middle name, and last name. To make this data easier to manipulate, we would typically populate a Java object with this data; for example, we could parse the JSON data and populate an instance of the following Java class:

```
package com.ensode.jakartaeebook.javajson.entity;
public class Customer {

    private Long id;
    private String firstName;
    private String middleName;
    private String lastName;

    public Customer() {
    }

    public Customer(Long id, String firstName,
        String middleName, String lastName) {
        //constructor body omitted for brevity
    }
    //getters,setters and toString() method omitted for brevity
}
```

Notice how the instance variable names of our `Customer` class match the names of the properties of our JSON data; Jakarta REST is smart enough to populate each variable with the corresponding JSON property. As long as the property names and variable names match, Jakarta REST can populate our Java object automatically (the types, needless to say, must match as well; an error would occur trying to populate a variable of the `Integer` type with a textual value, for example).

The following example illustrates how we can implement a RESTful web service that seamlessly converts the JSON data it receives to a Java object:

```
package com.ensode.jakartaeebook.javajson.service;
//imports omitted for brevity
@Path("customer")
public class CustomerResource {
    private static final Logger LOG =
        Logger.getLogger(CustomerResource.class.getName());

    private final Customer customer;
```

```java
public CustomerResource() {
  customer = new Customer(1L, "David",
    "Raymond", "Heffelfinger");
}


@GET
@Produces(MediaType.APPLICATION_JSON)
public Customer getCustomer() {
  LOG.log(Level.INFO, "{0}.getCustomer() invoked",
    this.getClass().getCanonicalName());

  return customer;
}


@POST
@Consumes(MediaType.APPLICATION_JSON)
public void updateCustomer(Customer customer) {
  LOG.log(Level.INFO, "got the following customer: {0}",
    customer);
}


@PUT
@Consumes(MediaType.APPLICATION_JSON)
public void createCustomer(Customer customer) {



  LOG.log(Level.INFO, "customer = {0}", customer);
}
}
```

Notice all we had to do was to change the type of the parameters for our methods to be of the Customer type (our simple example POJO); previously, they were of the String type. Similarly, we changed the type of the return value from String to Customer.

Notice we don't have to do anything special in our code to populate the Customer object, or to generate a JSON string to send as a response; it is all taken care of behind the scenes by Jakarta REST.

To illustrate this seamless conversion, let's use curl to send a request to our modified service:

```
curl -XPUT -HContent-type:application/json --data '{
  "id": 1,
  "firstName": "Bruce",
```

```
  "middleName": "Arnold",
  "lastName": "Stallone"
}' http://localhost:8080/jakartarestjavajson/resources/customer
```

Notice that in our `curl` command, we are sending JSON data to our Jakarta REST service. If we inspect the application server log, we can see the following output:

```
com.ensode.jakartaeebook.javajson.service.CustomerResource.
createCustomer() invoked|#]
  customer = Customer{id=1, firstName=Bruce, middleName=Arnold,
lastName=Stallone}|#]
```

In the application server log, we see the output of the `toString()` method of our `Customer` class, illustrating that the `createCustomer(Customer customer)` method in our service was invoked, and it seamlessly populated its customer parameter with the raw JSON data we sent it with our `curl` command.

When using non-Java clients, such as `curl`, or RESTful web service clients written in languages other than Java, we need to send raw JSON data to our service from the client side, as illustrated in our example. When writing clients in Java, we can take advantage of the Jakarta REST client API, which allows seamless conversion from Java to JSON on the client side as well. The following example illustrates how to do this:

```java
package com.ensode.jakartarestjavajsonclient;
//imports omitted for brevity
public class App {

  public static void main(String[] args) {
    App app = new App();
    app.insertCustomer();
  }

  public void insertCustomer() {
    Customer customer = new Customer(456L, "Daniel",
      "Robert","Hanson");
    Client client = ClientBuilder.newClient();

    client.target(
      "http://localhost:8080/"
      + "jakartarestjavajson/resources/customer").
      request().put(
        Entity.entity(customer, MediaType.APPLICATION_JSON),
      Customer.class);
  }
}
```

In this updated client, we simply create an instance of our `Customer` class. Then we can pass it as a parameter to the static `entity()` method of the `Entity` class, and pass the corresponding type (`Customer.class`, in our example) to the `put()` method.

After running our client code, we can see the following output in the application server log:

```
com.ensode.jakartaeebook.javajson.service.CustomerResource.
createCustomer() invoked|#]
    customer = Customer{id=456, firstName=Daniel, middleName=Robert,
lastName=Hanson}|#]
```

Our client seamlessly converted our `Customer` instance to a JSON string, and invoked our RESTful web service, which in turn converted the sent JSON back to a `Customer` instance; all behind the scenes, saving us a lot of drudge work.

So far, in all of our examples, we have been passing a JSON string (either directly or indirectly) as a body to the HTTP requests we have been sending to our RESTful web services. It is also possible to pass parameters to our RESTful web services. The following section illustrates how to do that.

Query and path parameters

In our previous examples, we have been working with a RESTful web service to manage a single customer object. In real life, this would obviously not be very helpful. The common case is to develop a RESTful web service to handle a collection of objects (customers, in our example). To determine what specific object in the collection we are working with, we can pass parameters to our RESTful web services. There are two types of parameters we can use: **query** and **path** parameters.

Query parameters

We can add parameters to methods that will handle HTTP requests in our web service. Parameters decorated with the `@QueryParam` annotation will be retrieved from the request URL.

The following example illustrates how to use query parameters in RESTful web services using Jakarta REST:

```
package com.ensode.jakartaeebook.queryparams.service;
//imports omitted for brevity
@Path("customer")
public class CustomerResource {

  private static final Logger LOG =
    Logger.getLogger(CustomerResource.class.getName());

  private final Customer customer;

  public CustomerResource() {
```

```
    customer = new Customer(1L, "Samuel",
        "Joseph", "Willow");
}

@GET
@Produces(MediaType.APPLICATION_JSON)
public Customer getCustomer(@QueryParam("id") Long id) {

    LOG.log(Level.INFO,
        "{0}.getCustomer() invoked, id = {1}", new Object[]
        {this.getClass().getCanonicalName(), id});
    return new Customer(id, "Dummy", null, "Customer");
}
@DELETE
@Consumes(MediaType.APPLICATION_JSON)
public void deleteCustomer(@QueryParam("id") Long id) {

LOG.log(Level.INFO,
        "{0}.deleteCustomer() invoked, id = {1}",
        new Object[]
    {this.getClass().getCanonicalName(), id});
}
//additional methods deleted for brevity
}
```

In our updated example, we added a parameter to the getCustomer() method, which, as we may recall, is decorated with the @GET annotation so that it is invoked when our RESTful web service receives an HTTP GET request. We annotated the parameter with the @QueryParam annotation; the value of this annotation (id in our example) is the name of the parameter to use when sending a request to our service.

We can pass a query parameter to the web service's URL just like we pass query parameters to any URL. For HTTP GET requests, we could simply type our RESTful web service's URL into the browser, or we could use curl as follows:

```
curl -XGET -HContent-type:application/json http://localhost:8080/
queryparams/resources/customer?id=1
```

Either way, we should see the corresponding output in the application server log:

```
com.ensode.jakartaeebook.queryparams.service.CustomerResource.
getCustomer() invoked, id = 1|#]
```

Plus, we should see the following response from our RESTful web service:

```
{"firstName":"Dummy","id":1,"lastName":"Customer"}
```

Notice the response is a JSON representation of the Customer object we return in our getCustomer() object. We didn't have to explicitly create the JSON data; Jakarta REST took care of it for us.

We added a deleteCustomer() method to our RESTful web service, and we annotated this method with @DELETE so that it responds to HTTP DELETE requests. Just like with getCustomer(), we added a parameter to this method and annotated it with the @QueryParam annotation.

We can send our RESTful web service using curl as follows:

```
curl -XDELETE -HContent-type:application/json http://localhost:8080/
queryparams/resources/customer?id=2
```

Our deleteCustomer() will be invoked as expected, as evidenced by the output in the application server log:

```
com.ensode.jakartaeebook.queryparams.service.CustomerResource.
deleteCustomer() invoked, id = 2|#]
```

Sending query parameters via the Jakarta REST client API

The Jakarta REST client API provides a straightforward way of sending query parameters to RESTful web services. The following example illustrates how to do this:

```
package com.ensode.jakartaeebook.queryparamsclient;
//imports omitted for brevity
public class App {

  public static void main(String[] args) {
    App app = new App();
    app.getCustomer();
  }

  public void getCustomer() {
    Client client = ClientBuilder.newClient();
    Customer customer = client.target(
      "http://localhost:8080/"
      + "queryparams/resources/customer").
      queryParam("id", 1L).
        request().get(Customer.class);
    System.out.println(String.format(
      "Received the following customer information:\n%s",
      customer));
    }
}
```

As we can see, all we need to do to pass a parameter is to invoke the `queryParam()` method on the `jakarta.ws.rs.client.WebTarget` instance returned by the `target()` method invocation on our `Client` instance. The first argument to this method is the parameter name and must match the value of the `@QueryParam` annotation on the web service. The second parameter is the value that we need to pass to the web service. If our web service accepts multiple parameters, we can chain `queryParam()` method invocations, using one for each parameter our RESTful web service expects.

Path parameters

Another way we can pass parameters to our RESTful web services is via path parameters. The following example illustrates how to develop a Jakarta REST web service that accepts path parameters:

```
package com.ensode.jakartaeebook.pathparams.service;
//imports omitted for brevity
@Path("/customer/")
public class CustomerResource {
  private static final Logger LOG =
    Logger.getLogger(CustomerResource.class.getName());
  private Customer customer;

  public CustomerResource() {
    customer = new Customer(1L, "William",
            "Daniel", "Graystone");
  }

  @GET
  @Produces(MediaType.APPLICATION_JSON)
  @Path("{id}/")
  public Customer getCustomer(@PathParam("id") Long id) {
    return customer;
  }
  @PUT
  @Consumes(MediaType.APPLICATION_JSON)
  public void createCustomer(Customer customer) {
    LOG.log(Level.INFO, "customer = {0}", customer);
  }

  @POST
  @Consumes(MediaType.APPLICATION_JSON)
  public void updateCustomer(Customer customer) {
    LOG.log(Level.INFO, "customer= {0}", customer);
  }
```

```
@DELETE
@Consumes(MediaType.APPLICATION_JSON)
@Path("{id}/")
public void deleteCustomer(@PathParam("id") Long id) {
  LOG.log(Level.INFO, "customer = {0}", customer);
}
}
```

Any method that accepts a path parameter must be annotated with the @Path annotation. The value attribute of this annotation must be formatted as "{paramName}/", where paramName is the parameter the method expects to receive. Additionally, method parameters must be decorated with the @PathParam annotation. The value of this annotation must match the parameter name declared in the @Path annotation for the method.

We can pass path parameters from the command line by adjusting our web service's URI as appropriate; for example, to pass an id parameter of 1 to the getCustomer() method (which handles HTTP GET requests), we could do it from the command line as follows:

```
curl -XGET -HContent-type:application/json http://localhost:8080/
pathparams/resources/customer/1
```

This returns the expected output of a JSON representation of the Customer object returned by the getCustomer() method, as seen in the following:

```
{"firstName":"William","id":1,"lastName":"Graystone",
"middleName":"Daniel"}
```

Sending path parameters via the Jakarta REST client API

Sending path parameters to a web service via the Jakarta REST client API is straightforward; all we need to do is add a couple of method invocations to specify the path parameter and its value. The following example illustrates how to do this:

```
package com.ensode.jakartaeebook.pathparamsclient;
//imports omitted for brevity
public class App {
  public static void main(String[] args) {
    App app = new App();
    app.getCustomer();
  }

  public void getCustomer() {
    Client client = ClientBuilder.newClient();
    Customer customer = client.target(
    http://localhost:8080/pathparams/resources/customer
```

```
      "http://localhost:8080/"
        + "pathparams/resources/customer").
      path("{id}").
      resolveTemplate("id", 1L).
      request().get(Customer.class);

      System.out.println("Received the following "
        + "customer information:");
      System.out.println("Id: " + customer.getId());
      System.out.println("First Name: " +
        customer.getFirstName());
      System.out.println("Middle Name: " +
        customer.getMiddleName());
      System.out.println("Last Name: " +
        customer.getLastName());
    }
  }
```

In this example, we invoke the `path()` method on the `WebTarget` instance returned by `client.target()`; this method appends the specified path to our `WebTarget` instance. The value of this method must match the value of the `@Path` annotation in our RESTful web service.

After invoking the `path()` method on our `WebTarget` instance, we then need to invoke `resolveTemplate()`. The first parameter for this method is the name of the parameter (without the curly braces), and the second parameter is the value we wish to pass as a parameter to our RESTful web service.

If we need to pass more than one parameter to one of our web services, we simply need to use the following format for the `@Path` parameter at the method level:

```
@Path("/{paramName1}/{paramName2}/")
```

Then annotate the corresponding method arguments with the `@PathParam` annotation as follows:

```
public String someMethod(
  @PathParam("paramName1") String param1,
  @PathParam("paramName2") String param2)
```

The web service can then be invoked by modifying the web service's URI to pass the parameters in the order specified in the `@Path` annotation. For example, the following URI would pass the values 1 and 2 for `paramName1` and `paramName2`:

```
http://localhost:8080/contextroot/resources/customer/1/2
```

This URI will work either from the command line or through a web service client we develop with the Jakarta REST client API.

All examples we've seen so far involve RESTful web services responding to an HTTP request from the client. We can have our RESTful web services send data to clients without necessarily having to respond to a request; this can be achieved via server-sent events.

Server-sent events

Typically, every interaction between a web service and its client is initiated by the client. The client sends a request (typically GET, POST, PUT, or DELETE), and then receives a response from the server. Server-sent events technology allows RESTful web services to "take the initiative" to send messages to clients; that is, to send data that is not a response to a client request. Server-sent events are useful for sending data continuously to a client for applications such as stock tickers, newsfeeds, and sports scores.

The following example illustrates how to implement this functionality into our Jakarta REST web services:

```
package com.ensode.jakartaeebook.serversentevents
// imports omitted for brevity

@ApplicationScoped
@Path("serversentevents")
public class SseResource {
  private  SseBroadcaster sseBroadcaster;
  private OutboundSseEvent.Builder eventBuilder;
  private ScheduledExecutorService scheduledExecutorService;
  private Double stockValue = 10.0;
  //initialization and cleanup methods omitted for brevity
  @Context
  public void setSse(Sse sse) {
    this.eventBuilder = sse.newEventBuilder();
    this.sseBroadcaster = sse.newBroadcaster();
  }

  @GET
  @Path("subscribe")
  @Produces(MediaType.SERVER_SENT_EVENTS)
  public void subscribe(@Context SseEventSink sseEventSink) {
    LOG.info(String.format("%s.subscribe() invoked",
      this.getClass().getName()));
    this.sseBroadcaster.register(sseEventSink);
  }

  public void sendEvents() {
    scheduledExecutorService.scheduleAtFixedRate(() -> {
      final OutboundSseEvent outboundSseEvent = eventBuilder
```

```
        .name("ENSD stock ticker value")
        .data(String.class, String.format("%.2f",
          stockValue))
        .build();
    LOG.info(String.format("broadcasting event: %.2f",
      stockValue));
    sseBroadcaster.broadcast(outboundSseEvent);
    stockValue += 0.9;
  }, 5, 5, TimeUnit.SECONDS);
  }
}
```

The preceding example simulates sending stock prices for a fictitious company to the client. To send server-sent events to the client, we need to utilize instances of the `SseEventSink` and `Sse` classes, as illustrated in our example.

We can inject an instance of `Sse` by creating a setter method and annotating it with the `@Context` annotation. We never invoke this setter method directly; instead, the Jakarta EE runtime invokes it, passing an instance of `Sse` we can use to send our events. We then invoke `newEventBuilder()` and `newBroadCaster()` methods on the injected `Sse` instance to obtain `OutboundSseEvent.Builder` and `SseBroadcaster` instances, which we will need to create and broadcast events.

In order to receive events, clients need to register with our Jakarta REST service; we implemented an endpoint in the `subscribe()` method of our example for this purpose. This endpoint has a "subscribe" path; clients sending an HTTP GET request to this endpoint will be subscribed to receive events from our service. Notice we annotated the `SseEventSink` parameter in our `subscribe()` method with `@Context`; this results in the Jakarta EE runtime injecting an `SseEventSink` instance we can use to register the client. We accomplish this by invoking the `broadcast()` method on our `SseBroadCaster` instance, and passing the injected `SseEventSink` instance as a parameter.

To broadcast an event, we first need to build an instance of `OutboundSseEvent` via our instance of `OutboundSseEvent.Builder`.

We give our event a name by invoking the `name()` method on our `OutboundSseEvent.Builder` instance, then set the data to send to the client via its `data()` method. The `data()` method takes two arguments; the first one is the type of data we are sending to the client (`String`, in our case), and the second one is the actual data we send to the client.

Once we have set our event's name and data via the corresponding method, we build an `OutboundSseEvent` instance by invoking the `build()` method on `OutboundSseEvent.Builder`.

Once we have built our `OutboundSseEvent` instance, we send it to the client by passing it as a parameter to the `broadcast()` method of `SseBroadcaster`. In our example, we calculate a new value for the simulated stock price (for simplicity, we simply increase the value by 0.9), and broadcast a new event with the updated value every five seconds.

Testing server-sent events

We can make sure our server-sent events are working properly by using `curl`; we can simply send an HTTP GET request to the endpoint we created for clients to subscribe to our events as follows:

```
curl -XGET http://localhost:8080/serversentevents/resources/
serversentevents/subscribe
```

As soon as we run this, we should see the output in the application server log confirming that the `subscribe()` method was invoked:

```
com.ensode.jakartaeebook.serversentevents.SseResource.subscribe()
invoked|#]
```

Within five seconds, we should start seeing output from `curl` indicating it is receiving events:

```
event: ENSD stock ticker value
data: 10.00

event: ENSD stock ticker value
data: 10.90

event: ENSD stock ticker value
data: 11.80
```

The value next to the `event` label is the name we gave to our event. `data` is the actual value we sent from our service as the event data.

By testing our server-sent events code with `curl`, we can rest assured that our server-side code is working properly. That way, if things are not working properly when developing a client, we can eliminate the server as a "suspect" when debugging our code.

Developing a server-sent events client

The Jakarta REST client API provides a way to consume server-sent events. The following example illustrates how to do this:

```
package com.ensode.jakartaeebook.serversenteventsclient;

//imports omitted for brevity

public class App {
  public static void main(String[] args) {
    App app = new App();
    app.listenForEvents();
  }
```

```java
public void listenForEvents() {
  final SseEventSource.Builder sseEventSourceBuilder;
  final SseEventSource sseEventSource;

  final Client client = ClientBuilder.newClient();
  final WebTarget webTarget = client.target(
    "http://localhost:8080/serversentevents/"
      + "resources/serversentevents/subscribe");

  sseEventSourceBuilder =
    SseEventSource.target(webTarget);
  sseEventSource = sseEventSourceBuilder.build();

  sseEventSource.register((inboundSseEvent) -> {
    System.out.println("Received the following event:");
    System.out.println(String.format("Event name: %s",
      inboundSseEvent.getName()));
    System.out.println(String.format("Event data: %s\n",
      inboundSseEvent.readData()));
  });

  sseEventSource.open();
  }
}
```

First, we need to obtain a `jakarta.ws.rs.client.Client` instance by invoking the static `ClientBuilder.newClient()` method.

We then obtain an instance of `jakarta.ws.rs.client.WebTarget` by invoking the `target()` method on the `Client` instance we retrieved in the previous step, and passing the URI of the endpoint we created for clients to subscribe as a parameter.

The next step is to obtain an `SseEventSource.Builder` instance by invoking the static `SseEventSource.target()` method, and passing our `WebTarget` instance as a parameter.

We then get an `SseEventSource` instance by invoking the `build()` method on our instance of `SseEventSource.Builder`.

Next, we register our client by invoking the `register()` method on our `sseEventSource` instance. This method takes an implementation of the functional interface `java.util.function.Consumer` as a parameter; for convenience, we implement this interface inline as a lambda expression. In our example, we simply output the event name and data we received to the console, via simple `System.out.println()` invocations.

Finally, we open the connection to our RESTful web service by invoking the `open()` method on our `SseEventSource` instance.

When we run our client, we see the expected output:

```
Received the following event:
Event name: ENSD stock ticker value
Event data: 10.00

Received the following event:
Event name: ENSD stock ticker value
Event data: 10.90

Received the following event:
Event name: ENSD stock ticker value
Event data: 11.80
```

For simplicity, our example is a stand-alone Java application we can run on the command line; the same principles apply when developing RESTful web services that act as clients for other RESTful web services.

JavaScript server-sent events client

So far, all of our client examples have either used the `curl` command-line utility or the Jakarta REST client API. It is very common to use JavaScript code running on a browser as a RESTful web service; therefore, in this section, we will take that approach. The following example illustrates an HTML/JavaScript client receiving server-sent events:

```html
<!DOCTYPE html>
<html>
    <head>
        <title>Stock Ticker Monitor</title>
        <meta http-equiv="Content-Type" content="text/html;
          charset=UTF-8">
    </head>
    <body onload="getStockTickerValues()">
        <h2>Super fancy stock ticker monitor</h2>
        <table cellspacing="0" cellpadding="0">
            <tr>
                <td>ENSD Stock Ticker Value: </td>
                <td> <span id="stickerVal"></span></td>
            </tr>
            <tr>
                <td></td><td><button>Buy!</button></td>
```

```
        </tr>
      </table>
      <script>
        function getStockTickerValues() {
          var source = new EventSource(
            "resources/serversentevents/subscribe");

          source.addEventListener(
            'ENSD stock ticker value', function (e) {
              console.log('event received', e);
              document.getElementById(
                "stickerVal").innerHTML =
                event.data;
          });
        }
      </script>
    </body>
</html>
```

The `getStockTickerValues()` JavaScript function creates an `EventSource` object. This constructor takes a `String` representing the URL used to subscribe to receive events as a parameter. In our case, we used a relative URL since the preceding HTML/JavaScript code is hosted in the same server as the server code; if this wasn't the case, we would have needed to use a complete URL.

We implement the functionality to be executed when the client receives an event by adding an event listener to our `EventSource` instance via its `addEventListener()` function. This function takes the event name (notice that the value matches the name we sent in the Java code for our RESTful web service), and a function to be executed when an event is received. In our example, we simply update the contents of a `<span>` tag with the data of the received message.

Summary

In this chapter, we discussed how to easily develop RESTful web services using Jakarta REST.

We covered the following topics:

- How to develop a RESTful web service by adding a few simple annotations to our code

- How to automatically generate JSON data

- How to automatically parse JSON data it receives as a request

- How to pass parameters to our RESTful web services via the `@PathParam` and `@QueryParam` annotations

- How to implement server-sent events and server-sent event clients

RESTful web services have become immensely popular in recent years; they are now the preferred way of developing web applications and are also heavily used when developing applications utilizing a microservices architecture. As seen in this chapter, Jakarta EE allows us to implement RESTful web services by adding a few simple annotations to our Java classes.

4

JSON Processing and JSON Binding

JavaScript Object Notation (**JSON**) is a human-readable data interchange format. As its name implies, JSON is derived from JavaScript. Jakarta EE provides support for two different APIs for JSON manipulation, namely **Jakarta JSON Processing**, which is a lower-level API allowing fine-grained control, and **Jakarta JSON Binding**, which is a higher-level API that allows us to easily populate Java objects from JSON data, as well as quickly generate JSON-formatted data from Java objects. In this chapter, we will cover both JSON Processing and JSON Binding.

JSON Processing includes two APIs for processing JSON: the **Model API** and the **Streaming API**. Both of these APIs will be covered in this chapter. JSON Binding transparently populates Java objects from JSON strings, as well as easily generates JSON strings from Java objects.

In this chapter, we will cover the following topics:

- Jakarta JSON Processing
- Jakarta JSON binding

> **Note**
>
> Example source code for this chapter can be found on GitHub at `https://github.com/PacktPublishing/Jakarta-EE-Application-Development/tree/main/ch04_src`.

Jakarta JSON Processing

In the following sections, we will discuss how to process JSON data using the two APIs provided by Jakarta JSON Processing, namely the Model and Streaming APIs. We will also discuss how to retrieve values from JSON data using JSON Pointer, as well as how to partially modify JSON data via JSON Patch.

The JSON Processing Model API

The JSON Processing Model API allows us to generate an in-memory representation of a JSON object. This API is more flexible than the Streaming API discussed later in this chapter. However, it is slower and requires more memory, which can be a concern when handling large volumes of data.

Generating JSON data with the Model API

At the heart of the JSON Processing Model API is the `JsonObjectBuilder` class. This class has several overloaded `add()` methods that can be used to add properties and their corresponding values to the generated JSON data.

The following code sample illustrates how to generate JSON data using the Model API:

```
package com.ensode.jakartaeebook.jsonpobject;
//imports omitted for brevity

@Path("jsonpmodel")
public class JsonPModelResource {

  private static final Logger LOG =
    Logger.getLogger(JsonPModelResource.class.getName());

  @Path("build")
  @GET
  @Produces(MediaType.APPLICATION_JSON)
  public String jsonpModelBuildJson() {
    JsonObject jsonObject = Json.createObjectBuilder().
      add("firstName", "Scott").
      add("lastName", "Gosling").
      add("email", "sgosling@example.com").
      build();
    StringWriter stringWriter = new StringWriter();
    try (JsonWriter jsonWriter = Json.createWriter(
      stringWriter)) {
      jsonWriter.writeObject(jsonObject);
    }
```

```
    return stringWriter.toString();
  }
}
```

As can be seen in the example, we generate an instance of `JsonObject` by invoking the `add()` method on an instance of `JsonObjectBuilder`. In our example, we see how we can add `String` values to our `JsonObject` by invoking the `add()` method on `JsonObjectBuilder`. The first parameter of the `add()` method is the property name of the generated JSON object, and the second parameter corresponds to the value of the said property. The return value of the `add()` method is another instance of `JsonObjectBuilder`; therefore, invocations to the `add()` method can be chained as shown in the example.

> **Note**
>
> The preceding example is a RESTful web service corresponding to a larger Jakarta RESTful Web Services application. Other parts of the application are not shown since they are not relevant to the discussion. The complete sample application can be obtained from this book's GitHub repository at `https://github.com/PacktPublishing/Jakarta-EE-Application-Development`.

Once we have added all the desired properties, we need to invoke the `build()` method of `JsonObjectBuilder`, which returns an instance of a class implementing the `JsonObject` interface.

In many cases, we will want to generate a `String` representation of the JSON object we created, so that it can be processed by another process or service. We can do this by creating an instance of a class implementing the `JsonWriter` interface, by invoking the static `createWriter()` method of the `Json` class, passing an instance of `StringWriter` as its sole parameter. Once we have an instance of the `JsonWriter` implementation, we need to invoke its `writeObject()` method, passing our `JsonObject` instance as its sole parameter.

At this point, our `StringWriter` instance will have the `String` representation of our JSON object as its value, so invoking its `toString()` method will return a `String` containing our JSON object.

Our specific example will generate a JSON string that looks like this:

```
{"firstName":"Scott","lastName":"Gosling","email":"sgosling@example.
com"}
```

Although in our example we added only `String` objects to our JSON object, we are not limited to this type of value; `JsonObjectBuilder` has several overloaded versions of its `add()` method, allowing us to add several different types of values to our JSON objects.

The following table summarizes all of the available versions of the add() method:

JsonObjectBuilder.add() method	Description
add(String name, BigDecimal value)	Adds a BigDecimal value to our JSON object.
add(String name, BigInteger value)	Adds a BigInteger value to our JSON object.
add(String name, JsonArrayBuilder value)	Adds an array to our JSON object. A JsonArrayBuilder implementation allows us to create JSON arrays.
add(String name, JsonObjectBuilder value)	Adds another JSON object to our original JSON object (property values for JSON objects can be other JSON objects). The added JsonObject implementation is built from the provided JsonObjectBuilder parameter.
add(String name, JsonValue value)	Adds another JSON object to our original JSON object (property values for JSON objects can be other JSON objects).
add(String name, String value)	Adds a String value to our JSON object.
add(String name, boolean value)	Adds a boolean value to our JSON object.
add(String name, double value)	Adds a double value to our JSON object.
add(String name, int value)	Adds an int value to our JSON object.
add(String name, long value)	Adds a long value to our JSON object.

Table 4.1 – JsonObjectBuilder add() methods

In all cases, the first parameter of the add() method corresponds to the name of the property in our JSON object, and the second parameter corresponds to the value of the property.

Parsing JSON data with the Model API

In the last section, we saw how to generate JSON data from our Java code with the object model API. In this section, we will see how we can read and parse existing JSON data. The following code sample illustrates how to do this:

```
package com.ensode.jakartaeebook.jsonpobject;
//imports omitted for brevity

@Path("jsonpmodel")
public class JsonPModelResource {
```

```
@Path("parse")
@POST
@Produces(MediaType.TEXT_PLAIN)
@Consumes(MediaType.APPLICATION_JSON)
public String jsonpModelParseJson(String jsonStr) {
  LOG.log(Level.INFO, String.format(
    "received the following JSON string: %s", jsonStr));
  Customer customer = new Customer();

  JsonObject jsonObject;
  try (JsonReader jsonReader = Json.createReader(new
  StringReader(jsonStr))) {
    jsonObject = jsonReader.readObject();
  }
  customer.setFirstName(
    jsonObject.getString("firstName"));
  customer.setLastName(jsonObject.getString("lastName"));
  customer.setEmail(jsonObject.getString("email"));

  return customer.toString();
  }
}
```

To parse an existing JSON string, we need to create a `StringReader` object, passing the `String` object containing the JSON to be parsed as a parameter. We then pass the resulting `StringReader` instance to the static `createReader()` method of the `Json` class. This method invocation will return an instance of `JsonReader`. We can then obtain an instance of `JsonObject` by invoking the `readObject()` method on it.

In this example, we use the `getString()` method to obtain the values for all properties in our JSON object. The first and only argument for this method is the name of the property we wish to retrieve; unsurprisingly, the return value is the value of the property.

In addition to the `getString()` method, there are several other similar methods to obtain values of other types. The following table summarizes these methods:

JsonObject method	Description
get(Object key)	Retrieves an instance of a class implementing the JsonValue interface
getBoolean(String name)	Retrieves a boolean value corresponding to the given key
getInt(String name)	Retrieves an int value corresponding to the given key
getJsonArray(String name)	Retrieves the instance of a class implementing the JsonArray interface corresponding to the given key

JsonObject method	Description
getJsonNumber(String name)	Retrieves the instance of a class implementing the JsonNumber interface corresponding to the given key
getJsonObject(String name)	Retrieves the instance of a class implementing the JsonObject interface corresponding to the given key
getJsonString(String name)	Retrieves the instance of a class implementing the JsonString interface corresponding to the given key
getString(String Name)	Retrieves a String corresponding to the given key

Table 4.2 – JsonObject methods to retrieve values from JSON data

In all cases, the String parameter of the method corresponds to the key name, and the return value is the JSON property value we wish to retrieve.

The JSON Processing Streaming API

The JSON Processing Streaming API allows sequential reading of a JSON object from a stream (a subclass of java.io.OutputStream or a subclass of java.io.Writer). It is faster and more memory efficient than the Model API; however, the trade-off is that it is less straightforward to access specific JSON properties directly when compared to the Model API. When using the Streaming API, we need to use JSON Pointer and JSON Patch to retrieve or modify specific values from JSON data.

Generating JSON data with the streaming API

The JSON Streaming API has a JsonGenerator class we can use to generate JSON data and write it to a stream. This class has several overloaded write() methods that can be used to add properties and their corresponding values to the generated JSON data.

The following code sample illustrates how to generate JSON data using the Streaming API:

```
package com.ensode.jakartaeebook.jsonpstreaming;
//imports omitted for brevity
@Path("jsonpstreaming")
public class JsonPStreamingResource {

    @Path("build")
    @GET
    @Produces(MediaType.APPLICATION_JSON)
    public String buildJson() {

        StringWriter stringWriter = new StringWriter();
        try (JsonGenerator jsonGenerator =
```

```
      Json.createGenerator(stringWriter)) {
      jsonGenerator.writeStartObject().
        write("firstName", "Larry").
        write("lastName", "Gates").
        write("email", "lgates@example.com").
        writeEnd();
    }

    return stringWriter.toString();
  }
}
```

We create an instance of `JsonGenerator` by invoking the `createGenerator()` static method of the `Json` class. The JSON Processing API provides two overloaded versions of this method; one takes an instance of a class that extends `java.io.Writer` (such as `StringWriter`, which we used in our example), and the other one takes an instance of a class that extends `java.io.OutputStream`.

Before we can start adding properties to the generated JSON stream, we need to invoke the `writeStartObject()` method on `JsonGenerator`. This method writes the JSON start object character (represented by an opening curly brace ({) in JSON strings) and returns another instance of `JsonGenerator`, allowing us to chain `write()` invocations to add properties to our JSON stream.

The `write()` method on `JsonGenerator` allows us to add properties to the JSON stream we are generating; its first parameter is a `String` corresponding to the name of the property we are adding, and the second parameter is the value of the property.

In our example, we are adding only `String` values to the JSON stream we are creating. However, we are not limited to strings; the Streaming API provides several overloaded `write()` methods that allow us to add several different types of data to our JSON stream. The following table summarizes all of the available versions of the `write()` method:

`JsonGenerator.write()` method	Description
`write(String name, BigDecimal value)`	Writes a `BigDecimal` value to our JSON stream
`write(String name, BigInteger value)`	Writes a `BigInteger` value to our JSON stream
`write(String name, JsonValue value)`	Writes a JSON object to our JSON stream (property values for JSON streams can be other JSON objects)
`write(String name, String value)`	Writes a `String` value to our JSON stream
`write(String name, boolean value)`	Writes a `boolean` value to our JSON stream

`JsonGenerator.write() method`	Description
`write(String name, double value)`	Writes a `double` value to our JSON stream
`write(String name, int value)`	Writes an `int` value to our JSON stream
`write(String name, long value)`	Writes a `long` value to our JSON stream

Table 4.3 – JsonGenerator write() method

In all cases, the first parameter of the `write()` method corresponds to the name of the property we are adding to our JSON stream, and the second parameter corresponds to the value of the property.

Once we are done adding properties to our JSON stream, we need to invoke the `writeEnd()` method on `JsonGenerator`; this method adds the JSON end object character (represented by a closing curly brace (}) in JSON strings).

At this point, our stream or reader is populated with the JSON data we generated. What we do with it depends on our application logic. In our example, we simply invoked the `toString()` method of our `StringReader` to obtain the `String` representation of the JSON data we created.

Parsing JSON data with the streaming API

In this section, we will cover how to parse JSON data we receive from a stream.

The following example illustrates how we can populate Java objects from JSON data using the streaming API.

```
package com.ensode.jakartaeebook.jsonpstreaming;
//imports omitted for brevity

@Path("jsonpstreaming")
public class JsonPStreamingResource {

    @Path("parse")
    @POST
    @Produces(MediaType.TEXT_PLAIN)
    @Consumes(MediaType.APPLICATION_JSON)
    public String parseJson(String jsonStr) {
        Customer customer = new Customer();
        StringReader stringReader = new StringReader(jsonStr);
        JsonParser jsonParser = Json.createParser(stringReader);
        Map<String, String> keyValueMap = new HashMap<>();
```

```
      String key = null;
      String value = null;

      while (jsonParser.hasNext()) {
        JsonParser.Event event = jsonParser.next();

        if (event.equals(Event.KEY_NAME)) {
          key = jsonParser.getString();
        } else if (event.equals(Event.VALUE_STRING)) {
          value = jsonParser.getString();
        }
        keyValueMap.put(key, value);
      }
      customer.setFirstName(keyValueMap.get("firstName"));
      customer.setLastName(keyValueMap.get("lastName"));
      customer.setEmail(keyValueMap.get("email"));
      return customer.toString();
    }
  }
```

The first thing we need to do to read JSON data using the Streaming API is to create an instance of `JsonParser` by invoking the static `createJsonParser()` method on the `Json` class. There are two overloaded versions of the `createJsonParser()` method: one takes an instance of a class that extends `java.io.InputStream`, and the other one takes an instance of a class that extends `java.io.Reader`. In our example, we use the latter, passing an instance of `java.io.StringReader`, which is a subclass of `java.io.Reader`.

The next step is to loop through the JSON data to obtain the data to be parsed. We can achieve this by invoking the `hasNext()` method on `JsonParser`, which returns true if there is more data to be read, and false otherwise.

We then need to read the next piece of data in our stream, the `JsonParser.next()` method returns an instance of `JsonParser.Event` that indicates the type of data that we just read. In our example, we check only for key names (i.e., `firstName`, `lastName`, and `email`), and the corresponding string values. We check for the type of data we just read by comparing the event returned by `JsonParser.next()` against several values defined in `JsonParser.Event`.

The following table summarizes all of the possible events that can be returned from `JsonParser.next()`:

JsonParser Event	Description
Event.START_OBJECT	Indicates the start of a JSON object
Event.END_OBJECT	Indicates the end of a JSON object
Event.START_ARRAY	Indicates the start of an array

JsonParser Event	Description
Event.END_ARRAY	Indicates the end of an array
Event.KEY_NAME	Indicates the name of a JSON property was read; we can obtain the key name by invoking getString() on JsonParser
Event.VALUE_TRUE	Indicates that a Boolean value of true was read
Event.VALUE_FALSE	Indicates that a Boolean value of false was read
Event.VALUE_NULL	Indicates that a null value was read
Event.VALUE_NUMBER	Indicates that a numeric value was read
Event.VALUE_STRING	Indicates that a string value was read

Table 4.4 – JsonParser events

As shown in the example, String values can be retrieved by invoking getString() on JsonParser. Numeric values can be retrieved in several different formats. The following table summarizes the methods in JsonParser that can be used to retrieve numeric values:

JsonParser method	Description
getInt()	Retrieves the numeric value as an int
getLong()	Retrieves the numeric value as a long
getBigDecimal()	Retrieves the numeric value as an instance of java.math.BigDecimal

Table 4.5 – JsonParser methods used to retrieve numeric values

JsonParser also provides a convenient isIntegralNumber() method that returns true if the numeric value can be safely cast to an int or long.

What we do with the values we obtain from the stream depends on our application logic; in our example, we place them in a Map and then use said Map to populate a Java class.

Retrieving values from data with JSON Pointer

Jakarta JSON Processing supports JSON Pointer, an **Internet Engineering Task Force (IETF)** standard that defines a string syntax for identifying a specific value within a JSON document, similar to what XPath provides for XML documents.

The syntax for JSON Pointer is straightforward. For example, let us suppose that we have the following JSON document:

```
{
  "dateOfBirth": "1997-03-03",
  "firstName": "David",
```

```
    "lastName": "Heffelfinger",
    "middleName": "Raymond",
    "salutation": "Mr"
}
```

If we would like to obtain the value of the lastName property of the document, the JSON Pointer expression to use would be "/lastName".

If our JSON document consisted of an array, then we would have to prefix the property with the index in the array; for example, say we want to obtain the lastName property of the second element in the following JSON array:

```
[
    {
        "dateOfBirth": "1997-01-01",
        "firstName": "David",
        "lastName": "Delabassee",
        "salutation": "Mr"
    },
    {
        "dateOfBirth": "1997-03-03",
        "firstName": "David",
        "lastName": "Heffelfinger",
        "middleName": "Raymond",
        "salutation": "Mr"
    }
]
```

The JSON Pointer expression to do so would be "/1/lastName". The "/1" at the beginning of the expression refers to the element index in the array. Just like in Java, JSON arrays are 0 indexed; therefore, in this example, we are obtaining the value of the lastName property in the second element of the array. Let's now look at an example of how we would use the JSON Pointer API to perform this task:

```
package com.ensode.jakartaeebook.jsonpointer;
//imports omitted for brevity
@Path("jsonpointer")
public class JsonPointerDemoService {

  private String jsonString; //initialization omitted

  @GET
  @Produces(MediaType.TEXT_PLAIN)
  public String jsonPointerDemo() {
    JsonReader jsonReader = Json.createReader(
```

```
        new StringReader(jsonString));
        JsonArray jsonArray = jsonReader.readArray();
        JsonPointer jsonPointer = Json.createPointer("/1/lastName");

        return jsonPointer.getValue(jsonArray).toString();
    }
}
```

The preceding code sample is a RESTful web service written using Jakarta RESTful Web Services. In order to read property values from a JSON document, we first need to create an instance of `jakarta.json.JsonReader` by invoking the static `createReader()` method on `jakarta.json.Json.createReader()`. This takes an instance of any class implementing the `java.io.Reader` interface as an argument. In our example, we are creating a new instance of `java.io.StringReader` on the fly and passing our JSON string as a parameter to its constructor.

> **Note**
>
> There is an overloaded version of `JSON.createReader()` that takes an instance of any class implementing `java.io.InputStream`.

In our example, our JSON document consists of an array of objects; therefore, we populate an instance of `jakarta.json.JsonArray` by invoking the `readArray()` method on the `JsonReader` object we created. (If our JSON document had consisted of a single JSON object, we would have invoked `JsonReader.readObject()` instead.)

Now that we have populated our `JsonArray` variable, we create an instance of `jakarta.json.JsonPointer`, and initialize it with the JSON Pointer expression we want to use to obtain the value we are searching for. Recall we are looking for the value of the `lastName` property in the second element of the array; therefore, the appropriate JSON Pointer expression is `/1/lastName`.

Now that we have created an instance of `JsonPointer` with the appropriate JSON Pointer expression, we simply invoke its `getValue()` method, passing our `JsonArray` object as a parameter; then, we invoke `toString()` on the result, and the return value of this invocation will be the value of the `lastName` property on the JSON document `"Heffelfinger`, in our example).

Updating JSON data values with JSON Patch

Jakarta JSON Processing includes support for JSON Patch, another IETF standard. This one provides a series of operations that can be applied to a JSON document. JSON Patch allows us to perform partial updates on a JSON object.

The following operations are supported by JSON Patch:

JSON Patch Operation	Description
add	Adds an element to a JSON document
remove	Removes an element from a JSON document
replace	Replaces a value in a JSON document with a new value
move	Moves a value in a JSON document from its current location in the document to a new position
copy	Copies a value in a JSON document to a new location in the document
test	Verifies that the value in a specific location in a JSON document is equal to the specified value

Table 4.6 – JSON Patch operations

Jakarta JSON Processing supports all of the preceding JSON Patch operations, which rely on JSON Pointer expressions to locate source and target locations in JSON documents.

The following example illustrates how we can use JSON Patch with Jakarta JSON Processing:

```
package com.ensode.jakartaeebook.jsonpatch

//imports omitted for brevity

@Path("jsonpatch")
public class JsonPatchDemoService {

  private String jsonString; //initialization omitted

  @GET
  public Response jsonPatchDemo() {
    JsonReader jsonReader = Json.createReader(
      new StringReader(jsonString));
    JsonArray jsonArray = jsonReader.readArray();
    JsonPatch jsonPatch = Json.createPatchBuilder()
      .replace("/1/dateOfBirth", "1977-01-01")
      .build();
    JsonArray modifiedJsonArray = jsonPatch.apply(
      jsonArray);

    return Response.ok(modifiedJsonArray.toString(),
      MediaType.APPLICATION_JSON).build();
  }
}
```

In this example, let's assume we are dealing with the same JSON document we used in our previous example, an array of two individual JSON objects, each with a `dateOfBirth` property (among other properties).

In our example, we create an instance of `JsonArray` as before and then modify the `dateOfBirth` of the second element in the array. In order to do this, we create an instance of `jakarta.json.JsonPatchBuilder` via the static `createPatchBuilder()` method in the `jakarta.json.Json` class. In our example, we are replacing the value of one of the properties with a new value; we use the `replace()` method of our `JsonPatch` instance to accomplish this. The first argument in the method is a JSON Pointer expression indicating the location of the property we are going to modify, and the second argument is the new value for the property. As its name implies, `JsonPatchBuilder` follows the `Builder` design pattern, meaning that most of its methods return another instance of `JsonPatchBuilder`; this allows us to chain method calls on the resulting instances of `JsonPatchBuilder` (in our example, we are performing only one operation, but this doesn't have to be the case). Once we are done specifying the operation(s) to perform on our JSON object, we create an instance of `jakarta.json.JsonPatch` by invoking the `build()` method on `JsonPatchBuilder`.

Once we have created the patch, we apply it to our JSON object (an instance of `JsonArray`, in our example) by invoking its `patch()` method and passing the JSON object as a parameter.

Our example shows how to replace the value of a JSON property with another via JSON Patch support in Jakarta JSON-Processing. All standard JSON Patch operations are supported by Jakarta JSONProcessing. For details on how to use other JSON Patch operations with JSON Processing, consult the Jakarta EE API documentation at `https://jakarta.ee/specifications/platform/10/apidocs/`.

Now that we've seen how to directly manipulate JSON data with JSON Processing, we will focus our attention on how to bind JSON data with Jakarta JSON Binding, a higher-level API that allows us to do common tasks quickly and easily.

Jakarta JSON Binding

Jakarta JSON Binding is a high-level API that allows us to almost seamlessly populate Java objects from JSON data, as well as easily generate JSON-formatted data from Java objects.

Populating Java objects from JSON with JSON Binding

A common programming task is to populate Java objects from JSON strings. It is such a common task that several libraries were created to transparently populate Java objects from JSON, freeing application developers from having to manually code this functionality. Several non-standard Java libraries that accomplish this task exist, such as Jackson (`https://github.com/FasterXML/jackson`), json-simple (`https://code.google.com/archive/p/json-simple/`), or Gson (`https://github.com/google/gson`). Jakarta EE includes a standard API providing this functionality, namely JSON Binding. In this section, we will cover how to transparently populate a Java object from a JSON string.

The following example shows a RESTful web service written using Jakarta RESTful Web Services. The service responds to HTTP POST requests in its addCustomer() method. The addCustomer() method takes a String as a parameter; it is expected for this string to contain valid JSON:

```
package com.ensode.jakartaeebook.jsonbjsontojava.service;
//imports omitted for brevity

@Path("/customercontroller")
public class CustomerControllerService {
  @POST
  @Consumes(MediaType.APPLICATION_JSON)
  public String addCustomer(String customerJson) {
    Jsonb jsonb = JsonbBuilder.create();
    Customer customer = jsonb.fromJson(customerJson,
      Customer.class);
    return customer.toString();
  }
}
```

The JSON Binding implementation provided by our application server provides an instance of a class implementing the JsonbBuilder interface; this class provides a static create() method that we can use to obtain an instance of Jsonb.

Once we have an instance of Jsonb, we can use it to parse a JSON string and automatically populate a Java object. This is done via its fromJson() method. The fromJson() method takes a String containing the JSON data we need to parse as its first parameter and the type of object we wish to populate as its second parameter. In our example, we are populating a simple Customer class containing fields such as firstName, middleName, lastName, and dateOfBirth. Jakarta JSON Binding will look for JSON property names matching the property names in the Java object, and automatically populate the Java object with the corresponding JSON properties. It couldn't get more simple than that!

Once we have populated our Java object, we can do whatever we need to do with it. In our example, we simply return a String representation of our Customer object to the client.

Generating JSON data from Java objects with JSON Binding

In addition to populating Java objects from JSON data, JSON Binding can also generate JSON strings from Java objects. The following example illustrates how to do this:

```
package com.ensode.jakartaeebook.jsonbjavatojson.service;
//imports omitted for brevity

@Path("/customercontroller")
public class CustomerControllerService {
  @GET
```

```java
public String getCustomerAsJson() {
  String jsonString;
  DateTimeFormatter dateTimeFormatter =
    DateTimeFormatter.ofPattern("d/MM/yyyy");

  Customer customer = new Customer("Mr", "David",
    "Raymond", "Heffelfinger",
    LocalDate.parse("03/03/1997", dateTimeFormatter));
  Jsonb jsonb = JsonbBuilder.create();

  jsonString = jsonb.toJson(customer);

  return jsonString;
  }
}
```

In this example, we are generating JSON data from a `Customer` object.

Just like before, we create an instance of `jakarta.json.bind.Jsonb` by invoking the static `jakarta.json.bind.JsonbBuilder.create()` method. Once we have our `Jsonb` instance, we simply invoke its `toJson()` method to convert the list of objects to its equivalent JSON representation.

Summary

In this chapter, we covered how to process JSON data using two Jakarta EE APIs, JSON Processing and JSON Binding.

We covered the following topics:

- We saw how we can generate and parse JSON data with JSON Processing's model API

- We also explored how to generate and parse JSON data with JSON Processing's streaming API

- Additionally, we covered how to extract values from JSON data with JSON Pointer

- Also, we saw how to update specific values in JSON data with JSON Patch

- Finally, we covered how to use Jakarta JSON Binding to easily populate Java objects from JSON data, as well as easily generate JSON data from Java objects

JSON-formatted data has become a de facto standard when working with RESTful web services and microservices. Jakarta JSON Processing and JSON Binding APIs provide excellent support for working with JSON-formatted data, as illustrated in this chapter.

5

Microservices Development with Jakarta EE

Microservices is an architectural style in which code is deployed in small, granular modules. The microservices architecture reduces coupling and increases cohesion. Typically, microservices are implemented as RESTful web services, using JSON to pass data to one another, by invoking HTTP methods (GET, POST, PUT or DELETE) on each other. Since communication between microservices is done via HTTP methods, microservices written in different programming languages can interact with each other. In this chapter, we will cover how we can use Jakarta EE to implement microservices.

In this chapter, we will cover the following topics:

- An introduction to microservices

- Microservices and Jakarta EE

- Developing microservices using Jakarta EE

> **Note**
>
> Example source code for this chapter can be found on GitHub at `https://github.com/PacktPublishing/Jakarta-EE-Application-Development/tree/main/ch05_src`.

An introduction to microservices

Architecting applications as a series of microservices offers some advantages over traditionally designed applications, as well as some disadvantages. When considering a microservices architecture for our applications, we must carefully weigh the advantages and disadvantages before we make our decision.

The advantages of a microservices architecture

Developing an application as a series of microservices offers several advantages over traditionally designed applications, such as the following:

- **Smaller code bases**: Since each microservice is a small, standalone unit, code bases for microservices tend to be smaller and easier to manage than traditionally designed applications.

- **Microservices encourage good coding practices**: A microservices architecture encourages loose coupling and high cohesion.

- **Greater resilience**: Traditionally designed applications act as a single point of failure; if any component of an application is down or unavailable, the whole application is unavailable. Since microservices are independent modules, one component (i.e., one microservice) being down does not necessarily make the whole application unavailable.

- **Scalability**: Since applications developed as a series of microservices are composed of a number of different modules, scalability becomes easier. We can focus only on those services that may need scaling, without having to waste effort on parts of an application that do not need to be scaled.

The disadvantages of a microservices architecture

Developing and deploying applications adhering to microservices architecture comes with its own set of challenges, regardless of what programming language or application framework is used to develop an application:

- **Additional operational and tooling overhead**: Each microservice implementation would require its own (possibly automated) deployment, monitoring systems, and so on.

- **Debugging microservices may be more involved than debugging traditional enterprise applications**: If an end user reports a problem with their application and the application utilizes multiple microservices internally, it is not always clear which of the microservices may be the culprit. This may be especially difficult if the microservices involved are developed by different teams with different priorities.

- **Distributed transactions may be a challenge**: Rolling back a transaction involving several microservices may be hard. A common approach to work around this is to isolate microservices as much as possible, treat them as single units, and then have local transaction management for each microservice. For example, if microservice A invokes microservice B and there is a problem with the latter, a local transaction in microservice B would roll back. Then, it would return a 500 HTTP status code (server error) to microservice A. It could then use this HTTP status code as a signal to initiate a compensating transaction, restoring the system to its initial state.

- **Network latency**: Since microservices rely on HTTP method calls for communication, performance may suffer due to network latency.

- **The potential for complex interdependencies**: While independent microservices tend to be simple, they are dependent on each other. A microservices architecture can potentially create a complex dependency graph. This situation can be worrisome if some of our services depend on microservices developed by other teams that may have conflicting priorities (i.e., we find a bug in their microservice, but fixing the bug may not be a priority for the other team).

- **Susceptibility to the fallacies of distributed computing**: Applications developed following a microservices architecture may make some incorrect assumptions, such as network reliability, zero latency, and infinite bandwidth.

Now that we've talked about microservices in general, we'll focus our attention on how Jakarta EE can be leveraged to develop applications adhering to a microservices architecture.

Microservices and Jakarta EE

Some may think that Jakarta EE is "too heavyweight" for microservices development. This is simply not the case. Because of this misconception, some may also think that Jakarta EE may not be suitable for a microservices architecture when, in reality, Jakarta EE fits microservices development well. Some time ago, Java EE applications were deployed to a "heavyweight" application server. Nowadays, most Jakarta EE application server vendors offer lightweight application servers that use very little memory or disk space. Some examples of these Jakarta EE-compliant lightweight application servers include IBM's Open Liberty, Red Hat's WildFly Swarm, Apache TomEE, and Payara Micro. Jakarta EE 10 introduced the core profile, which is ideal for microservices development using Jakarta EE.

Developing microservices with the Jakarta EE core profile involves writing standard Jakarta EE applications, while limiting yourself to the subset of Jakarta EE APIs supported by the core profile, namely Jakarta REST, JSON-P, JSON-B, and CDI. If interacting with a relational database, we may need transaction support and likely would like an object-relational mapping API, such as Jakarta Persistence. To interact with a relational database, we would need the Jakarta EE web profile, as the core profile does not include Jakarta Persistence or transaction support. Only microservices needing to directly interact with a relational database would need the web profile; other microservices can be developed against the core profile.

Jakarta EE developers can leverage their existing expertise when developing microservices. When developing microservices, the main requirement is the development of RESTful web services, which can be easily implemented using Jakarta REST. These RESTful web services would be packaged in a WAR file and deployed to a lightweight Jakarta EE runtime.

When using modern, embeddable Jakarta EE implementations, usually only one application is deployed to each instance of the application server, and, in some cases, the "tables are turned" so to speak, by making the Jakarta EE implementation just a library that the application uses as a dependency. With these modern Jakarta EE implementations, several instances of the Jakarta EE runtime are often deployed to a server, making modern Jakarta EE very suitable for microservices development. Many modern, lightweight Jakarta EE application servers are embeddable, allowing the creation of an "uber jar," which includes both the application code and the application server libraries. This "uber jar" is then transferred to the server and run as a standalone application. In addition to "uber jars," modern application servers can be added to a container image (such as Docker). Then, our application can be deployed as a thin WAR, typically only a few kilobytes in size; this approach has the advantage of very fast deployments, usually under two seconds.

By deploying to a contemporary, Jakarta EE core profile-compliant application server (or, as explained in the previous paragraph, creating an "uber jar"), Jakarta EE developers can certainly leverage their existing expertise to develop applications adhering to a microservices architecture.

Developing microservices using Jakarta EE

Now that we have briefly introduced you to microservices, we are ready to show an example of a microservices application written using Jakarta EE. Our example application should be very familiar to most Jakarta EE developers. It is a simple **CRUD (Create, Read, Update, Delete)** application developed as a series of microservices. The application will follow the familiar MVC design pattern, with the "View" and "Controller" developed as microservices. The application will also utilize the very common **Data Access Object (DAO) pattern**, with our DAO developed as a microservice as well.

> **DAO Pattern**
>
> The **DAO** design pattern is one that allows us to separate data access code from the rest of our application. Allowing us to switch the implementation of the data access code without impacting the rest of the application code.

Our application will be developed as three modules – first, a microservices client, followed by a microservices implementation of a controller in the MVC design pattern, and then an implementation of the DAO design pattern implemented as a microservice.

> **Note**
>
> The example code is not a full CRUD application. For simplicity, we only implemented the "create" part of our CRUD application.

Developing microservices client code

Before delving into developing our services, we will first develop a microservices client using plain HTML and JavaScript. The JavaScript code will invoke the controller microservice, passing a JSON representation of user-entered data. The controller service will then invoke the persistence service and save the data to a database. Each microservice will return an HTTP code indicating success or error condition.

The most relevant parts of our client code are the HTML form and the JavaScript code to submit it to our Controller microservice.

The form in our HTML page contains the following input fields:

```
<form id="customerForm">
  <!-- layout markup omitted for brevity -->
  <label for="salutation">Salutation</label>
  <select id="salutation" name="salutation" >
    <option value=""> </option>
    <option value="Mr">Mr</option>
    <option value="Mrs">Mrs</option>
    <option value="Miss">Miss</option>
    <option value="Ms">Ms</option>
    <option value="Dr">Dr</option>
  </select>
  <label for="firstName">First Name</label>
  <input type="text" maxlength="10" id="firstName"
    name="firstName" placeholder="First Name">
  <label for="middleName">Middle Name</label>
  <input type="text" maxlength="10"  id="middleName"
    name="middleName" placeholder="Middle Name">
  <label for="lastName">Last Name</label>
  <input type="text" maxlength="20"  id="lastName"
    name="lastName" placeholder="Last Name">
  <button type="submit" id="submitBtn" >Submit</button>
</form>
```

Our web client form contains a number of input fields to collect data from the user. It is implemented using plain HTML, with no additional CSS or JavaScript libraries. Our page also has a script to send form data to the controller microservice using JavaScript, as illustrated in the following code block:

```
<script>
  async function createCustomer(json) {
    try {
      const response = await fetch(  'http://localhost:8080/
        CrudController/resources/customercontroller/', {
```

```
        method: 'POST',
        body: json,
        headers: {
          'Content-Type': 'application/json'
        }
      });
      document.querySelector("#msg").innerHTML =
        "Customer saved successfully."
    } catch (error) {
      document.querySelector("#msg").innerHTML =
        "There was an error saving customer data.";
    }
  }

  function handleSubmit(event) {
    event.preventDefault();
    console.log("form submitted");
    const formData = new FormData(event.target);

    var formDataObject = {};
    formData.forEach(function (value, key) {
      formDataObject[key] = value;
    });
    var json = JSON.stringify(formDataObject);

    createCustomer(json);
  }
  const form = document.querySelector('#customerForm');
  form.addEventListener('submit', handleSubmit);
</script>
```

When the form is submitted, our script generates a JSON-formatted representation of the user-entered data and then sends an HTTP POST request to our controller service, using the JavaScript fetch API. In our example, our controller service is deployed to a Jakarta EE runtime on our local workstation, listening on port 8080; therefore, our client code sends a POST request to http://localhost:8080/CrudController/resources/customercontroller/.

We can now point our browser to our CrudView application URL (http://localhost:8080/CrudView in our example). After entering some data, the page will look as shown in the following screenshot.

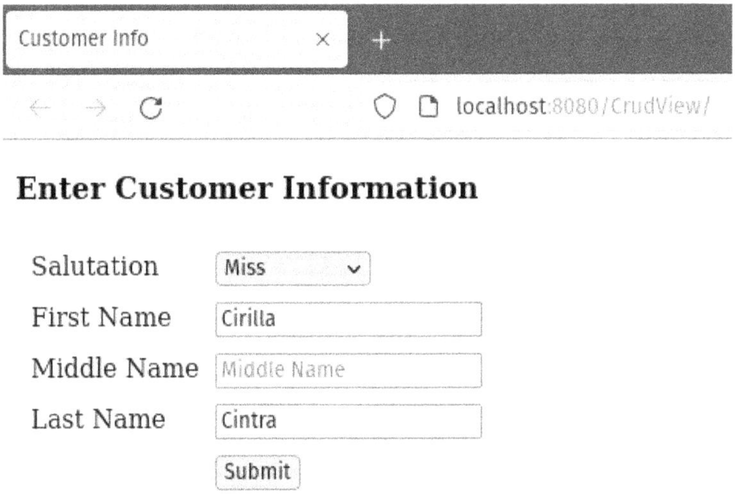

Figure 5.1 – The HTML/JavaScript RESTful web service client

When the user clicks on the **Submit** button, the client passes a JSON representation of user-entered data to the controller service.

The controller service

The controller service is a standard RESTful web service implementation of a controller in the MVC design pattern, implemented using Jakarta REST:

```
package com.ensode.jakartaeebook.microservices.crudcontroller.service;

//imports omitted for brevity

@Path("/customercontroller")
public class CustomerControllerService {
  @OPTIONS
  public Response options() {
    LOG.log(Level.INFO, "CustomerControllerService.options()
      invoked");
    return Response.ok("")
      .header("Access-Control-Allow-Origin",
        "http://localhost:8080")
      .header("Access-Control-Allow-Headers",
        "origin, content-type, accept, authorization")
      .header("Access-Control-Allow-Credentials", "true")
      .header("Access-Control-Allow-Methods",
        "GET, POST, PUT, DELETE, OPTIONS, HEAD")
```

```
            .header("Access-Control-Max-Age", "1209600")
              .build();
    }
    @POST
    @Consumes(MediaType.APPLICATION_JSON)
    public Response addCustomer(Customer customer) {
      Response response;
      Response persistenceServiceResponse;

      CustomerPersistenceClient client = new
        CustomerPersistenceClient();

      persistenceServiceResponse = client.create(customer);
      client.close();

      if (persistenceServiceResponse.getStatus() == 201) {
        response = Response.ok("{}").
          header("Access-Control-Allow-Origin",
          "http://localhost:8080").build();
      } else {
        response = Response.serverError().
          header("Access-Control-Allow-Origin",
          "http://localhost:8080").build();
      }
      return response;
    }
}
```

The `options()` method, annotated with the `jakarta.ws.rs.OPTIONS` annotation is necessary, since the browser automatically calls it, before invoking the actual request containing the main logic of our server. In this method, we set some header values to allow **CORS** (**Cross-Origin Resource Sharing**), which in simple terms means we allow our service to be invoked from a different server than the one where our service is running. Note that we explicitly allow requests from `http://localhost:8080`, which is the host and port where our client code is deployed.

The main logic of our controller service is in the `addCustomer()` method. This method receives an instance of our `Customer` class as a parameter; Jakarta REST automatically populates the `Customer` parameter with the JSON-formatted data sent by the client.

> **Note**
>
> The `Customer` class is a simple **Data Transfer Object** (**DTO**), containing a few properties matching the input fields in the form in the client, plus the corresponding getters and setters. Since the class is quite simple, we decided not to show it.

In the `addCustomer()` method, we create an instance of `CustomerPersistenceClient()`, which is a client for the persistence service, implemented using the Jakarta REST client API.

Then, our `addCustomer()` method invokes the persistence service by invoking the `create()` method on `CustomerPersistenceClient`, checks the HTTP status code returned by the persistence service, and then sends an appropriate response to the client.

Now, let's take a look at the implementation of our Jakarta REST client code:

```
package com.ensode.jakartaeebook.microservices.crudcontroller.
restclient;

//imports omitted

public class CustomerPersistenceClient {

  private final WebTarget webTarget;
  private final Client client;
  private static final String BASE_URI =
   "http://localhost:8080/CrudPersistence/resources";

  public CustomerPersistenceClient() {
    client = ClientBuilder.newClient();
    webTarget = client.target(BASE_URI).path(
      "customerpersistence");
  }

  public Response create(Customer customer)
    throws ClientErrorException {
    return webTarget.request(
      MediaType.APPLICATION_JSON).post(
      Entity.entity(customer,
      MediaType.APPLICATION_JSON), Response.class);
  }

  public void close() {
    client.close();
  }
}
```

As we can see, our client code is a fairly simple class that makes use of the Jakarta REST client API. We declare a constant containing the base URI of the service we are invoking (our persistence service). In its constructor, we create a new instance of `jakarta.ws.rs.client.ClientBuilder`. We then set its base URI and path, matching the appropriate values for our persistence service. Our client class has a single method, which submits an HTTP POST request to the persistence service and then returns the response sent back from it.

Now that we have successfully developed our controller service, we are ready to explore the final component of our application – the persistence service.

The persistence service

Our persistence service is implemented as a simple RESTful web service using Jakarta REST. Its `create()` method is invoked when the service receives an HTTP POST request:

```
package com.ensode.jakartaeebook.microservices.crudpersistence.
service;

//imports omitted for brevity

@ApplicationScoped
@Path("customerpersistence")
public class CustomerPersistenceService {

  private static final Logger LOG =
    Logger.getLogger(
      CustomerPersistenceService.class.getName());

  @Context
  private UriInfo uriInfo;

  @Inject
  private CrudDao customerDao;

  @POST
  @Consumes(MediaType.APPLICATION_JSON)
  public Response create(Customer customer) {
    try {
      customerDao.create(customer);
    } catch (Exception e) {
      LOG.log(Level.SEVERE, "Exception caught", e);
      return Response.serverError().build();
    }

    return Response.created(uriInfo.getAbsolutePath()).build();
  }
}
```

Our `create()` method is invoked when the controller service sends an HTTP POST request to the persistence service. This method simply invokes a `create()` method on a class implementing the DAO design pattern. Our persistence service returns an HTTP response, `201` (Created). If everything goes well and the DAO's `create()` method throws an exception, then our service returns a `500` HTTP error (Internal Server Error).

Our DAO is implemented as a CDI-managed bean, using JPA to insert data into the database:

```
package com.ensode.jakartaeebook.microservices.crudpersistence.dao;

//imports omitted for brevity
@ApplicationScoped
@DataSourceDefinition(name =
    "java:app/jdbc/microservicesCrudDatasource",
        className = "org.h2.jdbcx.JdbcDataSource",
        url = "jdbc:h2:tcp://127.0.1.1:9092/mem:microservicescrud",
        user = "sa",
        password = "")
public class CrudDao {

  @PersistenceContext(unitName = "CustomerPersistenceUnit")
  private EntityManager em;

  @H2DatabaseWrapper
  public void create(Customer customer) {
    em.persist(customer);
  }
}
```

Our DAO couldn't be much simpler; it implements a single method that invokes the `persist()` method on an injected instance of `EntityManager`. Note that we took advantage of the `@DataSourceDefinition` annotation to create a data source pointing to our database. This annotation is a standard Jakarta EE annotation that allows us to define data sources in an implementation-independent way.

> **Note**
>
> In our persistence service project, the `Customer` class is a trivial JPA entity.

Now that we have developed all three components of our application, we are ready to see it in action.

Once a user enters some data and clicks the submit button, we should see a "success" message at the top of our page (see *Figure 5.2*).

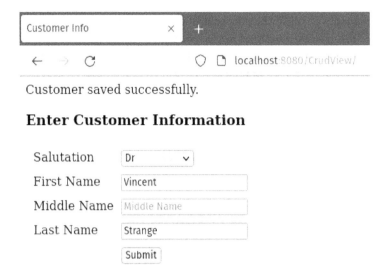

Figure 5.2 – User-entered data

If we look at the database, we should see that the user-entered data persisted successfully, as shown in *Figure 5.3*.

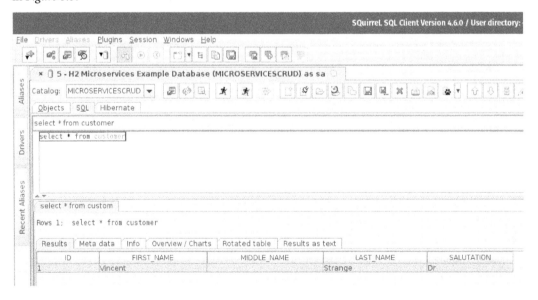

Figure 5.3 – Data inserted into the database

As shown by our example code, developing applications following microservices architecture in Jakarta EE is very simple. It doesn't require any special knowledge. Microservices are developed using standard Jakarta EE APIs and deployed to a lightweight Jakarta EE runtime.

Summary

As seen in this chapter, Jakarta EE is quite suitable for microservices development.

In this chapter, we covered the following topics:

- We introduced you to microservices, listing the advantages and disadvantages of a microservices architecture

- We explained how to develop microservices using standard Jakarta EE technologies, such as Jakarta REST

Jakarta EE developers can leverage their existing knowledge to develop microservices architecture – deploying modern, lightweight application servers. Traditional Jakarta EE applications can interact with microservices quite well, and they can also be refactored iteratively into a microservices architecture when it makes sense. Whether developing new applications following a microservices architecture, refactoring an existing application to microservices, or modifying existing applications to interact with microservices, Jakarta EE developers can leverage their existing skills for the task at hand.

6
Jakarta Faces

In this chapter, we will cover **Jakarta Faces**, the standard component framework of Jakarta EE. Jakarta Faces is used to develop user interfaces, typically rendered on a web browser. Faces relies a lot on convention over configuration, if we follow Faces conventions then we don't need to write a lot of configuration. In most cases, we don't need to write any configuration at all. This fact combined with the fact that web.xml has been optional since Java EE 6 means that in many cases we can write complete web applications without having to write a single line of XML.

In this chapter, we will cover the following topics:

- Introduction to Jakarta Faces
- Developing our first Faces application
- Custom data validation
- Customizing default messages

> **Note**
>
> Example source code for this chapter can be found on GitHub at https://github.com/PacktPublishing/Jakarta-EE-Application-Development/tree/main/ch06_src.

Introduction to Jakarta Faces

In this section, we will give a general overview of what developing web applications with Jakarta Faces entails, providing some background information necessary before digging into the nitty gritty of Jakarta Faces.

Facelets

Facelets is the default Jakarta Faces view technology. Facelets are written using standard **Extensible Hypertext Markup Language** (**XHTML**), using Jakarta Faces-specific XML namespaces that provide Jakarta Faces-specific tags we can use to develop the user interface of our web applications.

Optional faces-config.xml

In most cases, configuring a Jakarta Faces application is not necessary, as it follows a convention over configuration approach.

For some specific cases, when overriding Jakarta Faces' default error messages for example, we still need to configure Jakarta Faces via a `faces-config.xml` configuration file.

Standard resource locations

Resources are artifacts a page or Jakarta Faces component needs to render properly. Resource examples are CSS stylesheets, JavaScript files, and images.

When working with Jakarta Faces, resources can be placed in a subdirectory in a folder called `resources` either at the root of the WAR file or in its `META-INF` directory. By convention, Jakarta Faces components know they can retrieve resources from one of these two locations.

In order to avoid cluttering the resources directory, resources are typically placed in a subdirectory. This subdirectory is referred to from the `library` attribute of Faces components.

For example, we could place a CSS stylesheet called `styles.css` in `/resources/css/styles.css`.

In our Faces pages, we could retrieve this CSS file using the `<h:outputStylesheet>` tag, as follows:

```
<h:outputStylesheet library="css"  name="styles.css"/>
```

The value of the `library` attribute must match the subdirectory where our stylesheet is located.

Similarly, we could have a JavaScript file at `/resources/scripts/somescript.js` and an image at `/resources/images/logo.png`, and we could access these resources as follows:

```
<h:graphicImage library="images" name="logo.png"/>
<h:outputScript library="scripts" name="somescript.js"/>
```

Notice that in each case, the value of the `library` attribute matches the corresponding subdirectory name in the `resources` directory, and the value of the name attribute matches the resource's filename.

Developing our first Faces application

To illustrate basic Jakarta Faces concepts, we will develop a simple application consisting of two Facelet pages and a single **Contexts and Dependency Injection (CDI)** named bean.

Facelets

As we mentioned in this chapter's introduction, the default view technology for Jakarta Faces is called Facelets. Facelets need to be written using standard XML. The most popular way of developing Facelet pages is to use XHTML in conjunction with Jakarta Faces-specific XML namespaces. The following example shows what a typical Facelet page looks like:

```
<!-- XML declaration and doctype omitted -->
<html xmlns="http://www.w3.org/1999/xhtml"
      xmlns:h="jakarta.faces.html"
   xmlns:f="jakarta.faces.core">
  <h:head>
    <title>Enter Customer Data</title>
  </h:head>
  <h:body>
    <h:outputStylesheet library="css" name="styles.css"/>
    <h:form id="customerForm">
      <h:messages/>
      <h:panelGrid columns="2"
        columnClasses="rightAlign,leftAlign">
        <h:outputLabel for="firstName" value="First Name:">
        </h:outputLabel>
        <h:inputText id="firstName"
          label="First Name"
          value="#{customer.firstName}"
          required="true">
          <f:validateLength minimum="2" maximum="30"/>
        </h:inputText>
        <h:outputLabel for="lastName" value="Last Name:">
        </h:outputLabel>
        <h:inputText id="lastName"
                     label="Last Name"
                     value="#{customer.lastName}"
                     required="true">
          <f:validateLength minimum="2" maximum="30"/>
```

```
      </h:inputText>
      <h:outputLabel for="email" value="Email:">
      </h:outputLabel>
      <h:inputText id="email"
        label="Email"
        value="#{customer.email}">
        <f:validateLength minimum="3" maximum="30"/>
      </h:inputText>
      <h:panelGroup></h:panelGroup>
      <h:commandButton action="confirmation" value="Save">
      </h:commandButton>
    </h:panelGrid>
  </h:form>
 </h:body>
</html>
```

Figure 6.1 illustrates how our Facelets page renders in the browser after deploying our code and entering some data.

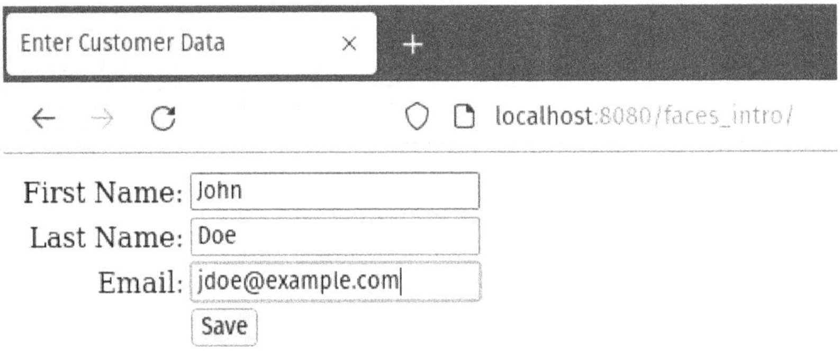

Figure 6.1 – Rendered Facelets page

Pretty much any Facelet page will include the two namespaces illustrated in the example. The first namespace (xmlns:h="jakarta.faces.html") is for tags that render HTML components. By convention, the prefix h (for HTML) is used when using this tag library.

The second namespace (xmlns:f="jakarta.faces.core") is the core Faces tag library. By convention, the prefix f (for Faces) is used when using this tag library.

The first Faces-specific tags we see in the preceding example are the <h:head> and the <h:body> tags. These tags are analogous to the standard HTML <head> and <body> tags and are rendered as such when the page is displayed in the browser.

The <h:outputStylesheet> tag is used to load a CSS stylesheet from a well-known location (Jakarta Faces standardizes the locations of resources, such as CSS stylesheets and javascript files, as previously discussed in this chapter). The value of the library attribute must correspond to the directory where the CSS file resides (this directory must be in the resources directory). The name attribute must correspond to the name of the CSS stylesheet we wish to load.

The next tag we see is the <h:form> tag. This tag generates an HTML form when the page is rendered. As can be seen in the example, unlike regular HTML, there is no need to specify an action or a method attribute for this tag. As a matter of fact, there is no action attribute or method attribute for this tag. The action attribute for the rendered HTML form will be generated automatically, and the method attribute will always be "post". The id attribute of <h:form> is optional; however, it is a good idea to always add it since it makes debugging Faces applications easier.

The following tag we see is the <h:messages> tag. As its name implies, this tag is used to display any messages. As we will see shortly, Faces can automatically generate validation messages; they will be displayed inside this tag. Additionally, arbitrary messages can be added programmatically via the addMessage() method defined in jakarta.faces.context.FacesContext.

The next Jakarta Faces tag we see is <h:panelGrid>. This tag is roughly equivalent to an HTML table, but it works a bit differently. Instead of declaring rows (<tr>) and cells (<td>), the <h:panelGrid> tag has a columns attribute. The value of this attribute indicates the number of columns in the table rendered by this tag. As we place components inside this tag, they will be placed in a row until the number of columns defined in the columns attribute is reached, then the next component will be placed in the next row. In the example, the value of the columns attribute is 2, therefore the first two tags will be placed in the first row, the next two will be placed in the second row, and so forth.

> **Note**
>
> Using HTML tables for page layout was a popular practice in the early days of web development. This practice fell out of favor with the advent of CSS. Most modern Facelets pages use CSS for layout, but we thought it was worth pointing out the layout capabilities provided by Jakarta Faces.

Another interesting attribute of <h:panelGrid> is the columnClasses attribute. This attribute assigns a CSS class to each column in the rendered table. In the example, two CSS classes (separated by a comma) are used as the value for this attribute. This has the effect of assigning the first CSS class to the first column and the second one to the second column. Had there been three or more columns, the third one would have gotten the first CSS class, the fourth one the second one, and so on, alternating between the first one and the second one.

> **Viewing generated HTML markup**
>
> We can view the generated HTML markup of our Facelets page by right-clicking on the browser window and selecting **View Page Source**.

To clarify how this works, the next code snippet illustrates a portion of the source of the HTML markup generated by the preceding page:

```
<form id="customerForm" name="customerForm" method="post" action="/
faces_intro/faces/index.xhtml" enctype="application/x-www-form-
urlencoded">
  <table>
    <tbody>
      <tr>
        <td class="rightAlign">
          <label for="customerForm:firstName">
            First Name:</label>
        </td>
        <td class="leftAlign">
          <input id="customerForm:firstName" type="text"
            name="customerForm:firstName" value="" />
        </td>
      </tr>
      <tr>
        <td class="rightAlign">
          <label for="customerForm:lastName">
            Last Name:</label></td>
        <td class="leftAlign">
          <input id="customerForm:lastName"
          type="text" name="customerForm:lastName"
            value="" /></td>
      </tr>
      <!-- Additional table rows omitted for brevity -->
    </tbody>
  </table>
</form>
```

Notice how each <td> tag has an alternating CSS tag of "rightAlign" or "leftAlign", we achieved this by assigning the value "rightAlign, leftAlign" to the columnClasses attribute of <h:panelGrid>. We should note that the CSS classes we are using in our example are defined in the CSS stylesheet we loaded via <h:outputStylesheet>, which we discussed earlier. The values of all the name and id attributes of the generated HTML tags are a combination of the ID we gave to the <h:form> component, plus the ID of each individual component. Notice that we didn't assign an ID to the <h:commandButton> component near the end of the page, so the Faces runtime assigned one automatically and used it to populate the name attribute of the generated submit button.

At this point in the example, we start adding components inside `<h:panelGrid>`. These components will be rendered inside the table rendered by `<h:panelGrid>`. As we mentioned before, the number of columns in the rendered table is defined by the `columns` attribute of `<h:panelGrid>`. Therefore, we don't need to worry about columns (or rows) we just start adding components and they will be placed in the right place.

The next tag we see is the `<h:outputLabel>` tag. This tag is rendered as an HTML `label` element. Labels are associated with other components via the `for` attribute, whose value must match the ID of the component that the label is for.

Next, we see the `<h:inputText>` tag. This tag generates a text field on the rendered page; its `label` attribute is used for any validation messages. It lets the user know what field the message refers to.

> **Note**
>
> Although it is not required for the value of the `label` attribute of `<h:inputText>` to match the label displayed on the page, it is highly recommended. If there is an error, this will let the user know exactly what field the error message is referring to.

Of particular interest is the tag's `value` attribute. What we see as the value for this attribute is a **value-binding expression**. What this means is that this value is tied to a property of one of the application's CDI named beans. In the example, this particular text field is tied to a property called `firstName` in a named bean called `customer`. When a user enters a value for this text field and submits the form, the corresponding property in the named bean is updated with this value. The tag's `required` attribute is optional and valid values for it are `true` and `false`. If this attribute is set to `true`, the container will not let the user submit the form until the user enters some data for the text field. If the user attempts to submit the form without entering a required value, the page will be reloaded and an error message will be displayed inside the `<h:messages>` tag, as illustrated in *Figure 6.2*.

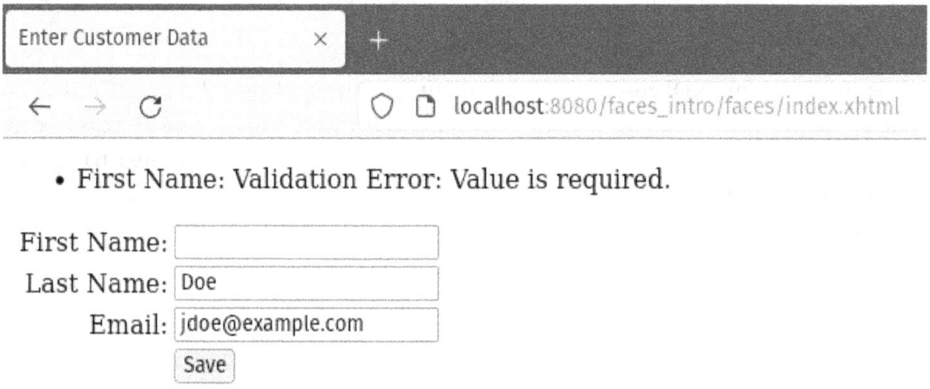

Figure 6.2 – Required field data validation

Figure 6.2 illustrates the default error message shown when the user attempts to save the form in the example without entering a value for the customer's first name. The first part of the message (**First Name**) is taken from the value of the `label` attribute of the corresponding `<h:inputTextField>` tag. The text of the message can be customized, as well as its style (font, color, etc.). We will cover how to do this later in this chapter.

Project stages

Having an `<h:messages>` tag on every Jakarta Faces page is a good idea. Without it, the user might not see validation messages and will have no idea why the form submission is not going through. By default, Jakarta Faces validation messages do not generate any output in the application server log. A common mistake new Jakarta Faces developers make is failing to add an `<h:messages>` tag to their pages. Without it, if validation fails, then navigation seems to fail for no reason (the same page is rendered if navigation fails, and without an `<h:messages>` tag, no error messages are displayed in the browser).

To avoid this situation, we can take advantage of Jakarta Faces **project stages**.

The following project stages are defined in Jakarta Faces:

- Production
- Development
- UnitTest
- SystemTest

We can define the project stage as an initialization parameter to the Faces servlet in `web.xml` or as a custom **Java Naming and Directory Interface** (**JNDI**) resource. The preferred way of setting the project stage is through a custom JNDI resource, as no modifications to `web.xml` are needed between environments.

How you set up a custom JNDI resource is dependent on your application server. Consult your application server documentation for details. For example, if we are using `GlassFish` to deploy our application, we can set up a custom JNDI resource by logging in to the web console, navigating to **JNDI | Custom Resources**, and then clicking the **New...** button, which allows us to add our custom JNDI resource, as illustrated in *Figure 6.3*.

New Custom Resource

Create a custom JNDI resource so that applications can gain access to resources stored in a local repository.

JNDI Name: *	jakarta.faces.PROJECT_STA(
Resource Type:	◉ java.lang.String ⌄
	○
	Enter a fully qualified type following the format xxx.xxx (for example, jakarta.jms.Topic)
Factory Class: *	org.glassfish.resources.custom.factory.PrimitivesAndStringFactory
	Factory class for resource; implements javax.naming.spi.ObjectFactory
Description:	
Status:	✔

Additional Properties (1)

[▦] [▣] | Add Property | Delete Properties

Select	Name	Value
☐	value	Development

Figure 6.3 – Defining Jakarta Faces project stage in GlassFish as a JNDI resource

To define the Jakarta Faces project stage, we need to enter the following information:

JNDI Name	`jakarta.faces.PROJECT_STAGE`
Resource Type	`java.lang.String`

Table 6.1 – Setting the Jakarta Faces project stage in GlassFish

After entering the two preceding values, the **Factory Class** field will be automatically populated with the following value:

```
org.glassfish.resources.custom.factory.PrimitivesAndStringFactory.
```

After entering the values, we need to add a new property with a name of `value` and a value corresponding to the project stage we wish to use (**Development**, our example).

Once we add our custom JNDI resource, we need to update our `web.xml` configuration file to read it, this step is the same across Jakarta EE implementations.

The following example `web.xml` configuration file illustrates how to do the Jakarta Faces project stage so that our application can use it successfully:

```
<?xml version="1.0" encoding="UTF-8"?>
<web-app xmlns="https://jakarta.ee/xml/ns/jakartaee"
  xmlns:xsi="http://www.w3.org/2001/XMLSchema-instance"
  xsi:schemaLocation="https://jakarta.ee/xml/ns/jakartaee
  https://jakarta.ee/xml/ns/jakartaee/web-app_6_0.xsd"
  version="6.0">
```

```
<resource-ref>
  <res-ref-name>faces/ProjectStage</res-ref-name>
  <res-type>java.lang.String</res-type>
  <mapped-name>jakarta.faces.PROJECT_STAGE</mapped-name>
</resource-ref>
<servlet>
  <servlet-name>Faces Servlet</servlet-name>
  <servlet-class>
      jakarta.faces.webapp.FacesServlet
  </servlet-class>
  <load-on-startup>1</load-on-startup>
</servlet>
<servlet-mapping>
  <servlet-name>Faces Servlet</servlet-name>
  <url-pattern>/faces/*</url-pattern>
</servlet-mapping>
<welcome-file-list>
  <welcome-file>faces/index.xhtml</welcome-file>
</welcome-file-list>
</web-app>
```

The <resource-ref> tag in web.xml allows us to access JNDI resources defined in our application server. In our case, we want to access the project stage of our Faces application.

<res-ref-name> gives our JNDI resource a name our code can use to look up our JNDI resource. Our Jakarta Faces implementation will look for a JNDI resource named faces/ProjectStage, and, if one is found, will use it to determine our project stage.

<res-type> allows us to specify the type of the resource we are looking for, as arbitrary Java objects can be looked up via JNDI. When setting the Jakarta Faces project stage, the value of this tag must always be java.lang.String.

We specify the name of the resource in the application server JNDI tree via the <mapped-name> tag. By convention, this value must always be jakarta.faces.PROJECT_STAGE when setting up the Jakarta Faces project stage via JNDI.

Setting the project stage allows us to perform some logic only if we are running in a specific stage. For instance, in one of our named beans, we could have code that looks like this:

```
FacesContext facesContext =
    FacesContext.getCurrentInstance();
Application application = facesContext.getApplication();

if (application.getProjectStage().equals(
    ProjectStage.Production)) {
  //do production stuff
```

```
    } else if (application.getProjectStage().equals(
       ProjectStage.Development)) {
     //do development stuff
    } else if (application.getProjectStage().equals(
       ProjectStage.UnitTest)) {
     //do unit test stuff
    } else if (application.getProjectStage().equals(
       ProjectStage.SystemTest)) {
     //do system test stuff
    }
```

As we can see, project stages allow us to modify our code's behavior for different environments. More importantly, setting the project stage allows Jakarta Faces to behave differently based on the project stage setting. In this context, setting the project stage to development results in additional debugging information to be displayed on the rendered page. Therefore, if we forget to add an <h:messages> tag to our page; our project stage is Development, and validation fails, a validation error will be displayed on the page even if we omit the <h:messages> component. This is illustrated in *Figure 6.4*.

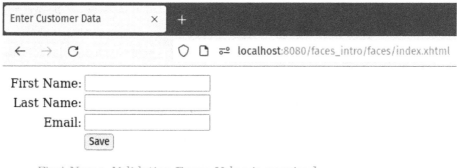

Figure 6.4 – Debugging information displayed when the project stage is in Development

In the default Production stage, this error message is not displayed on the page, leaving us confused as to why our page navigation doesn't seem to be working.

Validation

Notice that each <h:inputField> tag has a nested <f:validateLength> tag. As its name implies, this tag validates that the entered value for the text field is between a minimum and maximum length. Minimum and maximum values are defined by the tag's minimum and maximum attributes. <f:validateLength> is one of the standard validators included with Jakarta Faces. Just like with the required attribute of <h:inputText>, Jakarta Faces will automatically display a default error message when a user attempts to submit a form with a value that does not validate, as illustrated in *Figure 6.5*.

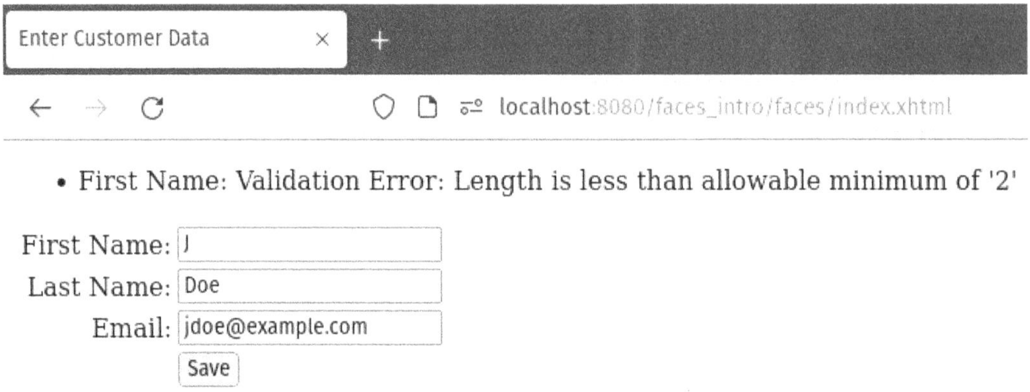

Figure 6.5 – Length validation

The default message text and CSS style for any Jakarta Faces validation message can be overridden; we will cover how to do this later in this chapter.

In addition to `<f:validateLength>`, Jakarta Faces includes other standard validators, which are listed in the following table:

Validation Tag	Description
`<f:validateBean>`	Bean validation allows us to validate named bean values by using annotations in our named beans without having to add validators to our Jakarta Faces tags. This tag allows us to fine-tune Bean Validation if necessary.
`<f:validateDoubleRange>`	Validates that the input is a valid `Double` value between the two values specified by the tag's `minimum` and `maximum` attributes, inclusive
`<f:validateLength>`	Validates that the input's length is between the values specified by the tag's `minimum` and `maximum` values, inclusive
`<f:validateLongRange>`	Validates that the input is a valid `Double` value between the values specified by the tag's `minimum` and `maximum` attributes, inclusive
`<f:validateRegex>`	Validates that the input matches a regular expression pattern specified in the tag's `pattern` attribute
`<f:validateRequired>`	Validates that the input is not empty. This tag is equivalent to setting the `required` attribute to `true` in the parent input field

Table 6.2 – Jakarta Faces validation tags

Notice that in the description for `<f:validateBean>`, we briefly mentioned **Bean Validation**. The Bean Validation API aims to standardize JavaBean validation. JavaBeans are used by several other APIs that previously had to implement their own validation logic. Jakarta Faces leverages Bean Validation to help validate named bean properties.

If we wish to take advantage of Bean Validation, all we need to do is annotate the desired field with the appropriate Bean Validation annotation, without having to explicitly use a Jakarta Faces validator.

> **Note**
>
> For the complete list of Bean Validation annotations, refer to the `jakarta.validation.constraints` package in the Jakarta EE 10 API documentation at `https://jakarta.ee/specifications/platform/10/apidocs/`.

Grouping components

`<h:panelGroup>` is the next new tag in the example. Typically, `<h:panelGroup>` is used to group several components together so that they occupy a single cell in `<h:panelGrid>`. This can be accomplished by adding components inside `<h:panelGroup>` and adding `<h:panelGroup>` to `<h:panelGrid>`. As can be seen in the example, this particular instance of `<h:panelGroup>` has no child components. In this particular case, the purpose of `<h:panelGroup>` is to have an empty cell and make the next component, `<h:commandButton>`, align with all other input fields in the form.

Form submission

`<h:commandButton>` renders an HTML submit button in the browser. Just like with standard HTML, its purpose is to submit the form. Its `value` attribute simply sets the button's label. This tag's `action` attribute is used for navigation, the next page to show is based on the value of this attribute. The `action` attribute can have a string constant or a **method binding expression**, meaning that it can point to a method in a named bean that returns a string.

If the base name of a page in our application matches the value of the `action` attribute of a `<h:commandButton>` tag, then we navigate to this page when clicking the button. In our example, our confirmation page is called `confirmation.xhtml`, therefore by convention, this page will be shown when the button is clicked, since the value of its `action` attribute (`"confirmation"`) matches the base name of the page.

> **Note**
>
> Even though the label for the button reads **Save**, in our simple example, clicking on the button won't actually save any data.

Named beans

Jakarta Faces includes tight integration with **CDI**. CDI beans can be given a name so that they can be referenced by Jakarta Faces pages. To make a Java class a CDI named bean, all we need to do is make sure the class has a public, no argument constructor (one is created implicitly if there are no other constructors declared, which is the case in our example) and add the @Named annotation at the class level. Here is the named bean for our example:

```
package com.ensode.jakartaeebook.faces;

import jakarta.enterprise.context.RequestScoped;
import jakarta.inject.Named;

@Named
@RequestScoped
public class Customer {

  private String firstName;
  private String lastName;
  private String email;

  //getters and setters omitted for brevity
}
```

The @Named class annotation designates this bean as a CDI named bean. This annotation has an optional value attribute we can use to give our bean a logical name to use in our Jakarta Faces pages. However, by convention, the value of this attribute is the same as the class name (Customer, in our case), with its first character switched to lowercase. In our example, we let this default behavior take place, therefore we access our bean's properties via the customer logical name. Notice the value attribute of any of the input fields in our example page to see this logical name in action.

Notice that, other than the @Named and @RequestScoped annotations, there is nothing special about this bean. It is a standard JavaBean with private properties and corresponding getter and setter methods. The @RequestScoped annotation specifies that the bean should live through a single request. The different scopes available to CDI named beans are covered in the next section.

Named bean scopes

Named beans always have a scope. A named bean scope defines the lifespan of the application. The named bean scope is defined by a class-level annotation. The following table lists all valid named bean scopes.

Named Bean Scope Annnotation	Description
`@ApplicationScoped`	The same instance of application-scoped named beans is available to all of our application's clients. If one client modifies the value of an application-scoped named bean, the change is reflected across clients.
`@SessionScoped`	An instance of each session-scoped named bean is assigned to each of our application's clients. A session-scoped named bean can be used to hold client-specific data across requests.
`@RequestScoped`	Request-scoped named beans only live through a single HTTP request.
`@Dependent`	Dependent-scoped named beans are assigned the same scope as the bean they are injected into.
`@ConversationScoped`	The conversation scope can span multiple requests but is typically shorter than the session scope.
`@ClientWindowScoped`	Client Window scoped beans are kept in memory until the current web browser window or tab is closed.

Table 6.3 – CDI scope annotations

Named bean scopes allow us to dictate the life cycle of CDI named beans. By using one of the named bean scopes listed in the preceding table, we can control when our named beans are created and destroyed.

Static navigation

As can be seen in our input page, when clicking on the **Save** button in the `customer_data_entry.xhtml` page, our application will navigate to a page called `confirmation.xhtml`. This happens because we are taking advantage of the convention over configuration capabilities of Jakarta Faces, in which if the value of the `action` attribute of a command button or link matches the base name of another page, then this navigation takes us to this page. This behavior is known as static navigation. Jakarta Faces also supports dynamic navigation, in which the landing page can be determined based on some business logic, we discuss dynamic navigation in the next section.

> **Same page reloading when clicking on a button or Link that should navigate to another page?**
>
> If navigation does not seem to be working properly, chances are there is a typo in the value of this attribute. Remember that by convention, Jakarta Faces will look for a page whose base name matches the value of the `action` attribute of a command button or link.

The source for `confirmation.xhtml` looks like this:

```
<!-- XML declaration and doctype omitted -->
<html xmlns="http://www.w3.org/1999/xhtml"
      xmlns:h="jakarta.faces.html">
  <h:head>
    <title>Customer Data Entered</title>
  </h:head>
  <h:body>
    <h:panelGrid columns="2"
      columnClasses="rightAlign,leftAlign">
      <h:outputText value="First Name:"/>
      <h:outputText value="#{customer.firstName}"/>
      <h:outputText value="Last Name:"></h:outputText>
      <h:outputText value="#{customer.lastName}"/>
      <h:outputText value="Email:"/>
      <h:outputText value="#{customer.email}"/>
    </h:panelGrid>
  </h:body>
</html>
```

The `<h:outputText>` we see on the confirmation page is the only tag we haven't covered before. This tag simply displays the value of its value attribute to the rendered page, its `value` attribute can be a simple string or a value binding expression. Since the value binding expressions in our `<h:outputText>` tags are the same expressions used in the previous page for the `<h:inputText>` tags, their values will correspond to the data the user entered. We can see how the page is rendered in *Figure 6.6*.

Figure 6.6 – Example confirmation page

In traditional (i.e. non-Jakarta Faces) Java web applications, we define URL patterns to be processed by specific servlets. Specifically for Jakarta Faces, the suffix `.faces` is commonly used. Another commonly used URL mapping for Faces is the `/faces` prefix. Under certain conditions, modern application servers automatically add all both mappings to the `faces` servlet. If these conditions are met, we don't have to specify any URL mappings at all.

If any of the following conditions is met, then the `FacesServlet` will be automatically mapped:

- There is a `faces-config.xml` file in the `WEB-INF` directory of our web application

- There is a `faces-config.xml` file in the `META-INF` directory of one of the dependencies of our web application

- There is a filename ending in `.faces-config.xml` in the `META-INF` directory of one of the dependencies of our web application

- We declare a context parameter named `jakarta.faces.CONFIG_FILES` in our `web.xml` or a `web-fragment.xml` in one of the dependencies

- We pass a non-empty set of classes when invoking the `onStartup()` method of `ServletContextInitializer`

When none of these conditions are met, we need to explicitly map the Jakarta Faces servlet in our `web.xml` deployment descriptor, as illustrated here:

```xml
<?xml version="1.0" encoding="UTF-8"?>
<web-app xmlns="https://jakarta.ee/xml/ns/jakartaee"
  xmlns:xsi="http://www.w3.org/2001/XMLSchema-instance"
  xsi:schemaLocation="https://jakarta.ee/xml/ns/jakartaee
  https://jakarta.ee/xml/ns/jakartaee/web-app_6_0.xsd"
  version="6.0">
  <servlet>
    <servlet-name>Faces Servlet</servlet-name>
    <servlet-class>
      jakarta.faces.webapp.FacesServlet
    </servlet-class>
    <load-on-startup>1</load-on-startup>
  </servlet>
  <servlet-mapping>
    <servlet-name>Faces Servlet</servlet-name>
    <url-pattern>/faces/*</url-pattern>
  </servlet-mapping>
</web-app>
```

The URL we used for the pages in our application was the name of our Facelets pages prefixed by `/faces`. We specify this in our `<servlet-mapping>` tag in our `web.xml` configuration file.

Dynamic navigation

In some cases, we may not know ahead of time what the next page in the application workflow would be, we need to run some business logic to determine what page to display next. For example, we may want to navigate to a confirmation page if everything went as expected when submitting our data, or we may want to navigate to an error page, or even back to the input page if there was an error processing the data.

The following example illustrates how we can implement dynamic navigation in Jakarta Faces:

```
<!-- XML declaration and doctype omitted -->
<html xmlns="http://www.w3.org/1999/xhtml"
      xmlns:h="jakarta.faces.html"
      xmlns:f="jakarta.faces.core">
  <h:head>
    <title>Enter Customer Data</title>
  </h:head>
  <h:body>
    <h:outputStylesheet library="css" name="styles.css"/>
    <h:form id="customerForm">
      <h:messages/>
      <h:panelGrid columns="2"
                   columnClasses="rightAlign,leftAlign">
        <!- input fields omitted for brevity -->
        <h:commandButton
          action="#{customerController.saveCustomer()}"
          value="Save"/>
      </h:panelGrid>
    </h:form>
  </h:body>
</html>
```

To achieve dynamic navigation, we need to modify the action attribute of our command button to be a Jakarta Expression Language method expression, that is, an expression that maps to a method in one of our CDI named beans. For dynamic navigation, the method in the expression must take no arguments and return a string. In our example, we are using a method called saveCustomer() in a CDI named bean named customerController, therefore our expression is #{customerController. saveCustomer}. We'll take a look at the implementation of our saveCustomer() method next:

```
package com.ensode.jakartaeebook.faces;
//imports omitted for brevity
@Named
@RequestScoped
```

```java
public class CustomerController {

  //instance variables omitted for brevity

    public String saveCustomer() throws IOException {
      String landingPage = "confirmation";
      String tmpDir = System.getProperty("java.io.tmpdir");
      Path customerFile;
      try {
        customerFile = Path.of(tmpDir, "customer-file.txt");
        if (!Files.exists(customerFile)) {
          customerFile = Files.createFile(Path.of(tmpDir,
                "customer-file.txt"));
        }
        //force an exception every other run
        customerFile.toFile().setWritable(
          !customerFile.toFile().canWrite());
        Files.writeString(customerFile, customer.toString(),
                StandardOpenOption.APPEND);
      } catch (IOException ex) {
        landingPage = "index";
        FacesMessage facesMessage = new FacesMessage(
                "Error saving customer");
        facesContext.addMessage(null, facesMessage);
      }
      return landingPage;
    }
}
```

Our example application adheres to the Model-View-Controller design pattern. Our CDI named bean serves as a controller and decides what page to navigate to when the user submits the form. If everything goes well, we navigate to the confirmation page as usual. If there is a problem (an exception is caught), we navigate back to the input page (named index.xhtml) and display an error message to the user.

For illustration purposes, our saveCustomer() method simply saves the string representation of the Customer object to a file in the filesystem to force an exception and allow us to illustrate dynamic navigation. Our code flips the read-only attribute of the file in question (makes it read-only if it is writeable, and vice versa), then attempts to write to the file. When attempting to write to the file when it is read-only, an exception is thrown and we navigate back to the input page, as illustrated in *Figure 6.7*.

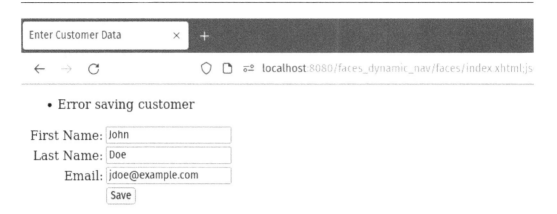

Figure 6.7 – Dynamic navigation

Sometimes we need to provide custom business logic validation or implement validation rules not included with the standard Jakarta Faces validators. In cases like this, we can take advantage of Jakarta Faces custom validation functionality.

Custom data validation

In addition to providing standard validators for our use, Jakarta Faces allows us to create custom validators. This can be done in one of two ways: by creating a custom validator class or by adding validation methods to our named beans.

Creating custom validators

In addition to the standard validators, Jakarta Faces allows us to create custom validators by creating a Java class implementing the `jakarta.faces.validator.Validator` interface.

The following class implements an email validator, which we will use to validate the email text input field in our customer data entry screen:

```
package com.ensode.jakartaeebook.facescustomval;
//imports ommitted for brevity
@FacesValidator(value = "emailValidator")
public class EmailAddressValidator implements Validator {
  @Override
  public void validate(FacesContext facesContext,
          UIComponent uiComponent,
          Object value) throws ValidatorException {
    EmailValidator emailValidator =
```

```
    EmailValidator.getInstance();
  HtmlInputText htmlInputText =
    (HtmlInputText) uiComponent;

  String emailAddress = (String) value;

  if (!StringUtils.isEmpty(emailAddress)) {
    if (!emailValidator.isValid(emailAddress)) {
      FacesMessage facesMessage =
        new FacesMessage(htmlInputText.getLabel()
        + ": email format is not valid");
      throw new ValidatorException(facesMessage);
    }
  }
 }
}
```

The `@FacesValidator` annotation registers our class as a Jakarta Faces custom validator class. The value of its `value` attribute is the logical name that Facelets' pages use to refer to it.

As can be seen in the example, the only method we need to implement when implementing the `Validator` interface is a method called `validate()`. This method takes three parameters, an instance of `jakarta.faces.context.FacesContext`, an instance of `jakarta.faces.component.UIComponent` and an object. Typically, application developers only need to be concerned with the last two. The second parameter is the component whose data we are validating and the third parameter is the actual value. In our example validator, we cast `uiComponent` to `jakarta.faces.component.html.HtmlInputText`. This way, we get access to its `getLabel()` method, which we can use as part of the error message.

If the entered value is not a valid email address format, a new instance of `jakarta.faces.application.FacesMessage` is created, passing the error message to be displayed in the browser as its constructor parameter. We then throw a new `jakarta.faces.validator.ValidatorException`. The error message is then displayed in the browser. How it gets there is done behind the scenes by the Jakarta Faces API.

Apache Commons Validator

Our custom validator uses **Apache Commons Validator** to do the actual validation. This library includes many common validations, such as dates, credit card numbers, ISBN numbers, and emails. When implementing a custom validator, it is worth investigating if this library already has a validator that we can use.

In order to use our validator on our page, we need to use the `<f:validator>` tag in our Facelets pages, nested inside the field we wish to validate. The following code snippet illustrates the changes we had to make to our email input field to incorporate our custom validator.:

```
<h:inputText label="Email" value="#{customer.email}">
  <f:validator validatorId="emailValidator" />
</h:inputText>
```

In order to validate our email input field, we added an `<f:validator>` tag nested inside its markup. Notice that the value of the `validatorId` attribute of `<f:validator>` matches the value we used in the `@FacesValidator` annotation in our custom email validator.

After writing our custom validator and modifying our page to take advantage of it, we can see our validator in action, as illustrated in *Figure 6.8*.

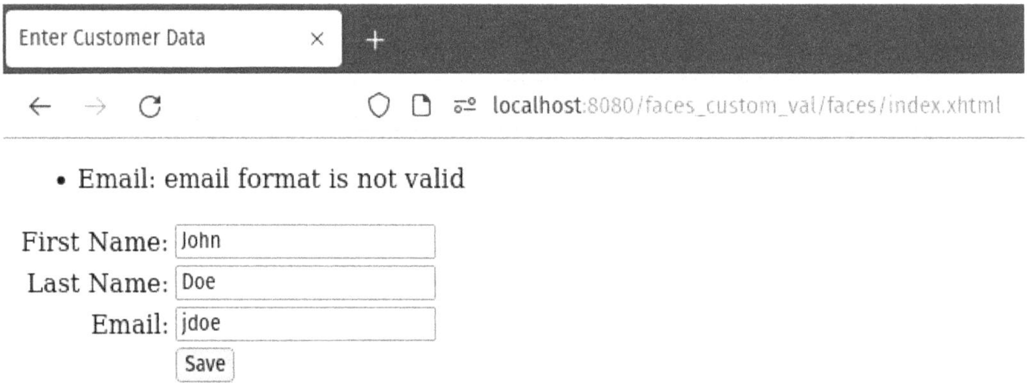

Figure 6.8 – Custom Jakarta Faces validator in action

Now that we've seen how to write custom validators, we will focus our attention to the other way we can implement custom validation in Jakarta Faces, by writing validator methods.

Validator methods

Another way we can implement custom validation is by adding validation methods to one or more of the application's named beans. The following Java class illustrates the use of validator methods for Faces validation:

```
package com.ensode.jakartaeebook.facescustomval;

//imports omitted for brevity

@Named
@RequestScoped
```

```
public class AlphaValidator {

  public void validateAlpha(FacesContext facesContext,
    UIComponent uiComponent,
    Object value) throws ValidatorException {
    if (!StringUtils.isAlphaSpace((String) value)) {
      HtmlInputText htmlInputText =
        (HtmlInputText) uiComponent;
      FacesMessage facesMessage =
        new FacesMessage(htmlInputText.
        getLabel()
        + ": only alphabetic characters are allowed.");
      throw new ValidatorException(facesMessage);
    }
  }
}
```

In this example, the class contains only the validator method, but that does not always have to be the case. We can give our validator method any name we want, but its return value must be void, and it must take the three parameters illustrated in the example, in that order. In other words, except for the method name, the signature of a validator method must be identical to the signature of the `validate()` method defined in the `jakarta.faces.validator.Validator` interface.

As we can see, the body of the preceding validator method is nearly identical to the body of our custom validator's `validate()` method. We check the value entered by the user to make sure it contains only alphabetic characters and/or spaces. If it doesn't, then we throw a `ValidatorException` passing an instance of `FacesMessage` containing an appropriate error message string.

> **StringUtils**
>
> In the example, we used `org.apache.commons.lang3.StringUtils` to perform the actual validation logic. In addition to the method used in the example, this class contains several methods for verifying that a `string` is numeric or alphanumeric. This class, part of the Apache Commons Lang library, is very useful when writing custom validators.

Since every validator method must be in a named bean, we need to make sure the class containing our validator method is annotated with the `@Named` annotation, as illustrated in our example.

The last thing we need to do to use our validator method is to bind it to our component via the tag's `validator` attribute:

```
<h:outputText value="First Name:"/>
<h:inputText label="First Name"
  value="#{customer.firstName}"
  required="true"
```

```
    validator="#{alphaValidator.validateAlpha}">
    <f:validateLength minimum="2" maximum="30"/>
  </h:inputText>
  <h:outputText value="Last Name:"/>
  <h:inputText label="Last Name"
    value="#{customer.lastName}"
    required="true"
    validator="#{alphaValidator.validateAlpha}">
    <f:validateLength minimum="2" maximum="30"/>
  </h:inputText>
```

Since neither the first name nor the last name fields should accept anything other than alphabetic characters or spaces, we added our custom validator method to both of these fields.

Notice that the value of the validator attribute of the <h:inputText> tag is an expression written in the Jakarta expression language, it uses the default named bean name for the bean containing our validation method. alphaValidator is the name of our bean, and validateAlpha is the name of our validator method.

After modifying our page to use our custom validator, we can now see it in action, as seen in *Figure 6.9*.

- First Name: only alphabetic characters are allowed.
- First Name: Validation Error: Length is less than allowable minimum of '2'

Figure 6.9 – Custom validation via validator methods

Notice how for the **First Name** field, both our custom validator message and the standard length validator were executed.

Implementing validator methods has the advantage of not having the overhead of creating a whole class just for a single validator method (our example does just that, but in many cases, validator methods are added to an existing named bean containing other methods). However, the disadvantage is that each component can only be validated by a single validator method. When using validator classes, several <f:validator> tags can be nested inside the tag to be validated, therefore multiple validations, both custom and standard, can be done on the field.

Now that we've seen how to create our own custom validation, we'll see how we can customize our Jakarta Faces validation messages, we'll see how we can change how they are formatted (font, color, etc.), and how to customize error message text for standard Jakarta Faces validators.

Customizing default messages

As we mentioned earlier, it is possible to customize the style (font, color, text, etc.) of Jakarta Faces default validation messages. Additionally, it is possible to modify the text of the default Jakarta Faces validation messages. In the following sections, we will explain how to modify error message formatting and text.

Customizing message styles

Customizing message styles can be done with **Cascading Style Sheets** (**CSS**). This can be accomplished by using the `<h:message>` `style` or `styleClass` attributes. The `style` attribute is used when we want to declare the CSS style inline. The `styleClass` attribute is used when we want to use a predefined style in a CSS style sheet or inside a `<style>` tag on our page.

The following `markup` illustrates using the `styleClass` attribute to alter the style of error messages. It is a modified version of the input page we saw in the previous section.

```
<h:body>
  <h:outputStylesheet library="css" name="styles.css" />
  <h:form>
    <h:messages styleClass="errorMsg"/>

    <!-- additional markup omitted for brevity →

  </h:form>
</h:body>
</html>
```

The only difference between this page and the previous one is the use of the `styleClass` attribute of the `<h:messages>` tag. As we mentioned earlier, the value of the `styleClass` attribute must match the name of a CSS style defined in a cascading stylesheet that our page has access to.

In our case, we defined a CSS style for messages as follows:

```
.errorMsg {
  color: red;
}
```

Then used this style as the value of the `styleClass` attribute of our `<h:messages>` tag.

Figure 6.10 illustrates how the validation error messages look after implementing this change.

Figure 6.10 – Custom styles for validation messages

In this particular case, we just set the color of the error message text to red, but we are only limited by CSS capabilities in setting the style of the error messages.

> **Note**
>
> Pretty much any standard Jakarta Faces component has both a `style` and a `styleClass` attribute that can be used to alter its style. The former is used for predefined CSS styles, the latter is used for inline CSS.

Customizing message text

Sometimes it is desirable to override the text of Jakarta Faces default validation messages. Default validation messages are defined in a resource bundle called `Messages.properties`. This file can typically be found inside one of the Faces JAR files included with your application server. For example, GlassFish includes it inside a JAR file called `jakarta.faces.jar` file under `[glassfish installation directory]/glassfish/modules`. The file contains several messages; we are only interested in validation errors at this point. The default validation error messages are defined as follows:

```
jakarta.faces.validator.DoubleRangeValidator.MAXIMUM={1}: Validation
Error: Value is greater than allowable maximum of "{0}"
jakarta.faces.validator.DoubleRangeValidator.MINIMUM={1}: Validation
Error: Value is less than allowable minimum of ''{0}''
jakarta.faces.validator.DoubleRangeValidator.NOT_IN_RANGE={2}:
Validation Error: Specified attribute is not between the expected
values of {0} and {1}.
jakarta.faces.validator.DoubleRangeValidator.TYPE={0}: Validation
Error: Value is not of the correct type
jakarta.faces.validator.LengthValidator.MAXIMUM={1}: Validation Error:
Length is greater than allowable maximum of ''{0}''
jakarta.faces.validator.LengthValidator.MINIMUM={1}: Validation Error:
```

```
Length is less than allowable minimum of ''{0}''
jakarta.faces.validator.LongRangeValidator.MAXIMUM={1}: Validation
Error: Value is greater than allowable maximum of ''{0}''
jakarta.faces.validator.LongRangeValidator.MINIMUM={1}: Validation
Error: Value is less than allowable minimum of ''{0}''
jakarta.faces.validator.LongRangeValidator.NOT_IN_RANGE={2}:
Validation Error: Specified attribute is not between the expected
values of {0} and {1}.
jakarta.faces.validator.LongRangeValidator.TYPE={0}: Validation Error:
Value is not of the correct type.
jakarta.faces.validator.NOT_IN_RANGE=Validation Error: Specified
attribute is not between the expected values of {0} and {1}.
jakarta.faces.validator.RegexValidator.PATTERN_NOT_SET=Regex pattern
must be set.
jakarta.faces.validator.RegexValidator.PATTERN_NOT_SET_detail=Regex
pattern must be set to non-empty value.
jakarta.faces.validator.RegexValidator.NOT_MATCHED=Regex Pattern not
matched
jakarta.faces.validator.RegexValidator.NOT_MATCHED_detail=Regex
pattern of ''{0}'' not matched
jakarta.faces.validator.RegexValidator.MATCH_EXCEPTION=Error in
regular expression.
jakarta.faces.validator.RegexValidator.MATCH_EXCEPTION_detail=Error in
regular expression, ''{0}''
jakarta.faces.validator.BeanValidator.MESSAGE={0}
```

In order to override the default error messages, we need to create our own resource bundle using the same keys used in the default one, but altering the values to suit our needs. Here is a very simple customized resource bundle for our application. For example, to overwrite the message for minimum length validation, we would add the following property to our custom resource bundle:

```
jakarta.faces.validator.LengthValidator.MINIMUM={1}: minimum allowed
length is ''{0}''
```

In this resource bundle, we override the error message for when the value entered for a field validated by the <f:validateLength> tag is less than the allowed minimum. In order to let our application know that we have a custom resource bundle for message properties, we need to modify the application's faces-config.xml file:

```
<?xml version='1.0' encoding='UTF-8'?>
<faces-config version="4.0"
  xmlns="https://jakarta.ee/xml/ns/jakartaee"
  xmlns:xsi="http://www.w3.org/2001/XMLSchema-instance"
  xsi:schemaLocation="https://jakarta.ee/xml/ns/jakartaee
  https://jakarta.ee/xml/ns/jakartaee/web-facesconfig_4_0.xsd">
  <application>
    <message-bundle>com.ensode.Messages</message-bundle>
  </application>
</faces-config>
```

As we can see, the only thing we need to do to the application's `faces-config.xml` file is to add a `<message-bundle>` element indicating the name and location of the resource bundle containing our custom messages.

After adding our custom message resource bundle and modifying the application's

`faces-config.xml` file, we can see our custom validation message in action, as illustrated in *Figure 6.11*.

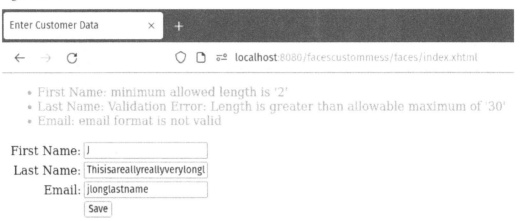

Figure 6.11 – Custom validation error message

If we haven't overridden a validation message, the default will still be displayed. In our resource bundle, we only overrode the minimum length validation error message, therefore our custom error message is shown for the **First Name** text field. Since we didn't override the error message for the other standard Jakarta Faces validators, the default error message is shown for each one of them. The email validator is the custom validator we developed previously in this chapter, since it is a custom validator its error message is not affected.

Summary

In this chapter, we covered how to develop web-based applications using Jakarta Faces, the standard component framework for the Jakarta EE.

In this chapter, we covered how to write a simple application by creating pages using Facelets as the view technology and CDI named beans. We saw how to implement static and dynamic navigation with Jakarta Faces. We also covered how to validate user input by using Faces standard validators and by creating our own custom validators or by writing validator methods. Additionally, we covered how to customize standard Faces error messages, both the message text and the message style (font, color, etc).

Jakarta Faces' tight integration with CDI allows us to efficiently develop web-based interfaces for our Jakarta EE applications.

7

Additional Jakarta Faces Features

In this chapter, we will cover the additional features of Jakarta Faces, the standard component framework for Jakarta EE. These additional features allow us to make our web application user-friendly, while providing features that are convenient for application developers.

In this chapter, we'll cover the following topics:

- Ajax-enabled Faces applications

- Jakarta Faces HTML5 support

- Faces Flows

- Faces WebSocket support

- Additional Faces component libraries

> **Note**
>
> The source code for this chapter can be found on GitHub at: `https://github.com/PacktPublishing/Jakarta-EE-Application-Development/tree/main/ch07_src`

Ajax-enabled Faces applications

Jakarta Faces allows us to easily implement **Asynchronous JavaScript and XML (Ajax)** functionality into our web applications by simply employing the `<f:ajax>` tag and CDI named beans, without needing to implement any JavaScript code or having to parse JSON strings.

The following markup illustrates the typical usage of the `<f:ajax>` tag.

```
<h:form>
  <h:messages/>
  <h:panelGrid columns="2">
    <h:outputText value="Echo input:"/>
    <h:inputText id="textInput"
      value="#{controller.text}">
      <f:ajax render="textVal" event="keyup"/>
    </h:inputText>
    <h:outputText value="Echo output:"/>
    <h:outputText id="textVal"
        value="#{controller.text}"/>
  </h:panelGrid>
  <hr/>
  <h:panelGrid columns="2">
    <h:outputText value="First Operand:"/>
    <h:inputText id="first"
      value="#{controller.firstOperand}" size="3"/>
    <h:outputText value="Second Operand:"/>
    <h:inputText id="second"
      value="#{controller.secondOperand}" size="3"/>
    <h:outputText value="Total:"/>
    <h:outputText id="sum" vaue="#{controller.total}"/>
    <h:commandButton
      actionListener="#{controller.calculateTotal}"
      value="Calculate Sum">
      <f:ajax execute="first second" render="sum"/>
    </h:commandButton>
  </h:panelGrid>
</h:form>
```

After deploying our application, the preceding markup renders as illustrated in *Figure 7.1*.

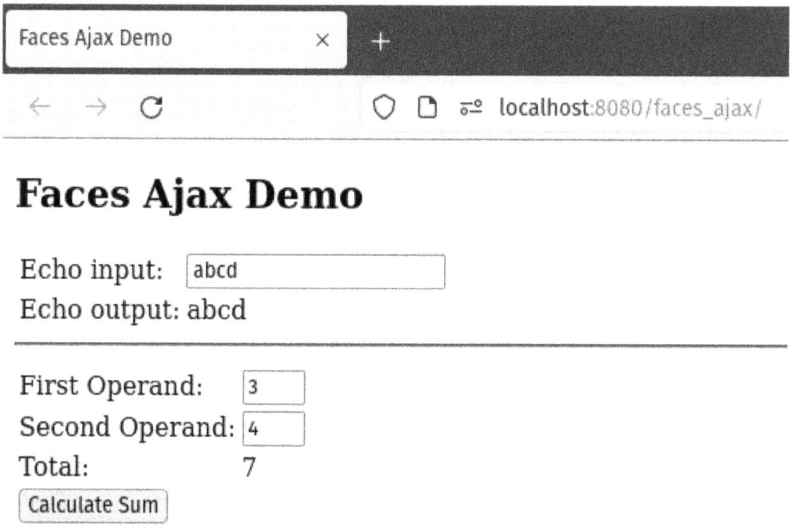

Figure 7.1 – Faces Ajax functionality in action

Our example illustrates two uses of the `<f:ajax>` tag. At the top of the page, we are using this tag by implementing a typical Ajax Echo example, in which we have an `<h:outputText>` component updating itself with the value of an input text component. Any time any character is entered into the input field, the value of the `<h:outputText>` component is automatically updated.

To implement the functionality described in the previous paragraph, we put an `<f:ajax>` tag inside an `<h:inputText>` tag. The value of the `render` attribute of the `<f:ajax>` tag must correspond to the ID of the component we wish to update after the Ajax request finishes. In our particular example, we wish to update the `<h:outputText>` component with an ID of `textVal`, therefore this is the value we use for the `render` attribute of our `<f:ajax>` tag.

> **Note**
>
> In some cases, we may need to render more than one Faces component after an Ajax event finishes. In order to accommodate for this, we can add several IDs as the value of the `render` attribute. We simply need to separate them with spaces.

The other `<f:ajax>` attribute we used in this instance is the `event` attribute. This attribute indicates the JavaScript event that triggers the Ajax event. In this particular case, we need to trigger the event any time a key is released while a user is typing into the input field. Therefore the appropriate event to use is `keyup`.

The following table lists all supported JavaScript events:

Event	Description
blur	The component loses focus
change	The component loses focus and its value has been modified
click	The component is clicked on
dblclick	The component is double-clicked on
focus	The component gains focus
keydown	A key is pressed down while the component has focus
keypress	A key is pressed or held down while the component has focus
keyup	A key is released while the component has focus
mousedown	The mouse button is depressed while the component has focus
mousemove	The mouse pointer is moved over the component
mouseout	The mouse pointer leaves the component
mouseover	The mouse pointer is placed over the component
mouseup	The mouse button is released while the component has focus
select	The component's text is selected
valueChange	Equivalent to change, the component loses focus and its value has been modified

Table 7.1 – <f:ajax> tag JavaScript event attributes

We use the <f:ajax> once again farther down the page to Ajax-enable a command button component. In this instance, we want to recalculate a value based on the values of two input components. In order to have the values on the server updated with the latest user input, we used the execute attribute of <f:ajax>. This attribute takes a space-separated list of component IDs to use as input. We then use the render attribute just like before to specify which components need to be re-rendered after the Ajax request finishes.

Notice we are using the actionListener attribute of <h:commandButton>. This attribute is typically used whenever we don't need to navigate to another page after clicking the button. The value for this attribute is an action listener method we wrote in one of our named beans. Action listener methods must return void, and take an instance of jakarta.faces.event.ActionEvent as their sole parameter.

The named bean for our application looks like this:

```
package com.ensode.jakartaeebook.facesajax;

//imports ommitted for brevity

@Named
```

```
@ViewScoped
public class Controller implements Serializable {

  private String text;
  private int firstOperand;
  private int secondOperand;
  private int total;

  @Inject
  private FacesContext facesContext;

  public void calculateTotal(ActionEvent actionEvent) {
    total = firstOperand + secondOperand;
  }

  //getters and setters omitted for brevity
}
```

The value of the `actionListener` attribute on our `commandButton` is a Jakarta Expression Language method expression resolving to the `calculateTotal()` method on our CDI named bean. As such, this method is automatically invoked when the user clicks on the button labeled **Calculate Sum**. The values of the `firstOperand` and `secondOperand` variables are bound to the **First Operand** and **Second Operand** input fields on our page, as evidenced by the Jakarta Expression Language expressions in the `value` attributes of those fields. As such, these variables are populated with the user-entered values on the page; our method simply adds those values and assigns them to the `total` variable. Then, the `outputText` component on the page bound to this variable is automatically updated.

Notice that we didn't have to do anything special in our named bean to enable Ajax in our application. It is all controlled by the `<f:ajax>` tag on the page.

As we can see from this example, Ajax-enabled Faces applications are very simple. We simply need to use a single tag to enable Ajax on our page, without having to write a single line of JavaScript, JSON, or XML.

Jakarta Faces HTML5 support

HTML5 is the latest version of the HTML specification. It includes several improvements over previous versions of HTML. Jakarta Faces includes several features to make Faces pages work nicely with HTML5. Jakarta Faces support for HTML5 includes the ability to develop our Jakarta Faces pages in HTML5 without using Faces-specific tags, along with the ability to add arbitrary HTML5 attributes to our Jakarta Faces pages.

HTML5-friendly markup

Through the use of pass-through elements, we can develop our Faces pages using HTML5, as opposed to using Faces-specific tags. Using HTML5 to develop our pages has the advantage that we can preview how our page renders in the browser without having to deploy our application to a Jakarta EE runtime. We can simply open the page in a web browser.

To do this, we need to specify at least one of the element attributes using the `jakarta.faces` XML namespace. The following example demonstrates this approach in action:

```
<!DOCTYPE html>
<html xmlns="http://www.w3.org/1999/xhtml"
      xmlns:faces="jakarta.faces">
  <head faces:id="head">
    <title>Jakarta Faces Page with HTML5 Markup</title>
    <link rel="stylesheet" type="text/css"
      href="resources/css/styles.css"/>
  </head>
  <body faces:id="body">
    <form faces:prependId="false">
      <div class="table">
        <div class="table-row">
          <div class="table-cell">
            <label faces:for="firstName">First Name</label>
          </div>
          <div class="table-cell">
            <input type="text" faces:id="firstName"
                   faces:value="#{customer.firstName}"/>
          </div>
        </div>
        <div class="table-row">
          <div class="table-cell">
            <label faces:for="lastName">Last Name</label>
          </div>
          <div class="table-cell">
            <input type="text" faces:id="lastName"
                   faces:value="#{customer.lastName}"/>
          </div>
        </div>
        <div class="table-row">
          <div class="table-cell">
            <label faces:for="email">Email Address</label></div>
          <div class="table-cell">
            <input type="email" faces:id="email"
```

```
                    faces:value="#{customer.email}"/>
        </div>
      </div>
      <div class="table-row">
        <div class="table-cell"></div>
        <div class="table-cell">
          <input type="submit" faces:action= "confirmation"
                 value="Submit"/>
        </div>
      </div>
    </div>
  </form>
</body>
</html>
```

The first thing we should notice about the preceding example is the XML namespace prefixed by faces near the top of the page. This namespace allows us to add Jakarta Faces-specific attributes to HTML5 pages. When the Faces runtime encounters attributes prefixed by faces in any of the tags on the page, it automatically converts the HTML5 tag to the equivalent Faces component. Faces-specific attributes are the same as in regular Faces pages, except they are prefixed with faces. Therefore, at this point, they should be self-explanatory and will not be discussed in detail.

The preceding example will render and behave just like the first example in this chapter.

The technique described in this section is useful if we have experienced HTML web designers in our team that prefer to have full control over the look of the page. The pages are developed using standard HTML5 with Faces-specific attributes so that the Faces runtime can manage user input.

If our team consists primarily of Java developers with limited CSS/HTML knowledge, then it is preferable to develop the web pages for our web application using Faces components.

HTML is an evolving standard; occasionally, attributes are added to HTML tags. To future-proof Faces components, Jakarta Faces supports pass-through attributes, which can be used to add arbitrary attributes to Jakarta Faces components. This technique is discussed in the next section.

Pass-through attributes

Jakarta Faces allows the definition of any arbitrary attributes (not processed by the Faces engine). These attributes are simply rendered as-is on the generated HTML displayed on the browser. The following example is a new version of an earlier example in this chapter, modified to take advantage of HTML5 pass-through attributes:

```
<?xml version='1.0' encoding='UTF-8' ?>
<!DOCTYPE html PUBLIC "-//W3C//DTD XHTML 1.0 Transitional//EN"
    "http://www.w3.org/TR/xhtml1/DTD/xhtml1-transitional.dtd">
```

```
<html xmlns="http://www.w3.org/1999/xhtml"
      xmlns:h="jakarta.faces.html"
      xmlns:f="jakarta.faces.core"
      xmlns:pt="jakarta.faces.passthrough">
  <!-- additional markup omitted for brevity -->
  <h:form id="customerForm">
    <h:messages/>
    <h:panelGrid columns="2"
                 columnClasses="rightAlign,leftAlign">
      <h:outputLabel for="firstName" value="First Name:">
      </h:outputLabel>
      <h:inputText id="firstName"
        label="First Name" value="#{customer.firstName}"
        required="true" pt:placeholder="First Name">
        <f:validateLength minimum="2" maximum="30"/>
      </h:inputText>
      <h:outputLabel for="lastName" value="Last Name:"/>
      <h:inputText id="lastName"
        label="Last Name" value="#{customer.lastName}"
        required="true" pt:placeholder="Last Name">
        <f:validateLength minimum="2" maximum="30"/>
      </h:inputText>
      <h:outputLabel for="email" value="Email:"/>
      <h:inputText id="email"
        label="Email" value="#{customer.email}"
        pt:placeholder="Email Address">
        <f:validateLength minimum="3" maximum="30"/>
      </h:inputText>
      <h:panelGroup/>
      <h:commandButton action="confirmation"
        value="Save"/>
    </h:panelGrid>
  </h:form>
  <!-- additional markup omitted -->
</html>
```

The first thing we should notice about this example is the addition of the `xmlns:pt="jakarta.faces.passthrough"` namespace. This namespace allows us to add any arbitrary attributes to our Faces components.

In our example, we added the HTML5 `placeholder` attribute to all input text fields on our page. As we can see, passthrough attributes need to be prefixed by the defined prefix for the namespace at the top of the application (`pt`, in our case). The `placeholder` HTML attribute simply adds some placeholder text to the input fields that are automatically deleted once the user starts typing on the input field (this technique was commonly implemented using JavaScript before the `placeholder` attribute was added to HTML5).

The following screenshot shows our updated page in action:

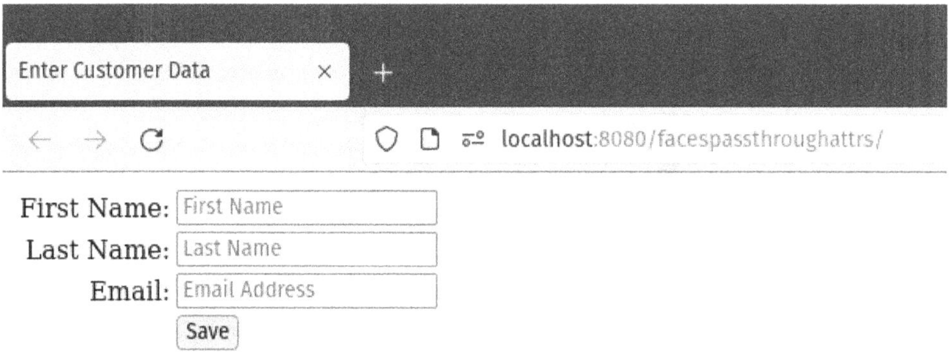

Figure 7.2 – Faces pass-through attributes

If we examine the generated HTML (by right-clicking on the web browser and selecting **View Source** or similar), we can see that the HTML placeholder attribute was added to it. For example, the generated markup for the **First Name** input field looks like this:

```
<input id="customerForm:firstName" type="text"
  name="customerForm:firstName" value=""
  placeholder="First Name" />
```

The placeholder attribute was placed there as a result of our pass-through attribute.

The next topic we'll discuss is Faces Flows, which provide a custom Jakarta Faces scope that is longer than the request scope, but shorter than the session scope.

Faces Flows

Faces Flows defines a scope that can span several pages. Flow-scoped beans are created when the user enters a flow (a set of web pages), and are destroyed when the user leaves the flow.

Faces Flows adopts the *convention-over-configuration* principle of Jakarta Faces. The following conventions are typically used when developing applications employing Faces Flows:

- All pages in the flow must be placed in a directory whose name defines the name of the flow.

- An XML configuration file named after the directory name and suffixed with -flow must exist inside the directory that contains the pages in the flow (the file may be empty, but it must exist)

- The first page in the flow must be named after the directory name that contains the flow

- The last page in the flow must not be located inside the directory containing the flow, and must be named after the directory name and suffixed with -return

Figure 7.3 illustrates these conventions:

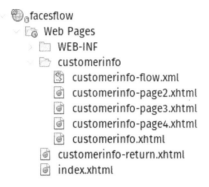

Figure 7.3 – Faces Flows conventions

In our example, we define a flow named "customerinfo". By convention, these files are inside a directory named "customerinfo", and the first page on the flow is named customerinfo.xhtml (there are no restrictions on the names of other pages in the flow). When we exit the flow, we navigate to a page named "flowname-return.xml" – in our case, since our flow is named "customerinfo", the name of the page in question is customerinfo-return.xhtml, which follows the naming convention and takes us out of the flow.

The markup for the pages doesn't illustrate anything we haven't seen before, so we will not examine it here – all example code is available as part of this book's code download bundle if you wish to review it yourself.

All of the preceding pages store data in a named bean named Customer, which has a flow scoped bean:

```
@Named
@FlowScoped("customerinfo")
public class Customer implements Serializable {
  //class body omitted
}
```

The @FlowScoped annotation has a value attribute that must match the name of the flow that the bean is meant to work with ("customerinfo", in this example).

This example creates a wizard-style set of pages in which data for a user is entered across several pages in the flow.

On the first page, we enter the customer's name information:

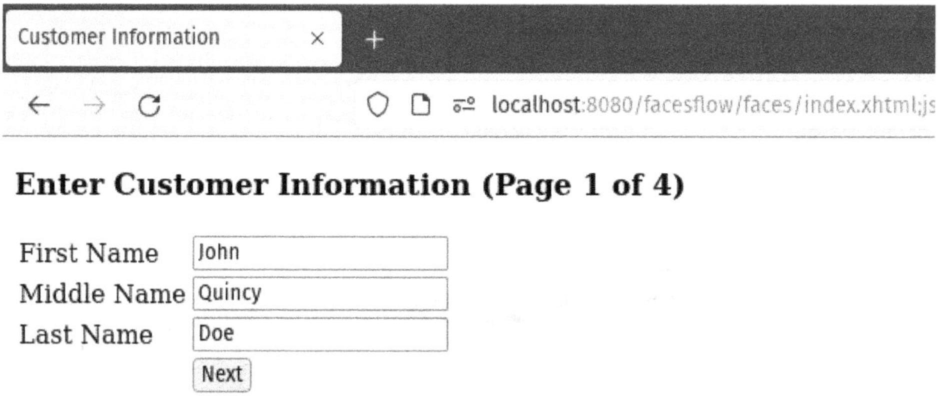

Figure 7.4 – First page of our Faces Flow example

On the second page, we enter the customer's address information:

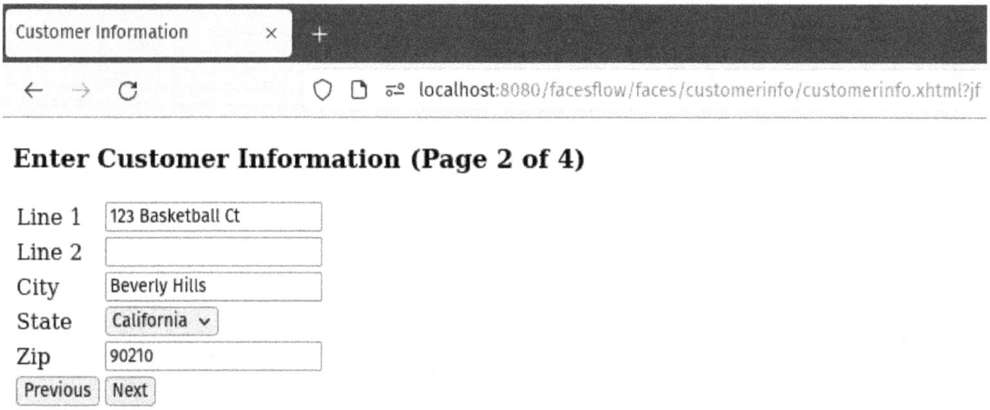

Figure 7.5 – Second page of our Faces Flow example

On the next page, we enter the customer's telephone contact details:

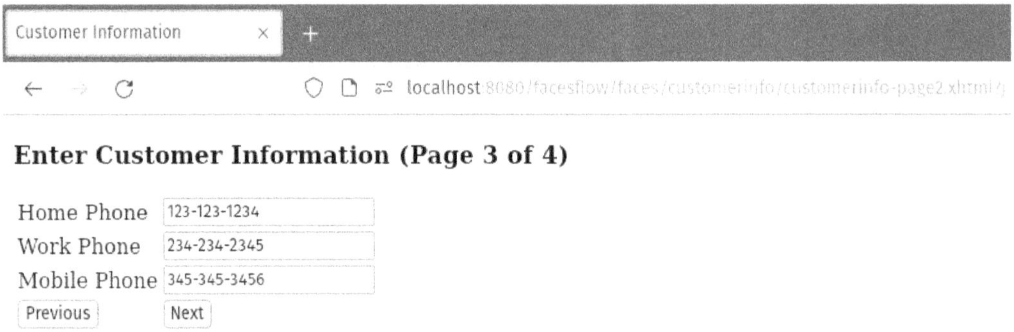

Figure 7.6 – Third page of our Faces Flow example

Finally, we display a confirmation page:

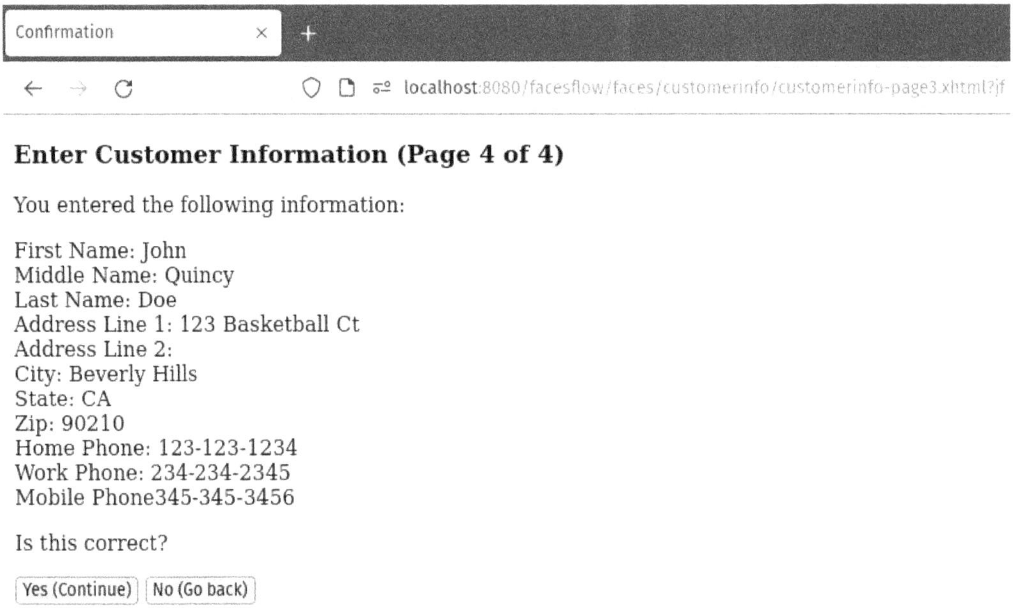

Figure 7.7 – Last page of our Faces Flow example

If the user verifies that the information is correct, we navigate outside the flow to `customerinfo-return.xhtml`; otherwise, we go back to the first page in the flow to allow the user to make any necessary corrections.

Faces WebSocket support

In typical web applications, servers always respond to requests from a browser. There is no way for a server to send data to the client browser without responding to a request. The **WebSocket** technology provides full duplex communication between a browser and a server, allowing servers to independently send data to a client without having to respond to a request. WebSocket allows myriad new applications to be developed for the web, including updating stock tickers, multiplayer online games, and chat applications.

> **Note**
> Although some of these types of web applications were developed before the advent of WebSockets, they relied on hacks to work around the limitations of HTTP. With WebSockets, these hacks are no longer necessary.

Traditionally, taking advantage of the WebSocket protocol when writing applications required a lot of JavaScript code. Faces' WebSocket supports abstracts out most of the JavaScript plumbing, allowing us to focus on developing the business logic of our applications.

The following example illustrates a simple chat application developed using Faces WebSocket support.

Note that Faces WebSocket support needs to be explicitly enabled. This can be done by adding a context parameter to our web.xml configuration file:

```xml
<?xml version="1.0" encoding="UTF-8"?>
<web-app xmlns="https://jakarta.ee/xml/ns/jakartaee"
         xmlns:xsi="http://www.w3.org/2001/XMLSchema-instance"
         xsi:schemaLocation="https://jakarta.ee/xml/ns/jakartaee
                   https://jakarta.ee/xml/ns/jakartaee/web-app_6_0.xsd"
         version="6.0">
  <servlet>
    <servlet-name>Faces Servlet</servlet-name>
    <servlet-class>
     jakarta.faces.webapp.FacesServlet
    </servlet-class>
    <load-on-startup>1</load-on-startup>
  </servlet>
  <servlet-mapping>
    <servlet-name>Faces Servlet</servlet-name>
    <url-pattern>/faces/*</url-pattern>
  </servlet-mapping>
  <context-param>
    <param-name>
    jakarta.faces.ENABLE_WEBSOCKET_ENDPOINT
```

```
        </param-name>
        <param-value>true</param-value>
    </context-param>
</web-app>
```

As illustrated in our example web.xml configuration file, to enable WebSocket support in our Faces applications, we need to set a context parameter named jakarta.faces.ENABLE_WEBSOCKET_ ENDPOINT and set its value to true.

Let's now take a look at how we can develop an application-scoped CDI named bean that is responsible for sending messages to all browser clients:

```
package com.ensode.jakartaeebook.faceswebsocket;

//imports omitted for brevity

@Named
@ApplicationScoped
public class FacesWebSocketMessageSender implements Serializable {

    private static final Logger LOG = Logger.getLogger(
            FacesWebSocketMessageSender.class.getName());

    @Inject
    @Push(channel = "websocketdemo")
    private PushContext pushContext;

    public void send(String message) {
        LOG.log(Level.INFO, String.format(""
                + "Sending message: %s", message));
        pushContext.send(message);
    }
}
```

As shown in the preceding example, in order to send data via WebSockets to the clients, we need to inject an instance of an implementation of the jakarta.faces.push.PushContext interface and annotate it with the @Push annotation. We can optionally specify a channel via the annotation's channel attribute. If we don't specify a channel name, then the name of the variable annotated with @Push will be used as the channel name by default.

To send the message to the WebSocket client, we need to invoke the send() method of the injected PushContext implementation. In our example, this is done in the send() method of our CDI named bean.

Further, in our example, there is a session-scoped CDI named bean that takes input from the user and passes it to the `send()` method of the preceding application-scoped CDI named bean. Our session-scoped CDI bean looks as follows:

```
package com.ensode.jakartaeebook.faceswebsocket;

//imports omitted for brevity

@Named
@SessionScoped
public class FacesWebSocketController implements Serializable {

    @Inject
    private FacesWebSocketMessageSender facesWebSocketMessageSender;

    private String userName;
    private String message;

    public void sendMessage() {
        facesWebSocketMessageSender.send(
                String.format("%s: %s", userName, message));
    }

    public String navigateToChatPage() {
        return "chat";
    }

    //setters and getters omitted for brevity
}
```

The `sendMessage()` method of the preceding class calls the `send()` method of the application-scoped CDI bean we discussed earlier, passing the name of the user and the message to be broadcasted to all browsers. The aforementioned `sendMessage()` method is invoked via Ajax when a user clicks a button on the corresponding page, as shown in the following markup:

```
<h:body>
  <h:form prependId="false">
    <h:panelGrid columns="2">
      <h:outputLabel for="chatWindow"
        value="Chat Window:"/>
      <textarea id="chatWindow" rows="10"/>
      <h:outputLabel for="chatInput"
        value="Type something here:"/>
      <h:inputText id="chatInput"
```

```
                value="#{facesWebSocketController.message}"/>
        <h:panelGroup/>
        <h:commandButton actionListener=
          "#{facesWebSocketController.sendMessage()}"
          value="Send message">
          <f:ajax execute="chatInput" render="chatWindow"/>
        </h:commandButton>
      </h:panelGrid>
    </h:form>

    <script type="text/javascript">
        function socketListener(message, channel, event) {
          var textArea =
            document.getElementById('chatWindow');
          var textAreaValue = textArea.value;
          if (textAreaValue.trim() !== '') {
            textAreaValue += "\n";
          }
          textAreaValue += message;
          textArea.value = textAreaValue;
          textArea.scrollTop = textArea.scrollHeight;
        }
    </script>
    <f:websocket id="webSocketTag" channel="websocketdemo"
                 onmessage="socketListener" />
  </h:body>
```

The `<f:websocket>` tag in the preceding markup is needed to enable WebSocket support for our page. The value of its `channel` attribute links the page to the corresponding `PushContext` instance on the server (in our example, it is defined in the application-scoped `FacesWebSocketMessageSender` CDI named bean). The value of this attribute must match the value of the corresponding attribute in the `@Push` annotation on the CDI bean (`"websocketdemo"` in our example).

After building and deploying our application, we can see it in action.

Figure 7.8 – Jakarta Faces WebSocket support

WebSocket technology allows us to develop two-way communication between web clients and servers. Jakarta Faces support for WebSocket makes it easy to implement WebSocket technologies in our Jakarta EE applications.

Additional Faces component libraries

In addition to the standard Jakarta Faces component libraries, there are a number of third-party libraries available. The following table lists two of the most popular.

Tag Library	Distributor	License	URL
ICEfaces	ICEsoft	MPL 1.1	`http://www.icefaces.org`
Primefaces	Prime Technology	Apache 2.0	`http://www.primefaces.org`

Table 7.2 – Jakarta Faces Component libraries

Using a third-party Jakarta Faces library allows us to develop elegant-looking applications without having to use much (if any) CSS. Most third-party Jakarta Faces contain drop-in replacements for standard Jakarta Faces components, such as `<h:inputText>` and `<h:commandButton>`, and also provide additional components that allow us to implement elaborate functionality with little effort. For example, most third-party libraries contain a table component with built-in pagination and sorting, freeing us from having to develop that functionality ourselves. Most real-life Jakarta Faces projects take advantage of a third-party component library, with PrimeFaces being the most popular one.

Summary

In this chapter, we covered how to develop web-based applications using Jakarta Faces, the standard component framework for the Jakarta EE:

- We covered how to develop Ajax-enabled Faces pages
- We explained how to integrate Faces and HTML5
- We covered how to develop wizard-like interfaces with Faces Flows
- We saw how to integrate WebSockets technology into our Jakarta Faces application
- We talked about third-party Jakarta Faces component libraries, which we can leverage to make our lives easier

In this chapter, we went beyond basic Jakarta Faces functionality, covering advanced Jakarta Faces features such as Ajax and WebSocket support.

8

Object Relational Mapping with Jakarta Persistence

Jakarta EE applications frequently need to persist data in a relational database. In this chapter, we will cover how to connect to a database and perform **Create, Read, Update, and Delete (CRUD) operations** via **Jakarta Persistence**.

Jakarta Persistence is the standard Jakarta EE **Object Relational Mapping (ORM)** tool. We will discuss this API in detail in this chapter.

The following are the topics covered in this chapter:

- The CUSTOMERDB database
- Configuring Jakarta Persistence
- Persisting data with Jakarta Persistence
- Entity relationships
- Composite primary keys
- Jakarta Persistence Query Language
- Criteria API
- Bean Validation support

Note

The source code used in this chapter can be found on GitHub at `https://github.com/PacktPublishing/Jakarta-EE-Application-Development/tree/main/ch08_src`.

The CUSTOMERDB database

Our examples in this chapter use a database called CUSTOMERDB. This database contains tables to track customers and order information for a fictitious store. For simplicity, the database uses an in-memory H2 database.

A simple utility that automatically starts the database and populates all reference tables is included with this book's example code. The utility can be found under ch08_src/customerdb. It is a Maven application. Therefore, it can be built from the command line via mvn install. It creates an executable JAR file with all dependencies included. The created JAR file can be found under the target directory, it can be run from the command line by issuing the following command:

```
java -jar customerdb-jar-with-dependencies.jar
```

The schema for the CUSTOMERDB database is depicted in *Figure 8.1*.

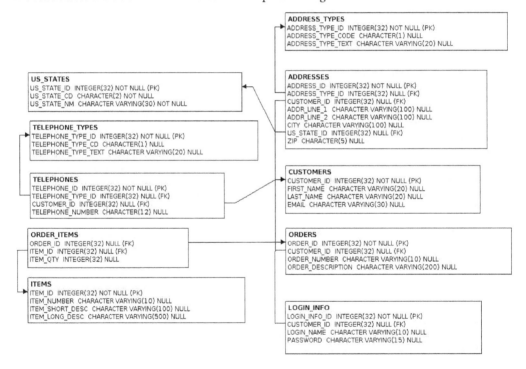

Figure 8.1 – CUSTOMERDB database schema

(The intent of this schema is to show the layout; the readability of the

text in the boxes, under the headings, is not essential.)

As can be seen in the diagram, the database contains tables to store customer information including their names, addresses, and email addresses. It also contains tables to store order and item information.

The ADDRESS_TYPES table stores values such as "Home", "Mailing" and "Shipping", to distinguish the type of address in the ADDRESSES table; similarly, the TELEPHONE_TYPES table stores the values "Cell", "Home", and "Work". These two tables are prepopulated when creating the database, as well as the US_STATES table.

> **Note**
>
> For simplicity, our database only deals with U.S. addresses.

Configuring Jakarta Persistence

Jakarta Persistence requires a bit of configuration before our code can work properly. A data source needs to be defined. The data source specifies information on how to reach the **Relational Database Management System** (**RDBMS**) system we are connecting to (server, port, database user credentials, etc.). There are two ways it can be set up. It can be done via the Jakarta EE implementation configuration, but how to do this is dependent on the specific implementation.

It can also be done by annotating an application-scoped CDI bean via the @DataSourceDefinition annotation.

There are advantages and disadvantages to each approach. Defining the data source as part of the Jakarta EE runtime configuration allows us to deploy our code to different environments (development, test, production) without having to make any modifications to our code. It also prevents adding any user credentials to our source. Using @DataSourceDefinition works across Jakarta EE implementations, and allows us to test and deploy our code without having to configure our Jakarta EE runtime.

For simplicity, our examples use @DataSourceDefinition, but for production code, configuring the Jakarta EE implementation is probably a better idea.

Typically, we use @DataSourceDefinition in an application-scoped CDI bean, as illustrated in the following example:

```
package com.ensode.jakartaeebook.beanvalidation.init;
//imports omitted for brevity

@ApplicationScoped
@DataSourceDefinition(name =
  "java:app/jdbc/customerdbDatasource",
  className = "org.h2.jdbcx.JdbcDataSource",
  url = "jdbc:h2:tcp://127.0.1.1:9092/mem:customerdb",
  user = "sa",
  password = "")
public class DbInitializer {
```

```
    private void init(@Observes @Initialized(ApplicationScoped.class)
Object object) {
        //This method will be invoked when the CDI application scope is
initialized, during deployment
        //No logic necessary, class level @DataSourceDefinition will
create a data source to be used by the application.
    }
}
```

The value of the name attribute in @DataSourceDefinition defines the JNDI name or our data source. The value of the url attribute of @DataSourceDefinition defines the **Java Database Connectivity (JDBC)** URL of our relational database, the exact format of the JDBC URL depends on the RDBMS we are using. For our examples, we are using an in-memory H2 database. The user and password attributes of @DataSourceDefinition define the user credentials needed to log in to our database.

Once a data source has been defined, an XML configuration file named persistence.xml must be deployed in the WAR file containing the aforementioned bean. This file must be placed in the WEB-INF/classes/META-INF/ directory inside the WAR file. An example persistence. xml configuration file is shown next:

```
<?xml version="1.0" encoding="UTF-8"?>
<persistence version="3.0" xmlns="http://xmlns.jcp.org/xml/ns/
persistence"
            xmlns:xsi="http://www.w3.org/2001/XMLSchema-
instance"
            xsi:schemaLocation="https://jakarta.ee/xml/ns/
persistence
                https://jakarta.ee/xml/ns/persistence/
persistence_3_0.xsd">
  <persistence-unit name="customerPersistenceUnit">
    <provider>org.eclipse.persistence.jpa.PersistenceProvider</
provider>
    <jta-data-source>java:app/jdbc/customerdbDatasource</jta-data-
source>
    <exclude-unlisted-classes>false</exclude-unlisted-classes>
  </persistence-unit>
</persistence>
```

persistence.xml must contain at least one <persistence-unit> element. Each <persistence-unit> element must provide a value for its name attribute and must contain a <jta-data-source> child element whose value is the JNDI name of the data source to be used for the persistence unit.

The value of the <jta-data-source> tag must come from a data source configured in our Jakarta EE implementation. Notice that in our example, the value of the <jta-data-source> tag matches the value of the name attribute in the data source we defined using @DataSourceDefinition.

The value of the `<provider>` tag must be an implementation of the `jakarta.persistence.spi.PersistenceProvider` interface. The exact value depends on the Jakarta Persistence implementation being used. In our example, we are using GlassFish as our Jakarta EE implementation, which includes EclipseLink as its Jakarta Persistence implementation. Therefore, we use the EclipseLink-provided PersistenceProvider implementation.

The reason more than one `<persistence-unit>` element is allowed is because an application may access more than one database. A `<persistence-unit>` element is required for each database the application will access. If the application defines more than one `<persistence-unit>` element, then the `@PersistenceContext` annotation used to inject `EntityManager` must provide a value for its `unitName` element. The value for this element must match the `name` attribute of the corresponding `<persistence-unit>` element in `persistence.xml`.

If our `persistence.xml` configuration class defines more than one persistence unit, we need to list the Jakarta Persistence entities managed by that persistence unit via a `<class>` tag inside each `<persistence-unit>` tag. Listing each Jakarta EE entity inside `<persistence-unit>` is a tedious task, but thankfully, most projects define a single persistence unit. We can avoid listing each and every Jakarta Persistence entity by using the `<exclude-unlisted-classes>` tag with a value of `false`, as illustrated in our example.

Persisting data with Jakarta Persistence

Jakarta Persistence is used to persist data to an RDBMS. Jakarta Persistence Entities are regular Java classes; the Jakarta EE runtime knows these classes are Entities because they are decorated with the `@Entity` annotation. Let's look at a Jakarta Persistence Entity mapping to the CUSTOMER table in the CUSTOMERDB database:

```
package com.ensode.jakartaeebook.persistenceintro.entity
//imports omitted for brevity
@Entity
@Table(name = "CUSTOMERS")
public class Customer implements Serializable {
  @Id
  @Column(name = "CUSTOMER_ID")
  private Long customerId;
  @Column(name = "FIRST_NAME")
  private String firstName;
  @Column(name = "LAST_NAME")
  private String lastName;
  private String email;
  //getters and setters omitted for brevity
}
```

In our example code, the `@Entity` annotation lets any other Jakarta EE-compliant runtime know that this class is a Jakarta Persistence entity.

The `@Table(name = "CUSTOMERS")` annotation lets the application server know what table to map the entity to. The value of the name element contains the name of the database table that the entity maps to. This annotation is optional. If the name of the class maps the name of the database table (case insensitive), then it isn't necessary to specify what table the entity maps to.

The `@Id` annotation indicates that the `customerId` field maps to the primary key.

The `@Column` annotation maps each field to a column in the table. If the name of the field matches the name of the database column, then this annotation is not needed. This is the reason why the `email` field is not annotated.

The `EntityManager` interface is used to persist entities to a database. The following example illustrates its usage:

```
package com.ensode.jakartaeebook.persistenceintro.namedbean;
//imports omitted for brevity
@Named
@RequestScoped
public class JakartaPersistenceDemoBean {
  @PersistenceContext
  private EntityManager entityManager;
  @Resource
  private UserTransaction userTransaction;
  public String updateDatabase() {
    String retVal = "confirmation";
    Customer customer = new Customer();
    Customer customer2 = new Customer();
    Customer customer3;

    customer.setCustomerId(3L);
    customer.setFirstName("James");
    customer.setLastName("McKenzie");
    customer.setEmail("jamesm@example.com");

    customer2.setCustomerId(4L);
    customer2.setFirstName("Charles");
    customer2.setLastName("Jonson");
    customer2.setEmail("cjohnson@example.org");

    try {
      userTransaction.begin();
      entityManager.persist(customer);
```

```
        entityManager.persist(customer2);
        customer3 = entityManager.find(Customer.class, 4L);
        customer3.setLastName("Johnson");
        entityManager.persist(customer3);
        entityManager.remove(customer);

        userTransaction.commit();
    } catch (Exception e) {
        retVal = "error";
        e.printStackTrace();
    }
    return retVal;
    }
}
```

Our example CDI named bean obtains an instance of a class implementing the `jakarta.persistence.EntityManager` interface via dependency injection. This is done by decorating the `EntityManager` variable with the `@PersistenceContext` annotation.

An instance of a class implementing the `jakarta.transaction.UserTransaction` interface is then injected via the `@Resource` annotation. This object is necessary, as without it, invoking calls to persist Entities to the database the code would throw a `jakarta.persistence.TransactionRequiredException`.

`EntityManager` instances perform many database-related tasks including finding entities in the database, updating them, and deleting them.

Since Jakarta Persistence entities are **plain old Java objects** (**POJOs**), they can be instantiated via the new operator.

Calls to the `persist()` method on `EntityManager` must be in a transaction, therefore it is necessary to start one by calling the `begin()` method on `UserTransaction`.

We then insert two new rows into the CUSTOMERS table by calling the `persist()` method on `EntityManager` for the two instances of the `Customer` class we populated earlier in the code.

After persisting the data contained in the `customer` and `customer2` objects, we search the database for a row in the CUSTOMERS table with a primary key of 4. We do this by invoking the `find()` method on `EntityManager`. This method takes the class of `Entity` we are searching for as its first parameter, and the primary key of the row corresponding to the object we want to obtain.

The primary key we set for the `customer2` object was 4, therefore what we have now is a copy of this object. The last name of this customer was misspelled when we originally inserted his data into the database, so we now correct Mr. Johnson's last name by invoking the `setLastName()` method on `customer3`, then update the information in the database by invoking `entityManager.persist()`.

We then delete the information for the customer object by invoking `entityManager.remove()` and passing the `customer` object as a parameter.

Finally, we commit the changes to the database by invoking the `commit()` method on `userTransaction`.

Cannot persist detached object exception

Frequently, an application will retrieve a Jakarta Persistence entity via the `EntityManager.find()` method, then pass this entity to a business or user interface layer, where it will potentially be modified, and later the database data corresponding to the entity will be updated. In cases like this, invoking `EntityManager.persist()` will result in an exception. In order to update Jakarta Persistence entities this way we need to invoke `EntityManager.merge()`. This method takes an instance of the Jakarta Persistence entity as its single argument and updates the corresponding row in the database with the data stored in it.

Now that we've seen how to handle single Jakarta Persistence entities, we'll focus our attention on how to define entity relationships.

Entity relationships

In the previous section, we saw how to retrieve, insert, update, and delete single entities from the database. Entities are rarely isolated – in the vast majority of cases, they are related to other entities.

Entities can have one-to-one, one-to-many, many-to-one, and many-to-many relationships.

In the CUSTOMERDB database, for example, there is a **one-to-one relationship** between the LOGIN_INFO and the CUSTOMERS tables. This means that each customer has exactly one corresponding row in the login info table. There is also a **one-to-many relationship** between the CUSTOMERS table and the ORDERS table. This is because a customer can place many orders, but each order belongs only to a single customer. There is also a **many-to-many relationship** between the ORDERS table and the ITEMS table. This is because an order can contain many items and an item can be in many orders.

In the next few sections, we discuss how to establish relationships between Jakarta Persistence entities.

One-to-one relationships

One-to-one relationships occur when an instance of an entity can have zero or one corresponding instance of another entity.

One-to-one entity relationships can be bidirectional (each entity is aware of the relationship) or unidirectional (only one of the entities is aware of the relationship). In the CUSTOMERDB database, the one-to-one mapping between the LOGIN_INFO and the CUSTOMERS tables is unidirectional, since the LOGIN_INFO table has a foreign key to the CUSTOMERS table, but not the other way around.

As we will soon see, this fact does not stop us from creating a bidirectional one-to-one relationship between the `Customer` entity and the `LoginInfo` entity.

The source code for the `LoginInfo` entity, which maps to the `LOGIN_INFO` table, is as follows:

```
package com.ensode.jakartaeebook.entityrelationship.entity;
//imports omitted for brevity
@Entity
@Table(name = "LOGIN_INFO")
public class LoginInfo {
  @Id
  @Column(name = "LOGIN_INFO_ID")
  private Long loginInfoId;
  @Column(name = "LOGIN_NAME")
  private String loginName;

  private String password;


  @OneToOne
  @JoinColumn(name = "CUSTOMER_ID")
  private Customer customer;


  //getters and setters omitted for brevity


}
```

The code for this entity is very similar to the code for the `Customer` entity; it defines fields that map to database columns. Each field whose name does not match the database column name is annotated with @Column, in addition to that, the primary key is annotated with @Id.

Where the preceding code gets interesting is in the declaration of the `customer` field. As can be seen in the code, the `customer` field is annotated with @OneToOne, this lets the Jakarta EE runtime know that there is a one-to-one relationship between this entity and the `Customer` entity. The customer field is also annotated with @JoinColumn. This annotation lets the container know what column in the LOGIN_INFO table is the foreign key corresponding to the primary key on the CUSTOMER table. Since LOGIN_INFO, the table that the `LoginInfo` entity maps to, has a foreign key to the CUSTOMER table, the `LoginInfo` entity owns the relationship. If the relationship was unidirectional, we wouldn't have to make any changes to the `Customer` entity. However, since we would like to have a bidirectional relationship between these two entities, we need to add a `LoginInfo` field to the `Customer` entity, along with the corresponding getter and setter methods.

As we mentioned before, in order to make the one-to-one relationship between the Customer and LoginInfo entities bidirectional, we need to make a few simple changes to the Customer entity:

```
package com.ensode.jakartaeebook.entityrelationship.entity;

//imports omitted for brevity

@Entity
@Table(name = "CUSTOMERS")
public class Customer implements Serializable {
  @Id
  @Column(name = "CUSTOMER_ID")
  private Long customerId;
  @Column(name = "FIRST_NAME")
  private String firstName;
  @Column(name = "LAST_NAME")
  private String lastName;
  private String email;

  @OneToOne(mappedBy = "customer")
  private LoginInfo loginInfo;

  public LoginInfo getLoginInfo() {
    return loginInfo;
  }

  public void setLoginInfo(LoginInfo loginInfo) {
    this.loginInfo = loginInfo;
  }

  //additional setters and getters omitted for brevity
}
```

The only change we need to make to the Customer entity to make the one-to-one relationship bidirectional is to add a LoginInfo field to it, along with the corresponding setter and getter methods. The loginInfo field is annotated with @OneToOne. Since the Customer entity does not own the relationship (the table it maps to does not have a foreign key to the corresponding table), the mappedBy element of the @OneToOne annotation needs to be added. This element specifies what field in the corresponding entity has the other end of the relationship. In this particular case, the customer field in the LoginInfo entity corresponds to the other end of this one-to-one relationship.

The following Java class illustrates the use of the preceding entity:

```java
package com.ensode.jakartaeebook.entityrelationship.namedbean;
//imports omitted for brevity
@Named
@RequestScoped
public class OneToOneRelationshipDemoBean {

  @PersistenceContext
  private EntityManager entityManager;
  @Resource
  private UserTransaction userTransaction;

  public String updateDatabase() {
    String retVal = "confirmation";
    Customer customer;
    LoginInfo loginInfo = new LoginInfo();
    loginInfo.setLoginInfoId(1L);
    loginInfo.setLoginName("charlesj");
    loginInfo.setPassword("iwonttellyou");

    try {
      userTransaction.begin();
      customer = entityManager.find(Customer.class, 4L);
      loginInfo.setCustomer(customer);
      entityManager.persist(loginInfo);
      userTransaction.commit();
    } catch (Exception e) {
      retVal = "error";
      e.printStackTrace();
    }

    return retVal;
  }
}
```

In this example, we first create an instance of the LoginInfo entity and populate it with some data. We then obtain an instance of the Customer entity from the database by invoking the find() method of EntityManager (data for this entity was inserted into the CUSTOMERS table in one of the previous examples). We then invoke the setCustomer() method on the LoginInfo entity, passing the customer object as a parameter. Finally, we invoke the EntityManager.persist() method to save the data in the database.

What happens behind the scenes is that the CUSTOMER_ID column of the LOGIN_INFO table gets populated with the primary key of the corresponding row in the CUSTOMERS table. This can be easily verified by querying the CUSTOMERDB database.

> **Note**
>
> Notice how the call to EntityManager.find() to obtain the customer entity is inside the same transaction where we call EntityManager.persist(). If this is not the case the database will not be updated successfully.

One-to-many relationships

Jakarta Persistence one-to-many entity relationships can be *bidirectional* (i.e., one entity contains a many-to-one relationship and the corresponding entity contains an inverse one-to-many relationship) or *unidirectional* (one entity contains a many-to-one relationship to another entity, which does not have a corresponding one-to-many relationship defined).

With SQL, one-to-many relationships are defined by foreign keys in one of the tables. The "many" part of the relationship is the one containing a foreign key to the "one" part of the relationship. One-to-many relationships defined in an RDBMS are typically unidirectional, since making them bidirectional usually results in denormalized data.

Just like when defining a unidirectional one-to-many relationship in an RDBMS, in Jakarta Persistence the "many" part of the relationship is the one that has a reference to the "one" part of the relationship, therefore the annotation used to define the relationship is @ManyToOne.

In the CUSTOMERDB database, there is a unidirectional one-to-many relationship between customers and orders. We define this relationship in the Order entity:

```
package com.ensode.jakartaeebook.entityrelationship.entity;

//imports omitted for brevity

@Entity
@Table(name = "ORDERS")
public class Order {
  @Id
  @Column(name = "ORDER_ID")
  private Long orderId;
  @Column(name = "ORDER_NUMBER")
  private String orderNumber;
  @Column(name = "ORDER_DESCRIPTION")
  private String orderDescription;
  @ManyToOne
```

```
    @JoinColumn(name = "CUSTOMER_ID")
    private Customer customer;

    //setters and getters omitted for brevity
}
```

If we were to define a unidirectional many-to-one relationship between the `Orders` entity and the `Customer` entity, we wouldn't need to make any changes to the `Customer` entity. To define a bidirectional one-to-many relationship between the two entities, a new field decorated with the @ `OneToMany` annotation needs to be added to the `Customer` entity, as illustrated in the next example:

```
package com.ensode.jakartaeebook.entityrelationship.entity;
//imports omitted for brevity
@Entity
@Table(name = "CUSTOMERS")
public class Customer implements Serializable {
    @Id
    @Column(name = "CUSTOMER_ID")
    private Long customerId;
    @Column(name = "FIRST_NAME")
    private String firstName;
    @Column(name = "LAST_NAME")
    private String lastName;
    private String email;

    @OneToOne(mappedBy = "customer")
    private LoginInfo loginInfo;

    @OneToMany(mappedBy = "customer")
    private Set<Order> orders;

    public Set<Order> getOrders() {
        return orders;
    }
    public void setOrders(Set<Order> orders) {
        this.orders = orders;
    }
    //additional getters and setters omitted for brevity
}
```

The only difference between this version of the `Customer` entity and the previous one is the addition of the orders field and related getter and setter methods. Of special interest is the @OneToMany annotation decorating this field. The mappedBy attribute must match the name of the corresponding field in the entity corresponding to the "many" part of the relationship. In simple terms, the value of the mappedBy attribute must match the name of the field decorated with the @ManyToOne annotation in the bean at the other side of the relationship.

The following example code illustrates how to persist one-to-many relationships to the database:

```
package com.ensode.jakartaeebook.entityrelationship.namedbean;

//imports omitted for brevity

@Named
@RequestScoped
public class OneToManyRelationshipDemoBean {
  @PersistenceContext
  private EntityManager entityManager;
  @Resource
  private UserTransaction userTransaction;

  public String updateDatabase() {
    String retVal = "confirmation";

    Customer customer;
    Order order1;
    Order order2;

    order1 = new Order();
    order1.setOrderId(1L);
    order1.setOrderNumber("SFX12345");
    order1.setOrderDescription("Dummy order.");

    order2 = new Order();
    order2.setOrderId(2L);
    order2.setOrderNumber("SFX23456");
    order2.setOrderDescription("Another dummy order.");

    try {
      userTransaction.begin();
      customer = entityManager.find(Customer.class, 4L);
      order1.setCustomer(customer);
      order2.setCustomer(customer);
      entityManager.persist(order1);
      entityManager.persist(order2);
      userTransaction.commit();
    }catch (NotSupportedException |
      SystemException |
```

```
            SecurityException |
            IllegalStateException |
            RollbackException |
            HeuristicMixedException |
            HeuristicRollbackException e) {
            retVal = "error";
            e.printStackTrace();
        }
            return retVal;
    }
}
```

Our example instantiates two instances of the `Order` entity, populates them with some data, then in a transaction, an instance of the `Customer` entity is located, and used as the parameter of the `setCustomer()` method of both instances of the `Order` entity. We then persist both `Order` entities by invoking `EntityManager.persist()` for each one of them.

Just like when dealing with one-to-one relationships, what happens behind the scenes is that the `CUSTOMER_ID` column of the `ORDERS` table in the `CUSTOMERDB` database is populated with the primary key corresponding to the related row in the `CUSTOMERS` table.

Since the relationship is bidirectional, we can obtain all orders related to a customer by invoking the `getOrders()` method on the `Customer` entity.

Many-to-many relationships

In the `CUSTOMERDB` database, there is a many-to-many relationship between the `ORDERS` table and the `ITEMS` table. We can map this relationship by adding a new `Collection<Item>` field to the `Order` entity and decorating it with the `@ManyToMany` annotation:

```
package com.ensode.jakartaeebook.entityrelationship.entity;
//imports omitted for brevity
@Entity
@Table(name = "ORDERS")
public class Order {
  @Id
  @Column(name = "ORDER_ID")
  private Long orderId;
  @Column(name = "ORDER_NUMBER")
  private String orderNumber;
  @Column(name = "ORDER_DESCRIPTION")
  private String orderDescription;

  @ManyToOne
```

```
@JoinColumn(name = "CUSTOMER_ID")
private Customer customer;

@ManyToMany
@JoinTable(name = "ORDER_ITEMS",
  joinColumns = @JoinColumn(name = "ORDER_ID",
    referencedColumnName = "ORDER_ID"),
  inverseJoinColumns = @JoinColumn(name = "ITEM_ID",
    referencedColumnName = "ITEM_ID"))
private Collection<Item> items;

public Collection<Item> getItems() {
  return items;
}
public void setItems(Collection<Item> items) {
  this.items = items;
}
//additional getters and setters omitted
}
```

As we can see in the preceding code, in addition to being annotated with @ManyToMany, the items field is also annotated with @JoinTable. As its name suggests, this annotation lets the application server know what table is used as a join table to create the many-to-many relationship between the two entities.

@JoinTable has three relevant elements: the name element, which defines the name of the join table, and the joinColumns and inverseJoinColumns elements, which define the columns that serve as foreign keys in the join table pointing to the entities' primary keys. Values for the joinColumns and inverseJoinColumns elements are yet another annotation, the @JoinColumn annotation. This annotation has two relevant elements, the name element, which defines the name of the column in the join table, and the referencedColumnName element, which defines the name of the column in the entity table.

The Item entity is a simple entity mapping to the ITEMS table in the CUSTOMERDB database:

```
package com.ensode.jakartaeebook.entityrelationship.entity;
//imports omitted for brevity
@Entity
@Table(name = "ITEMS")
public class Item {
  @Id
  @Column(name = "ITEM_ID")
  private Long itemId;
  @Column(name = "ITEM_NUMBER")
```

```
    private String itemNumber;
    @Column(name = "ITEM_SHORT_DESC")
    private String itemShortDesc;
    @Column(name = "ITEM_LONG_DESC")
    private String itemLongDesc;
    @ManyToMany(mappedBy = "items")
    private Collection<Order> orders;

    public Collection<Order> getOrders() {
      return orders;
    }
    public void setOrders(Collection<Order> orders) {
      this.orders = orders;
    }
    //addtional getters and setters omitted for brevity
}
```

Just like one-to-one and one-to-many relationships, many-to-many relationships can be unidirectional or bidirectional. Since we would like the many-to-many relationship between the Order and Item entities to be bidirectional, we added a Collection<Order> field and decorated it with the @ManyToMany annotation. Since the corresponding field in the Order entity already has the join table defined, it is not necessary to do it again here. The entity containing the @JoinTable annotation is said to own the relationship, in a many-to-many relationship, either entity can own the relationship. In our example, the Order entity owns it, since its Collection<Item> field is decorated with the @JoinTable annotation.

Just like with the one-to-one and one-to-many relationships, the @ManyToMany annotation on the non-owning side of a bidirectional many-to-many relationship must contain a mappedBy element indicating what field in the owning entity defines the relationship.

Now that we have seen the changes necessary to establish a bidirectional many-to-many relationship between the Order and Item entities, we can see the relationship in action in the following example:

```
package com.ensode.jakartaeebook.entityrelationship.namedbean;
//imports omitted for brevity
@Named
@RequestScoped
public class ManyToManyRelationshipDemoBean {
    @PersistenceContext
    private EntityManager entityManager;
    @Resource
    private UserTransaction userTransaction;

    public String updateDatabase() {
```

```
        String retVal = "confirmation";
        Order order;
        Collection<Item> items = new ArrayList<Item>();
        Item item1 = new Item();
        Item item2 = new Item();

        item1.setItemId(1L);
        item1.setItemNumber("BCD1234");
        item1.setItemShortDesc("Notebook Computer");

        item2.setItemId(2L);
        item2.setItemNumber("CDF2345");
        item2.setItemShortDesc("Cordless Mouse");

        items.add(item1);
        items.add(item2);

        try {
          userTransaction.begin();

          entityManager.persist(item1);
          entityManager.persist(item2);

          order = entityManager.find(Order.class, 1L);
          order.setItems(items);

          entityManager.persist(order);
          userTransaction.commit();
        } catch (Exception e) {
          retVal = "error";
          e.printStackTrace();
        }
        return retVal;
      }
  }
```

The preceding code creates two instances of the Item entity and populates them with some data. It then adds these two instances to a collection. A transaction is then started, the two Item instances are persisted in the database. Then an instance of the Order entity is retrieved from the database. The setItems() method of the Order entity instance is then invoked, passing the collection containing the two Item instances as a parameter. The Customer instance is then persisted into the database. At this point, two rows are created behind the scenes to the ORDER_ITEMS table, which is the join table between the ORDERS and ITEMS tables.

Composite primary keys

Most tables in the CUSTOMERDB database have a column with the sole purpose of serving as a primary key (this type of primary key is sometimes referred to as a surrogate primary key or as an artificial primary key). However, some databases are not designed this way. Instead, a column in the database that is known to be unique across rows is used as the primary key. If there is no column whose value is not guaranteed to be unique across rows, then a combination of two or more columns is used as the table's primary key. It is possible to map this kind of primary key to Jakarta Persistence entities by using a **primary key class**.

There is one table in the CUSTOMERDB database that does not have a surrogate primary key, this table is the ORDER_ITEMS table. This table serves as a join table between the ORDERS and ITEMS tables. In addition to having foreign keys for these two tables, this table has an additional column called ITEM_QTY, which stores the quantity of each item in an order. Since this table does not have a surrogate primary key, the Jakarta Persistence entity mapping to it must have a custom primary key class. In this table, the combination of the ORDER_ID and the ITEM_ID columns must be unique. Therefore, this is a good combination for a composite primary key, as illustrated in the following example:

```java
package com.ensode.jakartaeebook.compositeprimarykeys.entity;
import java.io.Serializable;
public class OrderItemPK implements Serializable {
  public Long orderId;
  public Long itemId;

  public OrderItemPK() {
  }
  public OrderItemPK(Long orderId, Long itemId) {
    this.orderId = orderId;
    this.itemId = itemId;
  }
  @Override
  public boolean equals(Object obj) {
    boolean returnVal = false;

    if (obj == null) {
      returnVal = false;
    } else if (!obj.getClass().equals(this.getClass())) {
      returnVal = false;
    } else {
      OrderItemPK other = (OrderItemPK) obj;
      if (this == other) {
        returnVal = true;
      } else if (orderId != null && other.orderId != null
          && this.orderId.equals(other.orderId)) {
```

```
          if (itemId != null && other.itemId != null
              && itemId.equals(other.itemId)) {
            returnVal = true;
          }
        } else {
          returnVal = false;
        }
      }
      return returnVal;
    }
    @Override
    public int hashCode() {
      if (orderId == null || itemId == null) {
        return 0;
      } else {
        return orderId.hashCode() ^ itemId.hashCode();
      }
    }
  }
}
```

A custom primary key class must satisfy the following requirements:

- The class must be public

- It must implement `java.io.Serializable`

- It must have a public constructor that takes no arguments

- Its fields must be `public` or `protected`

- Its field names and types must match those of the entity

- It must override the default `hashCode()` and `equals()` methods defined in the `java.lang.Object` class

The preceding `OrderPK` class meets all of these requirements. It also has a convenience constructor that takes two `Long` objects meant to initialize its `orderId` and `itemId` fields. This constructor was added for convenience; this is not a requirement for the class to be used as a primary key class.

When an entity uses a custom primary key class, it must be annotated with `@IdClass`. Since the `OrderItem` class uses `OrderItemPK` as its custom primary key class, it is annotated with said annotation:

```
package com.ensode.jakartaeebook.compositeprimarykeys.entity;
//imports omitted
@Entity
@Table(name = "ORDER_ITEMS")
@IdClass(value = OrderItemPK.class)
```

```
public class OrderItem {
  @Id
  @Column(name = "ORDER_ID")
  private Long orderId;
  @Id
  @Column(name = "ITEM_ID")
  private Long itemId;
  @Column(name = "ITEM_QTY")
  private Long itemQty;

  //getters and setters omitted
}
```

There are two differences between the `OrderItem` entity and the previous entities we have seen. The first difference is that this entity is annotated with `@IdClass`, indicating the primary key class corresponding to it. The second difference is that `OrderItem` has more than one field annotated with `@Id`. Since this entity has a composite primary key, each field that is part of the primary key must be annotated with this annotation.

Obtaining a reference of an entity with a composite primary key is not much different than obtaining a reference to an entity with a primary key consisting of a single field. The following example demonstrates how to do this:

```
package com.ensode.jakartaeebook.compositeprimarykeys.namedbean;
//imports omitted for brevity
@Named
@RequestScoped
public class CompositePrimaryKeyDemoBean {
  @PersistenceContext
  private EntityManager entityManager;
  private OrderItem orderItem;

  public String findOrderItem() {
    String retVal = "confirmation";

    try {
      orderItem = entityManager.find(OrderItem.class,
      new OrderItemPK(1L, 2L));
    } catch (Exception e) {
      retVal = "error";
      e.printStackTrace();
    }
    return retVal;
  }
  //getters and setters omitted
}
```

As can be seen in this example, the only difference between locating an entity with a composite primary key and an entity with a primary key consisting of a single field is that an instance of the custom primary key class must be passed as the second argument of the `EntityManager.find()` method; fields for this instance must be populated with the appropriate values for each field that is part of the primary key.

Jakarta Persistence Query Language

All of our examples that obtain entities from the database so far have conveniently assumed that the primary key for the entity is known ahead of time. We all know that frequently this is not the case. Whenever we need to search for an entity by a field other than the entity's primary key, we can use the **Jakarta Persistence Query Language (JPQL)**.

JPQL is an SQL-like language used for retrieving, updating, and deleting entities in a database. The following example illustrates how to use JPQL to retrieve a subset of states from the US_STATES table in the CUSTOMERDB database:

```
package com.ensode.jakartaeebook.jpql.namedbean;
//imports omitted for brevity
@Named
@RequestScoped
public class SelectQueryDemoBean {
  @PersistenceContext
  private EntityManager entityManager;
  private List<UsState> matchingStatesList;

  public String findStates() {
    String retVal = "confirmation";
    try {
      Query query = entityManager.createQuery(
          "SELECT s FROM UsState s WHERE s.usStateNm "
            + "LIKE :name");
      query.setParameter("name", "New%");
      matchingStatesList = query.getResultList();
    } catch (Exception e) {
      retVal = "error";
      e.printStackTrace();
    }

    return retVal;
  }
  //getters and setters omitted for brevity
}
```

The preceding code invokes the `EntityManager.createQuery()` method, passing a `String` containing a JPQL query as a parameter. This method returns an instance of `jakarta.persistence.Query`. The query retrieves all `UsState` entities whose names start with the word "New".

As can be seen in the preceding code, JPQL is similar to SQL, however, there are some differences that may confuse readers with SQL knowledge. The equivalent SQL code for the query in the code is as follows:

```
SELECT * from US_STATES s where s.US_STATE_NM like 'New%'
```

The first difference between JPQL and SQL is that in JPQL, we always reference entity names, whereas in SQL table names are referenced. The `s` after the entity name in the JPQL query is an alias for the entity. Table aliases are optional in SQL, but entity aliases are required in JPQL. Keeping these differences in mind, the JPQL query should now be a lot less confusing.

The `:name` in the query is a **named parameter**. Named parameters are meant to be substituted with actual values. This is done by invoking the `setParameter()` method in the instance of `jakarta.persistence.Query` returned by the call to `EntityManager.createQuery()`. A JPQL query can have multiple named parameters.

To actually run the query and retrieve the entities from the database, we can invoke the `getResultList()` method on the instance of `jakarta.persistence.Query` obtained from `EntityManager.createQuery()`. This method returns an instance of a class implementing the `java.util.List` interface, this list contains the entities matching the query criteria. If no entities match the criteria, then an empty list is returned.

If we are certain that the query will return exactly one entity, then the `getSingleResult()` method may be alternatively called on `Query`, this method returns an `Object` that must be cast to the appropriate entity.

The preceding example uses the `LIKE` operator to find entities whose name starts with the word "New". This is accomplished by substituting the query's named parameter with the value `New%`. The percent sign at the end of the parameter value means that any number of characters after the word "New" will match the expression. The percent sign can be used anywhere in the parameter value, for example, a value of `%Dakota` would match any entities whose names end in "Dakota", while a value of `A%a` would match any states whose names start with a capital "A" and end with a lowercase "a". There can be more than one percent sign in a parameter value. The underscore sign (_) can be used to match a single character, all the rules for the percent sign apply to the underscore as well.

In addition to the `LIKE` operator, there are other operators that can be used to retrieve entities from the database:

- The = operator will retrieve entities whose field on the left of the operator exactly match the value to the right of the operator

- The > operator will retrieve entities whose field on the left of the operator is greater than the value to the right of the operator

- The < operator will retrieve entities whose field on the left of the operator is less than the value to the right of the operator

- The >= operator will retrieve entities whose field on the left of the operator is greater than or equal to the value to the right of the operator

- The <= operator will retrieve entities whose field on the left of the operator is less than or equal to the value to the right of the operator

All of the preceding operators work the same way as the equivalent operators in SQL. Just like in SQL, these operators can be combined with the "AND" and "OR" operators. Conditions combined with the "AND" operator match if both conditions are true, while conditions combined with the "OR" operator match if at least one of the conditions is true.

If we intend to use a query many times, it can be stored in a **named query**. Named queries can be defined by decorating the relevant entity class with the @NamedQuery annotation. This annotation has two elements, a name element used to set the name of the query; and a query element defining the query itself. To execute a named query, the createNamedQuery() method must be invoked in an instance of EntityManager. This method takes a String containing the query name as its sole parameter, and returns an instance of jakarta.persistence.Query.

In addition to retrieving entities, JPQL can be used to modify or delete entities. However, entity modification and deletion can be done programmatically via the EntityManager interface, doing so results in code that tends to be more readable than when using JPQL. Because of this, we will not cover entity modification and deletion via JPQL. Readers interested in writing JPQL queries to modify and delete entities, as well as readers wishing to know more about JPQL are encouraged to review the Jakarta Persistence 3.1 specification. This specification can be found at https://jakarta.ee/specifications/persistence/3.1/jakarta-persistence-spec-3.1.

In addition to JPQL, Jakarta Persistence provides an API we can use to create queries, named, appropriately enough, the Criteria API.

Criteria API

The Jakarta Persistence **Criteria API** is meant as a complement to JPQL. The Criteria API allows us to write Jakarta Persistence queries programmatically, without having to rely on JPQL.

The Criteria API offers a few advantages over JPQL – for instance, JPQL queries are stored as Strings, and the compiler has no way of validating JPQL syntax. Additionally, JPQL is not type safe; we could write a JPQL query in which our where clause could have a string value for a numeric property, and our code would compile and deploy just fine.

The following code example illustrates how to use the Criteria API in our Jakarta EE applications:

```
package com.ensode.jakartaeebook.criteriaapi.namedbean;
//imports omitted for brevity
@Named
@RequestScoped
public class CriteriaApiDemoBean {
  @PersistenceContext
  private EntityManager entityManager;
  private List<UsState> matchingStatesList;

  public String findStates() {
    String retVal = "confirmation";
    try {
      CriteriaBuilder criteriaBuilder = entityManager.
          getCriteriaBuilder();
      CriteriaQuery<UsState> criteriaQuery =
        criteriaBuilder.createQuery(UsState.class);
      Root<UsState> root = criteriaQuery.from(
          UsState.class);

      Metamodel metamodel = entityManager.getMetamodel();
      EntityType<UsState> usStateEntityType =
        metamodel.entity(UsState.class);
      SingularAttribute<UsState, String> usStateAttribute =
       usStateEntityType.getDeclaredSingularAttribute(
          "usStateNm",String.class);
      Path<String> path = root.get(usStateAttribute);
      Predicate predicate = criteriaBuilder.like(
        path, "New%");
      criteriaQuery = criteriaQuery.where(predicate);
      TypedQuery typedQuery = entityManager.createQuery(
              criteriaQuery);
      matchingStatesList = typedQuery.getResultList();
    } catch (Exception e) {
      retVal = "error";
      e.printStackTrace();
    }
    return retVal;
  }

  //getters and setters omitted for brevity
}
```

The preceding example is equivalent to the JPQL example we saw earlier in this chapter. This example, however, takes advantage of the Criteria API instead of relying on JPQL.

When writing code using the Criteria API, the first thing we need to do is to obtain an instance of a class implementing the `jakarta.persistence.criteria.CriteriaBuilder` interface. As we can see in the preceding example, we need to obtain said instance by invoking the `getCriteriaBuilder()` method on our `EntityManager`.

From our `CriteriaBuilder` implementation, we need to obtain an instance of a class implementing the `jakarta.persistence.criteria.CriteriaQuery` interface. We do this by invoking the `createQuery()` method in our `CriteriaBuilder` implementation. Notice that `CriteriaQuery` is generically typed. The generic type argument dictates the type of result that our `CriteriaQuery` implementation will return upon execution. By taking advantage of generics in this way, the Criteria API allows us to write type-safe code.

Once we have obtained a `CriteriaQuery` implementation, from it we can obtain an instance of a class implementing the `jakarta.persistence.criteria.Root` interface. The Root implementation dictates what Jakarta Persistence entity we will be querying from. It is analogous to the FROM query in JPQL (and SQL).

The next two lines in our example take advantage of another feature of the Jakarta Persistence specification, the **Metamodel API**. In order to take advantage of the Metamodel API, we need to obtain an implementation of the `jakarta.persistence.metamodel.Metamodel` interface by invoking the `getMetamodel()` method on our `EntityManager`.

From our `Metamodel` implementation, we can obtain a generically typed instance of the `jakarta.persistence.metamodel.EntityType` interface. The generic type argument indicates the Jakarta Persistence entity our `EntityType` implementation corresponds to. `EntityType` allows us to browse the persistent attributes of our Jakarta Persistence entities at runtime. Which is exactly what we do in the next line in our example. In our case, we are getting an instance of `SingularAttribute`, which maps to a simple, singular attribute in our Jakarta Persistence entity. `EntityType` has methods to obtain attributes that map to collections, sets, lists, and maps. Obtaining these types of attributes is very similar to obtaining a `SingularAttribute`, therefore we won't be covering those directly. Please refer to the Jakarta EE API documentation at `https://jakarta.ee/specifications/platform/10/apidocs/` for more information.

As we can see in our example, `SingularAttribute` contains two generic type arguments. The first argument dictates the Jakarta Persistence entity we are working with, and the second one indicates the type of the attribute. We obtain our `SingularAttribute` by invoking the `getDeclaredSingularAttribute()` method on our `EntityType` implementation, and passing the attribute name (as declared in our Jakarta Persistence entity) as a String.

Once we have obtained our `SingularAttribute` implementation, we need to obtain an import `jakarta.persistence.criteria.Path` implementation by invoking the `get()` method in our `Root` instance, and passing our `SingularAttribute` as a parameter.

In our example, we will get a list of all the "new" states in the United States (that is, all states whose names start with "New"). This, of course, is a job for a "like" condition. We can do this with the Criteria API by invoking the `like()` method on our `CriteriaBuilder` implementation. The `like()` method takes our `Path` implementation as its first parameter, and the value to search for as its second parameter.

`CriteriaBuilder` has a number of methods that are analogous to SQL and JPQL clauses such as `equals()`, `greaterThan()`, `lessThan()`, `and()`, `or()`, and so on and so forth (for the complete list, refer to the online Jakarta EE documentation). These methods can be combined to create complex queries via the Criteria API.

The `like()` method in `CriteriaBuilder` returns an implementation of the `jakarta.persistence.criteria.Predicate` interface, which we need to pass to the `where()` method in our `CriteriaQuery` implementation. This method returns a new instance of `CriteriaBuilder`, which we assign to our `criteriaBuilder` variable.

At this point, we are ready to build our query. When working with the Criteria API, we deal with the `jakarta.persistence.TypedQuery` interface, which can be thought of as a type-safe version of the `Query` interface we use with JPQL. We obtain an instance of `TypedQuery` by invoking the `createQuery()` method in `EntityManager`, and passing our `CriteriaQuery` implementation as a parameter.

To obtain our query results as a list, we simply invoke `getResultList()` on our `TypedQuery` implementation. It is worth reiterating that the Criteria API is type safe, therefore attempting to assign the results of `getResultList()` to a List of the wrong type would result in a compilation error.

Let's look into how we can update data with the Criteria API.

Updating data with the Criteria API

We can update database data using the Criteria API using the `CriteriaUpdate` interface. The following example illustrates how to do so:

```
package com.ensode.jakartaeebook.criteriaupdate.namedbean;
//imports omitted for brevity
@Named
@RequestScoped
public class CriteriaUpdateDemoBean {
  @PersistenceContext
  private EntityManager entityManager;
  @Resource
  private UserTransaction userTransaction
  private int updatedRows;

  public String updateData() {
    String retVal = "confirmation";
```

```java
    try {
      userTransaction.begin();
      insertTempData();
      CriteriaBuilder criteriaBuilder =
        entityManager.getCriteriaBuilder();
      CriteriaUpdate<Address> criteriaUpdate =
        criteriaBuilder.createCriteriaUpdate(Address.class);
      Root<Address> root = criteriaUpdate.from(
          Address.class);
      criteriaUpdate.set("city", "New York");
      criteriaUpdate.where(criteriaBuilder.equal(
          root.get("city"), "New Yorc"));
      Query query = entityManager.createQuery(
          criteriaUpdate);
      updatedRows = query.executeUpdate();
      userTransaction.commit();
    } catch (Exception e) {
      retVal = "error";
      e.printStackTrace();
    }
    return retVal;
  }

  //getters and setters omitted
  private void insertTempData() throws Exception {
    //method body omitted
  }
}
```

What this example is doing is finding all of the database rows with entries of a city called "New Yorc" (a typo), and replacing the value with the correct spelling of "New York".

Just like in the previous example, we obtain an instance of a class implementing the `CriteriaBuilder` interface by invoking the `getCriteriaBuilder()` method on our `EntityManager` instance.

We then obtain an instance of a class implementing `CriteriaUpdate` by invoking `createCriteriaUpdate()` on our `CriteriaBuilder` instance.

The next step is to obtain an instance of a class implementing `Root` by invoking the `from()` method on our `CriteriaUpdate` instance.

We then invoke the `set()` method on `CriteriaUpdate` to specify the new values our rows will have after they have been updated. The first parameter of the `set()` method must be a `String` matching the property name in the Entity class, and the second parameter must be the new value.

At this point, we build the where clause by invoking the `where()` method on `CriteriaUpdate`, and passing the `Predicate` returned by the `equal()` method invoked in `CriteriaBuilder`.

Then we get a `Query` implementation by invoking `createQuery()` on `EntityManager`, and passing our `CriteriaUpdate` instance as a parameter.

Finally, we execute our query as usual by invoking `executeUpdate()` on our `Query` implementation.

Deleting data with the Criteria API

We can delete database data with the Jakarta Persistence Criteria API. This can be done with the `CriteriaDelete` interface. The following code snippet illustrates its usage:

```
package com.ensode.jakartaeebook.criteriadelete.namedbean;
//imports omitted
@Named
@RequestScoped
public class CriteriaDeleteDemoBean {
  @PersistenceContext
  private EntityManager entityManager;
  @Resource
  private UserTransaction userTransaction;
  private int deletedRows;

  public String deleteData() {
    String retVal = "confirmation";
    try {
      userTransaction.begin();
      CriteriaBuilder criteriaBuilder =
        entityManager.getCriteriaBuilder();
      CriteriaDelete<Address> criteriaDelete
        = criteriaBuilder.createCriteriaDelete(
          Address.class);
      Root<Address> root = criteriaDelete.from(
        Address.class);
      criteriaDelete.where(criteriaBuilder.or(
        criteriaBuilder.equal(
          root.get("city"), "New York"),
          criteriaBuilder.equal(root.get("city"),
            "New York")));
      Query query = entityManager.createQuery(
        criteriaDelete);
      deletedRows = query.executeUpdate();
      userTransaction.commit();
    } catch (HeuristicMixedException
            | HeuristicRollbackException
            | NotSupportedException
            | RollbackException
```

```
                    | SystemException
                    | IllegalStateException
                    | SecurityException e) {
        retVal = "error";
        e.printStackTrace();
      }
      return retVal;
    }

  //getters and setters omitted
}
```

To use `CriteriaDelete`, we first obtain an instance of `CriteriaBuilder` as usual, then invoke the `createCriteriaDelete()` method on our `CriteriaBuilder` instance to obtain an implementation of `CriteriaDelete`.

Once we have an instance of `CriteriaDelete`, we build the `where` clause as it is usually done with the Criteria API.

Once we have built our `where` clause, we obtain an implementation of the `Query` interface and invoke `executeUpdate()` on it as usual.

Now that we've seen how to insert and retrieve database data, we'll turn our attention to data validation via Bean Validation.

Bean Validation support

Bean Validation is a Jakarta EE specification consisting of a number of annotations used to simplify data validation. Jakarta Persistence Bean Validation support allows us to annotate our entities with Bean Validation annotations. These annotations allow us to easily validate user input and perform data sanitation.

Taking advantage of Bean Validation is very simple. All we need to do is annotate our Jakarta Persistence Entity fields or getter methods with any of the validation annotations defined in the `jakarta.validation.constraints` package. Once our fields are annotated as appropriate, `EntityManager` will prevent non-validating data from being persisted.

The following code example is a modified version of the `Customer` Jakarta Persistence entity we saw earlier in this chapter. It has been modified to take advantage of Bean Validation in some of its fields:

```
package com.ensode.jakartaeebook.beanvalidation.entity;

//imports omitted for brevity

@Entity
```

```
@Table(name = "CUSTOMERS")
public class Customer implements Serializable {
  @Id
  @Column(name = "CUSTOMER_ID")
  private Long customerId;
  @Column(name = "FIRST_NAME")
  @NotNull
  @Size(min = 2, max = 20)
  private String firstName;
  @Column(name = "LAST_NAME")
  @NotNull
  @Size(min = 2, max = 20)
  private String lastName;
  private String email;

  // getters and setters omitted for brevity
}
```

In this example, we used the `@NotNull` annotation to prevent the `firstName` and `lastName` of our entity from being persisted with `null` values. We also used the `@Size` annotation to restrict the minimum and maximum length of these fields.

That is all we need to do to take advantage of bean validation in Jakarta Persistence. If our code attempts to persist or update an instance of our entity that does not pass the declared validation, an exception of type `jakarta.validation.ConstraintViolationException` will be thrown, and the entity will not be persisted.

As we can see Bean Validation pretty much automates data validation, freeing us from having to manually write validation code.

In addition to the two annotations discussed in the previous example, the `jakarta.validation.constraints` package contains several additional annotations we can use to automate validation on our Jakarta Persistence entities. Please refer to the online Jakarta EE 10 API for the complete list.

Final notes

In the examples for this chapter, we demonstrated database access directly from CDI named beans serving as controllers. We did this to get the point across without bogging ourselves down with details; however, in general, this is not a good practice. Database access code should be encapsulated in **Data Access Objects (DAOs)**.

> **DAO design pattern**
>
> For more information on the DAO design pattern, see `http://www.oracle.com/technetwork/java/dao-138818.html`.

Named beans typically assume the role of controllers and/or models when using the **Model-View-Controller** (**MVC**) design pattern, a practice so common that it has become a de-facto standard for Jakarta EE applications.

> **MVC design pattern**
>
> For more information about the MVC design pattern, see `https://en.wikipedia.org/wiki/Model%E2%80%93view%E2%80%93controller`.

Additionally, we chose not to show any user interface code in our examples as it was irrelevant to the topic at hand. However, the code downloads for this chapter include Jakarta Faces pages that invoke the named beans in this chapter and display a confirmation page once the named-bean invocation finishes.

Summary

This chapter covered how to access data in a database via Jakarta Persistence, the standard object-relational mapping API of Jakarta EE.

In this chapter, we covered the following topics:

- How to mark a Java class as a Jakarta Persistence entity by decorating it with the `@Entity` annotation, and how to map it to a database table via the `@Table` annotation. We also covered how to map entity fields to database columns via the `@Column` annotation.

- Using the `jakarta.persistence.EntityManager` interface to find, persist, and update Jakarta Persistence entities.

- How to define unidirectional and bidirectional one-to-one, one-to-many, and many-to-many relationships between Jakarta Persistence entities.

- How to use composite primary keys by developing custom primary key classes.

- How to retrieve entities from a database by using the **Jakarta Persistence Query Language** (**JPQL**) and the Criteria API.

- Bean Validation, which allows us to easily validate input by simply annotating our Jakarta Persistence entity fields.

Jakarta Persistence abstracts out database access code and allows us to code against Java objects as opposed to database tables. It also works with every popular RDBMS system, making our code easily portable across different relational database management systems.

9
WebSockets

Traditionally, web applications have been developed using the request/response model followed by HTTP. In this traditional request/response model, the request is always initiated by the client, then the server sends a response back to the client.

There has never been any way for the server to send data to the client independently, that is, without having to wait for a request, until now. The WebSocket protocol allows full-duplex, two-way communication between the client (browser) and the server.

The Jakarta API for WebSocket allows us to develop WebSocket endpoints in Java.

In this chapter, we will cover the following topics:

- Developing WebSocket server endpoints

- Developing WebSocket clients in JavaScript

- Developing WebSocket clients in Java

> **Note**
> The source code for this chapter can be found on GitHub at `https://github.com/ PacktPublishing/Jakarta-EE-Application-Development/tree/main/ ch09_src`.

Developing WebSocket server endpoints

There are two ways we can implement a WebSocket server endpoint via the Jakarta API for WebSocket: we can either develop an endpoint programmatically, in which case we need to extend the `jakarta. websocket.Endpoint` class, or we can annotate **Plain Old Java Objects (POJOs)** with WebSocket-specific annotations. These two approaches are very similar, therefore we will be discussing in detail only the annotation approach, and will briefly explain how to develop WebSocket server endpoints programmatically later in the chapter.

In this chapter, we will develop a simple web-based chat application that takes full advantage of the Jakarta API for WebSocket.

Developing an annotated WebSocket server endpoint

The following Java class illustrates how we can develop a WebSocket server endpoint by annotating a Java class:

```
package com.ensode.jakartaeebook.websocketchat.serverendpoint;
//imports omitted
@ServerEndpoint("/websocketchat")
public class WebSocketChatEndpoint {
  private static final Logger LOG =
    Logger.getLogger(WebSocketChatEndpoint.class.getName());

  @OnOpen
  public void connectionOpened() {
    LOG.log(Level.INFO, "connection opened");
  }

  @OnMessage
  public synchronized void processMessage(Session session,
    String message) {
    LOG.log(Level.INFO, "received message: {0}", message);
    session.getOpenSessions().forEach(sess -> {
      if (sess.isOpen()) {
        try {
          sess.getBasicRemote().sendText(message);
        } catch (IOException ex) {
          LOG.log(Level.SEVERE, ex.getMessage(), ex);
        }
      }
    });
  }
  @OnClose
  public void connectionClosed() {
    LOG.log(Level.INFO, "connection closed");
  }
}
```

The class-level `@ServerEndpoint` annotation indicates that the class is a WebSocket server endpoint. The **URI (Uniform Resource Identifier)** of the server endpoint is the value specified between the parenthesis following the annotation (`"/websocketchat"`, in this example). WebSocket clients will use this URI to communicate with our endpoint.

The `@OnOpen` annotation is used to indicate a method that needs to be executed whenever a WebSocket connection is opened from any of the clients. In our example, we are simply sending some output to the server log, but of course, any valid server-side Java code can be placed here.

Any method annotated with the `@OnMessage` annotation will be invoked whenever our server endpoint receives a message from any of the clients. Since we are developing a chat application, our code simply broadcasts the message it receives to all connected clients.

In our example, the `processMessage()` method is annotated with `@OnMessage`, and it takes two parameters, an instance of a class implementing the `jakarta.websocket.Session` interface, and a `String` containing the message that was received. Since we are developing a chat application, our WebSocket server endpoint simply broadcasts the received message to all connected clients.

The `getOpenSessions()` method of the `Session` interface returns a `Set` of `Session` objects representing all open sessions, we iterate through this set to broadcast the received message back to all connected clients by invoking the `getBasicRemote()` method on each `Session` instance, then invoking the `sendText()` method on the resulting `RemoteEndpoint.Basic` implementation returned by this call.

The `getOpenSessions()` method on the `Session` interface returns all the open sessions at the time the method was invoked. It is possible for one or more of the sessions to have closed after the method was invoked, so it is recommended to invoke the `isOpen()` method on a `Session` implementation before attempting to send data back to the client.

Finally, we need to annotate a method with the `@OnClose` annotation to handle the event when a client disconnects from the server endpoint. In our example, we simply log a message to the server log.

There is one additional annotation we didn't use in our example. The `@OnError` annotation is used to indicate a method that needs to be invoked in case of an error when sending or receiving data to or from the client.

As we can see, developing an annotated WebSocket server endpoint is straightforward. We simply need to add a few annotations and the application server will invoke our annotated methods as necessary.

If we wish to develop a WebSocket server endpoint programmatically, we need to write a Java class that extends `jakarta.websocket.Endpoint`. This class has `onOpen()`, `onClose()`, and `onError()` methods that are called at the appropriate times during the endpoint's lifecycle. There is no method equivalent to the `@OnMessage` annotation – to handle incoming messages from the clients, the `addMessageHandler()` method needs to be invoked in the session, passing an instance of a class implementing the `jakarta.websocket.MessageHandler` interface (or one of its subinterfaces) as its sole parameter.

In general, it is more straightforward to develop annotated WebSocket endpoints as opposed to their programmatic counterparts. Therefore, we recommend the annotated approach whenever possible.

Now that we have seen how to develop WebSocket endpoints, we will focus our attention on developing WebSocket clients.

Developing WebSocket clientsin JavaScript

Most WebSocket clients are implemented as web pages taking advantage of the JavaScript WebSocket API. We will cover how to do this in the next section.

The Jakarta API for WebSocket provides a client API that allows us to develop WebSocket clients as standalone Java applications. We will be covering this capability later in the chapter.

Developing JavaScript client-side WebSocket code

In this section, we will cover how to develop client-side JavaScript code to interact with the WebSocket endpoint we developed in the previous section.

The client page for our WebSocket example is implemented as a JSF page using HTML5-friendly markup (as explained in *Chapter 7*).

As illustrated in *Figure 9.1*, our client page consists of a text area where we can see what the users of our application are saying (it is, after all, a chat application), and a text-input box that we can use to send messages to other users.

Figure 9.1 – Javascript WebSocket client

The JavaScript code for our client page looks like this:

```
<script type="text/javascript">
  var websocket;
  function init() {
    websocket = new WebSocket(
     'ws://localhost:8080/websocketchat/websocketchat');
    websocket.onopen = function (event) {
```

```
      websocketOpen(event)
    };
    websocket.onmessage = function (event) {
      websocketMessage(event)
    };
    websocket.onerror = function (event) {
      websocketError(event)
    };
  }
  function websocketOpen(event) {
    console.log("webSocketOpen invoked");
  }
  function websocketMessage(event) {
    console.log("websocketMessage invoked");
    document.getElementById('chatwindow').value += '\r' +
      event.data;
  }
  function websocketError(event) {
    console.log("websocketError invoked");
  }
  function sendMessage() {
    var userName = document.getElementById('userName').value;
    var msg = document.getElementById('chatinput').value;
    websocket.send(userName + ": " + msg);
  }
  function closeConnection() {
    websocket.close();
  }
  window.addEventListener("load", init, false);
</script>
```

The last line of our JavaScript code (window.addEventListener("load", init);) sets our JavaScript init() function to get executed as soon as the page loads.

In the init() function, we initialize a new JavaScript WebSocket object, passing the URI of our server endpoint as a parameter. This lets our JavaScript code know the location of our server endpoint.

The JavaScript WebSocket object has a number of function types used to handle different events such as opening the connection, receiving a message, and handling errors. We need to set these types to our own JavaScript functions so that we can handle these events, which is what we do in our init() method right after invoking the constructor for the JavaScript WebSocket object. In our example, the functions we assigned to the WebSocket object simply delegate their functionality to stand-alone JavaScript functions.

Our websocketOpen() function is called whenever the WebSocket connection is opened. In our example, we simply send a message to the browser's JavaScript console.

Our `webSocketMessage()` function is invoked whenever the browser receives a WebSocket message from our WebSocket endpoint. In our example, we update the contents of the text area that has the ID of the chat window with the contents of the message.

Our `websocketError()` function is called whenever there is a WebSocket-related error. In our example, we simply send a message to the browser's JavaScript console.

Our JavaScript `sendMessage()` function sends a message to the WebSocket server endpoint containing both the username and the contents of the text input with the ID of `chatinput`. This function is called when the user clicks on the button with the ID of `sendBtn`.

Our `closeConnection()` JavaScript function closes the connection to our WebSocket server endpoint.

As we can see from this example, writing client-side JavaScript code to interact with WebSocket endpoints is fairly straightforward.

Developing WebSocket clients in Java

Although developing web-based WebSocket clients is currently the most common way of developing WebSocket clients, the Jakarta API for WebSocket provides a client API we can use to develop WebSocket clients in Java.

In this section, we will be developing a simple graphical WebSocket client using the client API of the Jakarta API for WebSocket. *Figure 9.2* illustrates the GUI of our Java WebSocket client.

Figure 9.2 – WebSocket client developed in Java

Note

We won't be covering the GUI code, since it is not relevant to the discussion. The complete code for the example, including the GUI code, can be downloaded from the book's GitHub repository.

Just as with WebSocket server endpoints, Java WebSocket clients can be developed either programmatically or by using annotations. Once again, we will cover only the annotation approach. Developing a programmatic client is very similar to the way programmatic server endpoints are developed, which is to say, programmatic clients must extend jakarta.websocket.Endpoint and override the appropriate methods.

Without further ado, here is the code for our Java WebSocket client:

```
package com.ensode.websocketjavaclient;

//imports omitted
@ClientEndpoint
public class WebSocketClient {

  private static final Logger LOG =
    Logger.getLogger(WebSocketClient.class.getName());

  private String userName;
  private Session session;
  private final WebSocketJavaClientFrame webSocketJavaClientFrame;

  public WebSocketClient(WebSocketJavaClientFrame
    webSocketJavaClientFrame) {
    this.webSocketJavaClientFrame = webSocketJavaClientFrame;

    try {
      WebSocketContainer webSocketContainer =
      ContainerProvider.getWebSocketContainer();
      webSocketContainer.connectToServer(this, new URI(
      "ws://localhost:8080/websocketchat/websocketchat"));
    } catch (DeploymentException | IOException | URISyntaxException
  ex) {
      ex.printStackTrace();
    }
  }

  @OnOpen
  public void onOpen(Session session) {
   this.session = session;
  }

  @OnClose
  public void onClose(CloseReason closeReason) {
    LOG.log(Level.INFO, String.format(
```

```
      "Connection closed, reason: %s",
      closeReason.getReasonPhrase()));
  }

  @OnError
  public void onError(Throwable throwable) {
    throwable.printStackTrace();
  }

  @OnMessage
  public void onMessage(String message, Session session) {
    webSocketJavaClientFrame.getChatWindowTextArea().setText(
        webSocketJavaClientFrame.getChatWindowTextArea().getText()
        + ""
        + "\n" + message);
  }

  public void sendMessage(String message) {
    try {
      session.getBasicRemote().sendText(userName + ": " + message);
    } catch (IOException ex) {
      ex.printStackTrace();
    }
  }

  //setters and getters omitted

}
```

The class-level `@ClientEndPoint` annotation denotes our class as a WebSocket client. All Java WebSocket clients must be annotated with this annotation.

The code to establish a connection to the WebSocket server endpoint is in our class constructor. First, we need to invoke `ContainerProvider.getWebSocketContainer()` to obtain an instance of `jakarta.websocket.WebSocketContainer`. We then establish the connection by invoking the `connectToServer()` method on our `WebSocketContainer` instance, passing a class annotated with `@ClientEndpoint` as the first parameter (in our example, we use `this`, since the connection code is inside our WebSocket Java client code), and an `URI` object containing the WebSocket server endpoint URI as the second parameter.

After the connection is established, we are ready to respond to WebSocket events. Alert readers may have noticed that we are using the exact same annotations we used to develop our server endpoint again in our client code.

Any method annotated with the `@OnOpen` annotation will be invoked automatically when the connection to the WebSocket server endpoint is established, the method must return void and can have an optional parameter of type `jakarta.websocket.Session`. In our example, we initialize a class variable with the `Session` instance we received as a parameter.

Methods annotated with the `@OnClose` annotation are invoked whenever the WebSocket session is closed. The annotated method can have optional parameters of type `jakarta.websocket.Session` and type `CloseReason`. In our example, we chose to use only the `CloseReason` optional parameter, since this class has a handy `getReasonPhrase()` method that provides a short explanation of why the session was closed.

The `@OnError` annotation is used to indicate that a method will be called when an error occurs. Methods annotated with `@OnError` must have a parameter of type `java.lang.Throwable` (the parent class of `java.lang.Exception`), and can have an optional parameter of type `Session`. In our example, we simply send the stack trace of the `Throwable` parameter to `stderr`.

Methods annotated with `@OnMessage` are invoked whenever an incoming WebSocket message is received. `@OnMessage` methods can have different parameters depending on the type of message received and how we wish to handle it. In our example, we used the most common case, receiving a text message. In this particular case, we need a `String` parameter that will hold the contents of the message, and an optional `Session` parameter.

> **Note**
>
> Refer to the JavaDoc documentation for `@OnMessage` at `https://jakarta.ee/specifications/platform/10/apidocs/jakarta/websocket/onmessage` for information on how to handle other types of messages.

In our example, we simply update the chat window text area, appending the received message to its contents.

To send a WebSocket message, we invoke the `getBasicRemote()` method on our Session instance, then invoke the `sendText()` method on the resulting `RemoteEndpoint.Basic` implementation returned by this call (if this looks familiar, it is because we did exactly the same thing in the WebSocket server endpoint code). In our example, we do this in the `sendMessage()` method.

> **Additional information about the Jakarta API for WebSocket**
>
> In this chapter, we covered the bulk of the functionality provided by the Jakarta API for WebSocket. For additional information, refer to the user guide for Tyrus, a popular open source Jakarta API for WebSocket implementation, at `https://eclipse-ee4j.github.io/tyrus-project.github.io/documentation/latest/index/`.

Summary

In this chapter, we covered the Jakarta API for WebSocket, a Jakarta EE API for developing WebSocket server endpoints and clients:

- We first saw how to develop WebSocket server endpoints by taking advantage of the Jakarta API for WebSockets

- Then, we covered how to develop web-based WebSocket clients using JavaScript

- Finally, we explained how to develop WebSocket client applications in Java

WebSockets allow us to implement real-time, two-way communication between a web browser and a web server. As we saw in this chapter, the Jakarta EE WebSocket API takes care of the low-level details allowing us to develop WebSocket endpoints via a few simple annotations.

10

Securing Jakarta EE Applications

Jakarta EE Security standardizes application security across all Jakarta EE-compliant application servers. The API includes standardized access to identity stores, which allow a uniform way of retrieving user credentials from a relational or **Lightweight Directory Access Protocol** (**LDAP**) database, as well as allowing us to implement access to custom identity stores. Jakarta EE Security includes authentication mechanism support, allowing us to authenticate a user in a standard way. Several authentication mechanisms are supported, such as the basic authentication supported by most browsers, client certificates, and HTML forms.

The following topics will be covered in this chapter:

- Identity stores
- Authentication mechanisms

> **Note**
>
> Example source code for this chapter can be found on GitHub at the following link: `https://github.com/PacktPublishing/Jakarta-EE-Application-Development/tree/main/ch10_src`.

Identity stores

Identity stores provide access to a persistence storage system, such as a relational or LDAP database, where user credentials are stored. The Jakarta EE Security API supports relational and LDAP databases directly, and it allows us to integrate with custom identity stores, if necessary.

Setting up an identity store stored in a relational database

To authenticate a secured resource, such as a servlet or RESTful web service, against credentials stored in a relational database, annotate an application-scoped CDI bean with the `@DatabaseIdentityStoreDefinition` annotation, as illustrated in the following example:

```
package net.ensode.javaee8book.httpauthdatabaseidentitystore.security;
//imports omitted for brevity

@DatabaseIdentityStoreDefinition(
  dataSourceLookup = "java:global/jdbc/userauthdbDatasource",
    callerQuery =
      "select password from users where USERNAME = ?",
    groupsQuery =
      "select g.GROUP_NAME from USER_GROUPS ug, users u, "
        + "GROUPS g where ug.USER_ID = u.user_id and "
        + "g.GROUP_ID= ug.GROUP_ID and u.USERNAME=?"
)
@ApplicationScoped
public class ApplicationConfig {

}
```

In our example, the JNDI name for the JDBC connection for the relational database containing user credentials is `java:global/jdbc/userauthdbDatasource`, which is the value we provided to the `dataSourceLookup` attribute of the `@DatabaseIdentityStoreDefinition` annotation.

The `callerQuery` parameter of `@DatabaseIdentityStoreDefinition` is used to specify the SQL query used to retrieve the username and password for the user we are authenticating. The values retrieved from the database must match the values provided by the user (via an authentication mechanism, which we will discuss in the next section).

Most secured applications have different types of users, separated into roles; for example, an application could have "regular" users plus administrators. Administrators would be allowed to perform certain actions that regular users would not. For example, administrators could be able to reset user passwords and add or remove users from the system. The `groupsQuery` attribute of `@DatabaseIdentityStoreDefinition` allows us to retrieve all roles for the user.

Setting up an identity store stored in an LDAP database

To secure resources against credentials stored in an LDAP database, we need to annotate the resource to be secured (such as a servlet or RESTful web service) with the `@LdapIdentityStoreDefinition` annotation; the following example illustrates how to do this:

```
package com.ensode.jakartaeebook.httpauthdatabaseidentitystore.
servlet;

//imports omitted for brevity
@LdapIdentityStoreDefinition(
        url = "ldap://myldapserver:33389/",
        callerBaseDn = "ou=caller,dc=packtpub,dc=com",
        groupSearchBase = "ou=group,dc=packtpub,dc=com")
@WebServlet(name = "ControllerServlet", urlPatterns = {"/controller"})
public class ControllerServlet extends HttpServlet {
    @Override
    protected void doGet(HttpServletRequest req,
      HttpServletResponse res)
            throws ServletException, IOException {
        System.out.println("doGet() invoked");
    }
}
```

The `url` attribute of `@LdapIdentityStoreDefinition` is used to specify the URL of the LDAP server containing user credentials for our application; its `callerBaseDn` attribute is used to specify the LDAP base distinguished name to verify user credentials supplied by the user, and, finally, its `groupSearchBase` attribute is used to retrieve the roles for the user.

Custom identity stores

In some cases, we may need to integrate our application security with an identity store not directly supported by the Security API. For example, we may have a requirement to integrate with an existing commercial security product. For such cases, the Jakarta EE Security API allows us to roll out our own identity store definition.

To handle custom identity stores, we need to create an application-scoped CDI bean (refer to *Chapter 2*), and the bean must implement the `IdentityStore` interface, as illustrated in the following example:

```
package com.ensode.jakartaeebook.security.basicauthexample;
//imports omitted for brevity
@ApplicationScoped
public class DummyIdentityStore implements IdentityStore {

  Set<String> adminRoleSet;
```

```
Set userRoleSet;
Set userAdminRoleSet;

@PostConstruct
public void init() {
  adminRoleSet = new HashSet<>(Arrays.asList("admin"));
  userRoleSet = new HashSet<>(Arrays.asList("user"));
  userAdminRoleSet = new HashSet<>(Arrays.asList("user",
    "admin"));
}

@Override
public CredentialValidationResult validate(
 Credential credential) {
 UsernamePasswordCredential usernamePasswordCredential =
   (UsernamePasswordCredential) credential;
 CredentialValidationResult credentialValidationResult;
 if (usernamePasswordCredential.compareTo(
   "david", "secret")) {
   credentialValidationResult = new
     CredentialValidationResult("david", adminRoleSet);
 }
 else if (usernamePasswordCredential.compareTo(
   "alan", "iforgot")) {
   credentialValidationResult =
     new CredentialValidationResult("alan", userAdminRoleSet);
 }
 else if (usernamePasswordCredential.compareTo("alice",
  "password")) {
   credentialValidationResult = new
     CredentialValidationResult("alice", userRoleSet);
 }
 else {
   credentialValidationResult =
     CredentialValidationResult.INVALID_RESULT;
 }
 return credentialValidationResult;
 }
}
```

The validate() method is defined in the IdentityStore interface provided by the security API in our example. We implement this method so that we can use custom validation in our application.

> **Note**
>
> In our example, we are hard coding valid credentials into the code; do not do this for real applications as this would be a major security risk.

The `validate()` method defined in the `IdentityStore` interface accepts an instance of a class implementing the `Credential` interface as its sole argument. In the body of our method, we cast it down to `UserNamePasswordCredential`, and then we invoke its `compareTo()` method, passing the expected username and password. If the provided credentials match either one of the expected set of credentials, then we allow the user to successfully log in. We do this by returning an instance of `CredentialValidationResult` containing the username and `Set` containing all the roles that the user has in our application.

If the supplied credentials don't match either of the expected credentials, then we prevent the user from logging in by returning `CredentialValidationResult.INVALID_RESULT`.

Now that we have seen how to access user credential information via identity stores, we'll focus our attention on the different authentication mechanisms provided by Jakarta EE.

Authentication mechanisms

Authentication mechanisms provide a way for the user to provide their credentials so that they can be authenticated against an identity store.

The Jakarta EE Security API provides support for the HTTP Basic authentication mechanism provided by most browsers, as well as form authentication, which is the most common authentication mechanism where users provide their credentials via an HTML form.

Form authentication by default submits a form to the security servlet provided by the Jakarta EE implementation. If we need more flexibility or to better align with other Jakarta EE technologies, the Security API provides custom form authentication as well, which allows us as application developers to have more control over how to authenticate users attempting to access our application.

Basic authentication mechanism

A basic authentication mechanism can be achieved by annotating the resource as secure (i.e, a servlet or RESTful web service) with the `@BasicAuthenticationMechanismDefinition` annotation:

```
package com.ensode.jakartaeebook.security.basicauthexample;
//imports omitted for brevity
@BasicAuthenticationMechanismDefinition
@WebServlet(name = "SecuredServlet", urlPatterns = {"/
securedServlet"})
@ServletSecurity(
        @HttpConstraint(rolesAllowed = "admin"))
```

```
public class SecuredServlet extends HttpServlet {
  @Override
    protected void doGet(HttpServletRequest request,
        HttpServletResponse response) throws Exception {
        response.getOutputStream().print(
          "Congratulations, login successful.");
    }
}
```

We declare the user roles that are allowed to access the secured resource via the `@HttpConstraint` annotation, which is an attribute of the `@ServletSecurity` annotation. In our example, only users with the `admin` role are allowed to access the secured resource.

Using basic authentication will cause a window to pop up in the browser asking for a username and a password, as illustrated in *Figure 10.1*:

⊕ **localhost:8080**

This site is asking you to sign in.

Username

| david |

Password

| •••••• |

Cancel   **Sign in**

Figure 10.1 – Basic authentication login prompt

If the user enters the correct credentials and has the necessary role, access is granted to the protected resource, as shown in *Figure 10.2*:

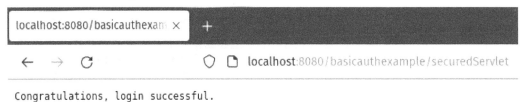

localhost:8080/basicauthexam ×   +

←   →   C   ○   🗋   localhost:8080/basicauthexample/securedServlet

Congratulations, login successful.

Figure 10.2 – Successful basic authentication

If the user enters incorrect credentials, the login popup will show up again, allowing the user to re-enter their credentials.

If the user enters the correct credentials but does not have the appropriate role to access the protected resource, the server will return an HTTP 403 error code, indicating that the user is forbidden from accessing the protected resource.

Form authentication mechanism

Another way we can authenticate our users is to develop an HTML form to collect the user's credentials, and then delegate authentication to the Jakarta EE Security API. The first step when following this approach is to develop an HTML page containing a form where the user can log in to the application, as illustrated in the following example:

```html
<form method="POST" action="j_security_check">
  <table cellpadding="0" cellspacing="0" border="0">
    <tr>
      <td align="right">Username: </td>
      <td><input type="text" name="j_username"></td>
    </tr>
    <tr>
      <td align="right">Password: </td>
      <td><input type="password" name="j_password"></td>
    </tr>
    <tr>
      <td></td>
      <td><input type="submit" value="Login"></td>
    </tr>
  </table>
</form>
```

As seen in the example, the HTML form used for logging in must submit an HTTP POST request, and the value for its action attribute must be j_security_check. Now, j_security_check maps to a servlet provided by the Jakarta EE Security API. We don't need to develop any validation logic ourselves. The form must have a couple of input fields, one for the username and one for the password. The names for these fields must be j_username and j_password respectively; the security servlet provided by the Jakarta EE API will retrieve these values and authenticate the user automatically.

Additionally, we need to provide an HTML page where the user will be redirected if login fails. The page can have any valid HTML markup. In our example, we simply provide an error message and a link to direct the user back to the login page so that they can try to log in again:

```html
<!DOCTYPE html>
<html>
  <head>
    <meta http-equiv="Content-Type" content="text/html;
      charset=UTF-8">
```

```
    <title>Login Error</title>
  </head>
  <body>
    There was an error logging in.
    <br />
    <a href="login.html">Try again</a>
  </body>
</html>
```

On the server side, all we need to do is annotate the secured resource with the @FormAuthenticationMechanismDefinition annotation, which will let the Jakarta EE Security API know we are using form-based authentication, and what HTML pages to use to log in or to display when logging in fails:

```
package com.ensode.jakartaeebook.httpauthdbidentitystore;
//imports omitted for brevity
@FormAuthenticationMechanismDefinition(
  loginToContinue = @LoginToContinue(
  loginPage = "/login.html",
  errorPage = "/loginerror.html")
)

@DatabaseIdentityStoreDefinition(
  //attributes omitted for brevity
)
@WebServlet("/securedServlet")
@ServletSecurity(
        @HttpConstraint(rolesAllowed = {"admin"}))
public class SecuredServlet extends HttpServlet {
  @Override
  protected void doGet(HttpServletRequest request, HttpServletResponse
    response)
          throws ServletException, IOException {
    response.getWriter().write("Congratulations, login successful.");
  }
}
```

The @FormAuthenticationMechanismDefinition annotation has a required loginToContinue attribute. The value of this attribute must be an instance of the @LoginToContinue annotation. @LoginToContinue has two required attributes: loginPage and errorPage. The value of these attributes must indicate the path for the login page and the path of the page to display in case of authentication failure, respectively.

After building and deploying our code, and then attempting to access a protected resource, the user is automatically redirected to our login page:

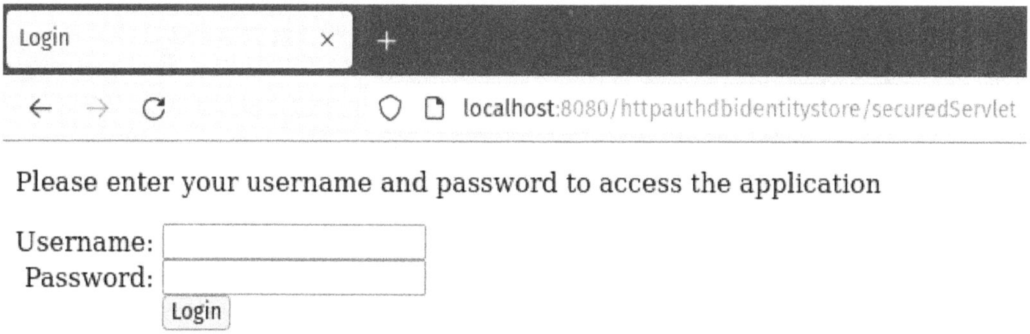

Figure 10.3 – Form authentication mechanism

If the user enters the correct credentials and has the appropriate role, then access to the protected resource is granted, as illustrated in *Figure 10.4*:

Figure 10.4 – Successful form authentication

If invalid credentials are entered, then the user is directed to our custom error page, as shown in *Figure 10.5*:

Figure 10.5 – Unsuccessful form authentication

Custom form authentication mechanism

Another way we can authenticate users in our application is to use a **custom form authentication mechanism**. This type of authentication mechanism is useful when we want to integrate our application with a web framework, such as Jakarta Faces. In our next example, we will illustrate how to do just that: integrating the Jakarta EE Security API with Jakarta Faces via custom form authentication.

To use custom form authentication in our applications, we need to use the aptly named @CustomFormAuthenticationMechanismDefinition annotation, as illustrated in the following example:

```
package com.ensode.jakartaeebook.httpauthdbidentitystore;
//imports omitted for brevity
@CustomFormAuthenticationMechanismDefinition(
    loginToContinue = @LoginToContinue(
        loginPage="/faces/login.xhtml",
        errorPage=""
    )
)

@DatabaseIdentityStoreDefinition(
  //attributes omitted for brevity
)
@WebServlet("/securedServlet")
@ServletSecurity(
        @HttpConstraint(rolesAllowed = {"admin"}))
public class SecuredServlet extends HttpServlet {
    @Override
    protected void doGet(HttpServletRequest request,
      HttpServletResponse response)
      throws ServletException, IOException {
        response.getWriter().write(
          "Congratulations, login successful.");
    }
}
```

Just like @FormAuthenticationMechanismDefinition we saw previously, the @CustomFormAuthenticationMechanismDefinition annotation has a loginToContinue attribute that takes an instance of the @LoginToContinue annotation as its value. In this case, since we are integrating with Jakarta Faces, the value of the loginPage attribute of @LoginToContinue must point to the path of a Facelets page used for the user to log in. When using Jakarta Faces to authenticate the user, it is expected that the login page will display an error message if authentication fails. Therefore, we need to leave the errorPage attribute of @LoginToContinue blank.

Our login page is a standard Facelets page that collects user credentials and redirects to a CDI bean that acts as a controller:

```
<h:form>
  <h:messages/>
  <h:panelGrid columns="2">
    <h:outputLabel for="userName" value="User Name:"/>
    <h:inputText id="userName" value="#{user.userName}"/>
    <h:outputLabel for="password" value="Password: "/>
    <h:inputSecret id="password" value="#{user.password}"/>
    <h:panelGroup/>
    <h:commandButton action="#{loginController.login()}"
    value="Login"/>
  </h:panelGrid>
</h:form>
```

Our login page has input fields for userName and password, and it stores those values in a CDI named bean (not shown as it is trivial) via value binding expressions. When the user clicks on the **Login** button, controls go to a loginController CDI named bean that performs the actual authentication:

```
package com.ensode.jakartaeebook.httpauthdbidentitystore.customauth;
//imports omitted for brevity
@Named
@RequestScoped
public class LoginController {
    @Inject
    private SecurityContext securityContext;
    @Inject
    private User user;
    public void login() {
        FacesContext facesContext = FacesContext.getCurrentInstance();
        ExternalContext externalContext = facesContext.
          getExternalContext();
        HttpServletRequest httpServletRequest =
          HttpServletRequest) externalContext.getRequest();
        HttpServletResponse httpServletResponse =
          (HttpServletResponse) externalContext.getResponse();
        UsernamePasswordCredential usernamePasswordCredential =
      new UsernamePasswordCredential(user.getUserName(),
      user.getPassword());

    AuthenticationParameters authenticationParameters =
      AuthenticationParameters.withParams().credential(
      usernamePasswordCredential);
```

```
        AuthenticationStatus authenticationStatus =
          securityContext.authenticate
          (httpServletRequest, httpServletResponse,
            authenticationParameters);

    if (authenticationStatus.equals(
      AuthenticationStatus.SEND_CONTINUE)) {
        facesContext.responseComplete();
    } else if(authenticationStatus.equals(
        AuthenticationStatus.SEND_FAILURE)) {
        FacesMessage facesMessage = new FacesMessage(
          "Login error");
            facesContext.addMessage(null, facesMessage);
      }
    }
  }
```

In our `LoginController` class, we need to inject an instance of `jakarta.security.enterprise.SecurityContext` since we will need it for authentication. We implement the authentication logic in our `login()` method. The first thing we need to do is create an instance of `UsernamePasswordCredential`, passing the user-entered username and password as parameters to its constructor.

We then create an instance of `jakarta.security.enterprise.authentication.mechanism.http.AuthenticationParameters` by invoking the static `withParams()` method on `AuthenticationParameters`, then invoking the `credential()` method on the resulting instance of `AuthenticationParameters`, and passing the instance of `UserNamePasswordCredential` we just created as a parameter. This returns yet another instance of `AuthenticationParameters`, which we can use to actually validate the user-entered credentials.

We validate user-entered credentials by invoking the `authenticate()` method on our `SecurityContext` instance, passing the HTTP Request and Response objects as parameters, as well as the instance of `AuthenticationParameters` containing the user-entered credentials. This method invocation will return an instance of `AuthenticationStatus`. We need to check the returned instance to determine whether the user entered valid credentials.

If `SecurityContext.authenticate()` returns `AuthenticationStatus.SEND_CONTINUE`, then the user-entered credentials are valid, and we can allow the user to access the requested resource. If instead, the method returns `AuthenticationStatus.SEND_FAILURE`, then the user-entered credentials are invalid, and we need to prevent the user from accessing the protected resource.

After deploying and running our application, when a user attempts to access a protected resource, he is automatically redirected to a login page, which in this case, since we are using custom form authentication, is implemented using Jakarta Faces. This is illustrated in *Figure 10.6*:

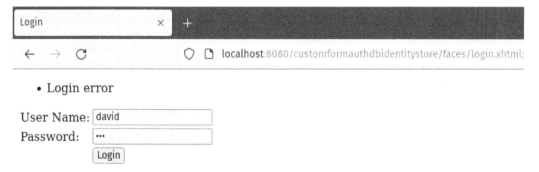

Figure 10.6 – Custom form authentication

Entering correct credentials directs the user to the protected resource (not shown) while entering incorrect credentials directs the user back to the login page, which should show an appropriate error message as shown in *Figure 10.7*.

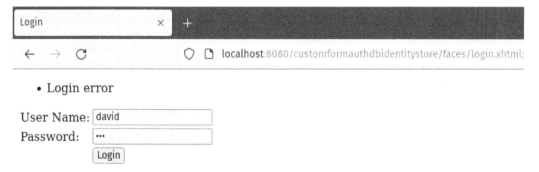

Figure 10.7 – Custom form authentication failure

It is worth noting that custom form authentication is flexible enough to integrate with any web application framework, although it is most commonly used with Jakarta Faces as discussed in this section.

Summary

In this chapter, we covered the Jakarta Security API. We discussed the following topics in this chapter:

- How to access different types of identity stores to retrieve user credentials, such as relational databases or LDAP databases

- How the Security API provides the ability to integrate with custom identity stores, in case we need to access one not directly supported, and how to use different authentication mechanisms to allow access to our secured Jakarta EE applications

- How to implement the basic authentication mechanism provided by all web browsers

- How to implement a form-based authentication mechanism, where we provide custom HTML pages used for authentication

- How to use custom form authentication, so that we can integrate our application security with a web framework such as Jakarta Faces

Using the security features provided by Jakarta EE allows us to develop secure applications. The API is flexible enough to allow integration with arbitrary data stores, as well as any Java web application framework.

11

Servlet Development
and Deployment

In this chapter, we will discuss how to develop and deploy Java EE Servlets. Servlets allow us as application developers to implement server-side logic in Java web and enterprise applications.

The topics covered include the following:

- What is a servlet?
- Request forwarding and response redirection
- Persisting application data across requests
- Passing initialization parameters to a servlet via annotations
- Servlet filters
- Servlet listeners
- Pluggability
- Configuring web applications programmatically
- Asynchronous processing
- HTTP/2 server push support

> **Note**
>
> Example source code for this chapter can be found on GitHub at `https://github.com/PacktPublishing/Jakarta-EE-Application-Development/tree/main/ch11_src`

What is a servlet?

A **servlet** is a Java class that is used to extend the capabilities of servers that host server-side web applications. Servlets can respond to requests and generate responses. The base class for all servlets is `jakarta.servlet.GenericServlet`. This class defines a generic, protocol-independent servlet.

By far the most common type of servlet is an HTTP servlet. This type of servlet is used when handling HTTP requests and generating HTTP responses. An HTTP servlet is a class that extends the `jakarta.servlet.http.HttpServlet` class, which is a subclass of `jakarta.servlet.GenericServlet`.

A servlet must implement one or more methods to respond to specific HTTP request types. These methods are overridden from the parent `HttpServlet` class. As can be seen in *Table 11.1*, these methods are named so that knowing which one to use is intuitive.

HTTP Request	HttpServlet Method
GET	`doGet(HttpServletRequest request, HttpServletResponse response)`
POST	`doPost(HttpServletRequest request, HttpServletResponse response)`
PUT	`doPut(HttpServletRequest request, HttpServletResponse response)`
DELETE	`doDelete(HttpServletRequest request, HttpServletResponse response)`

Table 11.1 – Servlet methods for different HTTP request types

Each of these methods takes the same two parameters, namely an instance of a class implementing the `jakarta.servlet.http.HttpServletRequest` interface and an instance of a class implementing `jakarta.servlet.http.HttpServletResponse`. These interfaces will be covered in detail later in this chapter.

> **Note**
>
> Application developers never call the above methods directly. They are called automatically by the application server whenever it receives the corresponding HTTP request.

Of the four methods listed above, `doGet()` and `doPost()` are, by far, the most commonly used.

An HTTP GET request is generated whenever a user types the servlet's URL in the browser, when a user clicks on a link pointing to the servlet's URL, or when a user submits an HTML form using generating an HTTP GET method where the form's action points to the servlet's URL. In any of these cases, the code inside the servlet's `doGet()` method gets executed.

An HTTP POST request is typically generated when a user submits an HTML form generating an HTTP POST method and an action pointing to the servlet's URL. In this case, the servlet's code inside the doPost() method gets executed.

Now that we've explained how a servlet works, let's take a look at how to develop servlets.

Writing our first servlet

In this section, we will develop a simple servlet to illustrate how to use the servlet API. The code for our servlet is as follows:

```
package com.ensode.jakartaeebook.simpleapp;
//imports omitted for brevity

@WebServlet(urlPatterns = {"/simpleservlet"})
public class SimpleServlet extends HttpServlet {
  @Override
  protected void doGet(HttpServletRequest req,
   HttpServletResponse res) {
    try {
      res.setContentType("text/html");
      PrintWriter printWriter = res.getWriter();
      printWriter.println("<h2>");
      printWriter
        .println("Hello servlet world!");
      printWriter.println("</h2>");
    } catch (IOException ioException) {
      ioException.printStackTrace();
    }
  }
}
```

The @WebServlet annotation specifies that our class is a servlet. Its urlPatterns attribute specifies the relative URL of our servlet.

> **Note**
>
> Servlets can also be configured via a web.xml deployment descriptor. However, since Java EE 6, annotation-based configuration is preferred.

Since this servlet is meant to execute when a user enters its URL in the browser window, we need to override the doGet() method from the parent HttpServlet class. As explained, this method takes two parameters, an instance of a class implementing the jakarta.servlet.http.HttpServletRequest interface, and an instance of a class implementing the jakarta.servlet.http.HttpServletResponse interface.

> **Note**
>
> Even though `HttpServletRequest` and `HttpServletResponse` are interfaces, application developers don't typically write classes implementing them. When control goes to a servlet from an HTTP request, the application server provides objects implementing these interfaces.

The first thing our `doGet()` method does is to set the content type for the `HttpServletResponse` object to `"text/html"`. If we forget to do this, the default content type used is `"text/plain"`, which means that the HTML tags used a couple of lines down will be displayed on the browser, as opposed to them being interpreted as HTML tags.

Then we obtain an instance of `java.io.PrintWriter` by calling the `HttpServletResponse.getWriter()` method. We can then send text output to the browser by calling the `PrintWriter.print()` and `PrintWriter.println()` methods (the preceding example uses `println()` exclusively). Since we set the content type to `"text/html"`, any HTML tags are interpreted properly by the browser.

Testing the web application

To verify that the servlet has been properly deployed, we need to point our browser to our application's URL, for example, `http://localhost:8080/simpleapp/simpleservlet`. After doing so, we should see a page like the one shown in *Figure 11.1*.

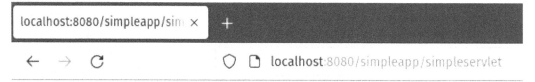

Hello servlet world!

Figure 11.1 – Simple servlet responding to an HTTP GET request

In this example, we simply displayed some static text in the browser. Servlets are typically used to process user-entered data in an HTML form, as illustrated in the next section.

Processing HTML forms

Servlets are rarely accessed by typing their URL directly in the browser. The most common use for servlets is to process data entered by users in an HTML form. In this section, we illustrate this process.

The relevant markup for the HTML file containing the form for our application looks like this:

```html
<form method="post" action="formhandlerservlet">
  <table cellpadding="0" cellspacing="0" border="0">
    <tr>
      <td>Please enter some text:</td>
      <td><input type="text" name="enteredValue" /></td>
    </tr>
    <tr>
      <td></td>
      <td><input type="submit" value="Submit"></td>
    </tr>
  </table>
</form>
```

The value for the form's `action` attribute must match the value of the servlet's `urlPatterns` attribute in its `@WebServlet` annotation. Since the value of the form's `method` attribute is `"post"`, our servlet's `doPost()` method will be executed when the form is submitted.

Now let's take a look at our servlet's code:

```java
package com.ensode.jakartaeebook.formhandling;
//imports omitted for brevity

@WebServlet(urlPatterns = {"/formhandlerservlet"})
public class FormHandlerServlet extends HttpServlet {
  @Override
  protected void doPost(HttpServletRequest request,
    HttpServletResponse response) {
    String enteredValue;
    enteredValue = request.getParameter("enteredValue");
    response.setContentType("text/html");

    PrintWriter printWriter;
    try {
      printWriter = response.getWriter();
      printWriter.println("<p>");
      printWriter.print("You entered: ");
      printWriter.print(enteredValue);
      printWriter.print("</p>");
    } catch (IOException e) {
      e.printStackTrace();
    }
  }

}
```

As can be seen in this example, we obtain a reference to the value the user typed by calling the `request.getParameter()` method. This method takes a single `String` object as its sole parameter. The value of this string must match the name of the input field in the HTML file. In this case, the HTML file has a text field named `"enteredValue"`:

```
<input type="text" name="enteredValue" />
```

Therefore, the servlet has this corresponding line:

```
enteredValue = request.getParameter("enteredValue");
```

This is to obtain the text entered by the user and store it in the `String` variable named `enteredValue` (the name of the variable does not need to match the input field name, but naming it that way is good practice to make it easy to remember what value the variable is holding).

After packaging the preceding three files in a WAR file called `formhandling.war`, followed by deploying the WAR file, we can see the rendered HTML file by entering a URL similar to the following in the browser (the exact URL will depend on the Jakarta EE application server being used): `http://localhost:8080/formhandling`.

The HTML form will be rendered as illustrated in *Figure 11.2*.

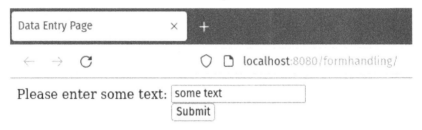

Figure 11.2 – HTML form

After the user enters `some text` in the text field and submits the form (either by hitting *Enter* or clicking on the **Submit** button), we should see the output of the servlet, as illustrated in *Figure 11.3*.

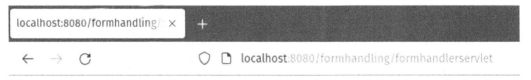

Figure 11.3 – Servlet form handling

The `HttpServletRequest.getParameter()` method can be used to obtain the value of any HTML input field that can only return one value (textboxes, text areas, single selects, radio buttons, hidden fields, etc.). The procedure to obtain any of these fields' values is identical. In other words, the servlet doesn't care if the user typed in the value in a text field, selected it from a set of radio buttons, and so on. As long as the input field's name matches the value passed to the `getParameter()` method, the preceding code will work.

> **Note**
>
> When dealing with radio buttons, all related radio buttons must have the same name. Calling the `HttpServletRequest.getParameter()` method and passing the name of the radio buttons will return the value of the selected radio button.

Some HTML input fields such as checkboxes and multiple select boxes allow the user to select more than one value. For these fields, instead of using the `HttpServletRequest.getParameter()` method, the `HttpServletRequest.getParameterValues()` method is used. This method also takes `String` containing the input field's name as its only parameter and returns an array of strings containing all the values that were selected by the user.

The following example illustrates this case. The relevant sections of our new HTML markup are shown here:

```html
<form method="post" action="multiplevaluefieldhandlerservlet">
<p>Please enter one or more options.</p>
<table cellpadding="0" cellspacing="0" border="0">
  <tr>
    <td>
      <input name="options" type="checkbox" value="option1" />
      Option 1</td>
  </tr>
  <tr>
    <td><input name="options" type="checkbox" value="option2" />
    Option 2</td>
  </tr>
  <tr>
    <td><input name="options" type="checkbox" value="option3" />
    Option 3</td>
  </tr>
  <tr>
    <td><input type="submit" value="Submit" /></td>
  </tr>
</table>
</form>
```

The new HTML file contains a simple form having three checkboxes and a submit button. Notice how every checkbox has the same value for its name attribute. As we mentioned before, any checkboxes that are clicked by the user will be sent to the servlet.

Let's now take a look at the doPost() method of the servlet that will handle the HTML form:

```
@Override
protected void doPost(HttpServletRequest request,
  HttpServletResponse response) {
  String[] selectedOptions =
    request.getParameterValues("options");

  response.setContentType("text/html");
  try {
    PrintWriter printWriter = response.getWriter();
    printWriter.println("<p>");
    printWriter.print("The following options were selected:");
    printWriter.println("<br/>");

    if (selectedOptions != null) {
      for (String option : selectedOptions) {
        printWriter.print(option);
        printWriter.println("<br/>");
      }
    } else {
      printWriter.println("None");
    }
    printWriter.println("</p>");
  } catch (IOException e) {
    e.printStackTrace();
  }
}
```

The preceding code calls the request.getParameterValues() method and assigns its return value to the selectedOptions variable. Farther down the doPost() method, the code traverses the selectedOptions array and prints the selected values in the browser.

If no checkboxes are clicked, the request.getParameterValues() method will return null, therefore it is a good idea to check for null before attempting to traverse through this method's return values.

After packaging our new servlet in a WAR file and deploying it, we can see the changes in action by typing its URL in the browser window. In most application servers, the URL will be http://localhost:8080/multiplevaluefields/. The form will be rendered as illustrated in *Figure 11.4*.

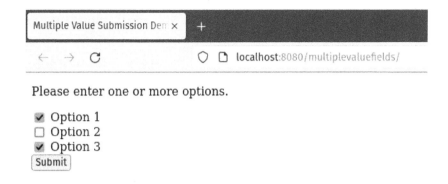

Figure 11.4 – HTML form with multiple value fields

After submitting the form, control goes to our servlet, and the browser window should look something like what's illustrated in *Figure 11.5*:

Figure 11.5 – Servlet handling fields with multiple values

Of course, the actual message seen in the browser window will depend on what checkboxes the user clicked on.

Now that we've seen how to process HTML form data, we'll focus our attention on automatically navigating to a different page via HTTP request forwarding and HTTP response redirection.

Request forwarding and response redirection

In many cases, one servlet processes form data, then transfers control to another servlet or JSP to do some more processing or displays a confirmation message on the screen. There are two ways of doing this: either the request can be forwarded or the response can be redirected to another servlet or page.

Request forwarding

Notice how the text displayed in the previous section's example matches the value of the value attribute of the checkboxes that were clicked, and not the labels displayed on the previous page. This might confuse the users. Let's modify the servlet to change these values so that they match the labels, then forward the request to another servlet that will display the confirmation message in the browser.

The doPost() method for the new version of MultipleValueFieldHandlerServlet is shown next:

```
protected void doPost(HttpServletRequest request, HttpServletResponse
response) {
  String[] selectedOptions =
    request.getParameterValues("options");
  ArrayList<String> selectedOptionLabels = null;

  if (selectedOptions != null) {
    selectedOptionLabels =
      new ArrayList<String>(selectedOptions.length);

    for (String selectedOption : selectedOptions) {
      if (selectedOption.equals("option1")) {
        selectedOptionLabels.add("Option 1");
      } else if (selectedOption.equals("option2")) {
        selectedOptionLabels.add("Option 2");
      } else if (selectedOption.equals("option3")) {
        selectedOptionLabels.add("Option 3");
      }
    }
  }
  request.setAttribute("checkedLabels", selectedOptionLabels);
  try {
    request.getRequestDispatcher("confirmationservlet").
      forward(request,response);
  } catch (ServletException | IOException e) {
    e.printStackTrace();
  }
}
```

This version of the servlet iterates through the selected options and adds the corresponding label to an ArrayList of strings. This string is then attached to the request object by calling the request.setAttribute() method. This method is used to attach any object to the request so that any other code we forward the request to can have access to it later.

After attaching ArrayList to the request, we then forward the request to the new servlet in the following line of code:

```
request.getRequestDispatcher("confirmationservlet").forward(
    request, response);
```

The `String` argument to this method must match the value of the `urlPatterns` tag of the target servlet's `@WebServlet` annotation.

At this point, control goes to our new servlet. Since we are forwarding an HTTP POST request, its `doPost()` method is automatically called. The code for this new servlet is shown in the following example:

```
package com.ensode.jakartaeebook.requestforward;
//imports omitted for brevity
@WebServlet(urlPatterns = {"/confirmationservlet"})
public class ConfirmationServlet extends HttpServlet {
  @Override
  protected void doPost(HttpServletRequest request,
    HttpServletResponse response) {
    try {
      PrintWriter printWriter;
      List<String> checkedLabels = (List<String>) request
        .getAttribute("checkedLabels");

      response.setContentType("text/html");
      printWriter = response.getWriter();
      printWriter.println("<p>");
      printWriter.print("The following options were selected:");
      printWriter.println("<br/>");

      if (checkedLabels != null) {
        for (String optionLabel : checkedLabels) {
          printWriter.print(optionLabel);
          printWriter.println("<br/>");
        }
      } else {
        printWriter.println("None");
      }
      printWriter.println("</p>");
    } catch (IOException ioException) {
      ioException.printStackTrace();
    }
  }
}
```

This code obtains `ArrayList` that was attached to the request by the previous servlet. This is accomplished by calling the `request.getAttribute()` method. The parameter for this method must match the value used to attach the object to the request.

Once the above servlet obtains the list of option labels, it traverses through it and displays them in the browser.

The following options were selected:
Option 1
Option 3

Figure 11.6 – Request forwarding in action

Forwarding a request as described only works for other resources (servlets and JSP pages) in the same context as the code doing the forwarding. In simple terms, the servlet or JSP we want to forward to must be packaged in the same WAR file as the code that is invoking the `request.getRequestDispatcher().forward()` method. If we need to direct the user to a page in another context (or even another server), we can do it by redirecting the response object.

Response redirection

One disadvantage of forwarding a request as described in the previous section is that requests can only be forwarded to other servlets or JSPs in the same context. If we need to direct the user to a page in a different context (deployed in another WAR file on the same server or deployed on a different server), we need to use the `HttpServletResponse.sendRedirect()` method.

To illustrate response redirection, let's develop a simple web application that asks the user to select their favorite search engine, and then direct the user to their search engine of choice. The HTML form for this application would look like this:

```html
<form method="post" action="responseredirectionservlet">
  <p>Please indicate your favorite search engine.</p>
  <table>
    <tr>
      <td><input type="radio" name="searchEngine"
            value="http://www.google.com"/>Google</td>
    </tr>
    <tr>
      <td><input type="radio" name="searchEngine"
            value="http://www.bing.com"/>Bing</td>
    </tr>
    <tr>
      <td><input type="radio" name="searchEngine"
            value="http://www.yahoo.com"/>Yahoo!</td>
```

```
      </tr>
      <tr>
        <td><input type="submit" value="Submit" /></td>
      </tr>
    </table>
  </form>
```

The HTML form in the markup code above contains three radio buttons. The value for each of them is the URL for the search engine corresponding to the user's selection. Notice how the value for the name attribute of each radio button is the same, namely "searchEngine". The servlet will obtain the value of the selected radio button by calling the request.getParameter() method and passing the "searchEngine" string as a parameter, as is demonstrated in the code here:

```
package com.ensode.jakartaeebook.responseredirection;
//imports omitted

@WebServlet(urlPatterns = {"/responseredirectionservlet"})
public class ResponseRedirectionServlet extends HttpServlet {
  @Override
  protected void doPost(HttpServletRequest request,
    HttpServletResponse response)
    throws IOException {
    String url = request.getParameter("searchEngine");

    if (url != null) {
      response.sendRedirect(url);
    } else {
      PrintWriter printWriter = response.getWriter();
      printWriter.println("No search engine was selected.");
    }
  }
}
```

By calling request.getParameter("searchEngine"), the code shown here assigns the URL of the selected search engine to the url variable. Then, (after checking for null, in case the user clicked on the **Submit** button without selecting a search engine), directs the user to the selected search engine by calling response.sendRedirect() and passing the url variable as a parameter.

After packaging the code and deploying it, we can see it in action by typing a URL similar to the following in the browser: http://localhost:8080/responseredirection/.

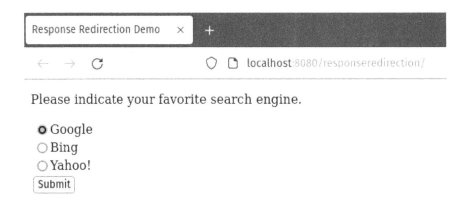

Figure 11.7 – Response redirection example

After clicking the **Submit** button, the user is directed to their favorite search engine.

It should be noted that redirecting the response as illustrated here creates a new HTTP request to the page we are redirecting to, therefore any request parameters and attributes are lost.

Persisting application data across requests

In the previous section, we saw how it is possible to store an object in the request by invoking the `HttpRequest.setAttribute()` method, and how later this object can be retrieved by invoking the `HttpRequest.getAttribute()` method. This approach only works if the request was forwarded to the servlet invoking the `getAttribute()` method. If this is not the case, the `getAttribute()` method will return null.

It is possible to persist an object across requests. In addition to attaching an object to the request object, an object can also be attached to the session object or to the servlet context. The difference between these two is that objects attached to the session will not be visible to different users, whereas objects attached to the servlet context are.

Attaching objects to the session and servlet context is very similar to attaching objects to the request. To attach an object to the session, the `HttpServletRequest.getSession()` method must be invoked. This method returns an instance of `jakarta.servlet.http.HttpSession`. We then call the `HttpSession.setAttribute()` method to attach the object to the session. The following code fragment illustrates the process:

```
protected void doPost(HttpServletRequest request,
  HttpServletResponse response) {
  .
  .
  .
  Foo foo = new Foo(); //theoretical object
```

```
    HttpSession session = request.getSession();
    session.setAttribute("foo", foo);
      .

      .

      .

}
```

We can then retrieve the object from the session by calling the HttpSession.getAttribute() method:

```
protected void doPost(HttpServletRequest request, HttpServletResponse
response)
{
    HttpSession session = request.getSession();

    Foo foo = (Foo)session.getAttribute("foo");
}
```

Notice how the return value of session.getAttribute() needs to be cast to the appropriate type. This is necessary since the return value of this method is java.lang.Object.

The procedure to attach and retrieve objects to and from the servlet context is very similar. The servlet needs to call the getServletContext() method (defined in the class called GenericServlet, which is the parent class of HttpServlet, which in turn is the parent class of our servlets). This method returns an instance of jakarta.servlet.ServletContext, which defines a setAttribute() and a getAttribute() method. These methods work the same way as their HttpServletRequest and HttpSessionResponse counterparts.

The procedure to attach an object to the servlet context is illustrated in the following code snippet:

```
protected void doPost(HttpServletRequest request,
    HttpServletResponse response) {
    //The getServletContext() method is defined higher in
    //the inheritance hierarchy.
    ServletContext servletContext = getServletContext();

    Foo foo = new Foo();
    servletContext.setAttribute("foo", foo);
      .

      .

      .

}
```

The preceding code attaches the `foo` object to the servlet context. This object will be available to any servlet in our application and will be the same across sessions. It can be retrieved by calling the `ServletContext.getAttribute()` method, as is illustrated next:

```
protected void doPost(HttpServletRequest request,
  HttpServletResponse response){
  ServletContext servletContext = getServletContext();
  Foo foo = (Foo)servletContext.getAttribute("foo");
    .
    .
    .
}
```

This code obtains the `foo` object from the request context. Again, a cast is needed since the `ServletContext.getAttribute()` method, like its counterparts, returns an instance of `java.lang.Object`.

> **Note**
>
> Objects attached to the servlet context are said to have a scope of *application*. Similarly, objects attached to the session are said to have a scope of *session*, and objects attached to the request are said to have a scope of *request*.

Passing initialization parameters to a servlet via annotations

Sometimes it is useful to pass some initialization parameters to a servlet. That way, we can make said servlet behave differently based on the parameters that are sent to it. For example, we may want to configure a servlet to behave differently in development and production environments.

In the old days, servlet initialization parameters were sent via the `<init-param>` parameter in `web.xml`. As of servlet 3.0, initialization parameters can be passed to the servlet as the value of the `initParams` attribute of the `@WebServlet` annotation. The following example illustrates how to do this:

```
package com.ensode.jakartaeebook.initparams;
//imports omitted for brevity

@WebServlet(name = "InitParamsServlet", urlPatterns = {
  "/InitParamsServlet"}, initParams = {
  @WebInitParam(name = "param1", value = "value1"),
  @WebInitParam(name = "param2", value = "value2")})
public class InitParamsServlet extends HttpServlet {
  @Override
```

```
protected void doGet(HttpServletRequest request,
        HttpServletResponse response)
        throws ServletException, IOException {
    ServletConfig servletConfig = getServletConfig();
    String param1Val = servletConfig.getInitParameter("param1");
    String param2Val = servletConfig.getInitParameter("param2");
    response.setContentType("text/html");
    PrintWriter printWriter = response.getWriter();

    printWriter.println("<p>");
    printWriter.println("Value of param1 is " + param1Val);
    printWriter.println("</p>");

    printWriter.println("<p>");
    printWriter.println("Value of param2 is " + param2Val);
    printWriter.println("</p>");
  }
}
```

As we can see, the value of the `initParams` attribute of the `@WebServlet` annotation is an array of `@WebInitParam` annotations. Each `@WebInitParam` annotation has two attributes: `name`, which corresponds to the parameter name, and `value`, which corresponds to the parameter value.

We can obtain the values of our parameters by invoking the `getInitParameter()` method on the `jakarta.servlet.ServletConfig` class. This method takes a single `String` argument as a parameter, corresponding to the parameter name, and returns `String` corresponding to the parameter value.

Each servlet has a corresponding instance of `ServletConfig` assigned to it. As we can see in this example, we can obtain this instance by invoking `getServletConfig()`, which is a method inherited from `jakarta.servlet.GenericServlet`, the parent class of `HttpServlet`, which our servlets extend.

After packaging and deploying our servlet, then pointing the browser to the servlet URL, we will see the following page rendered in the browser, as shown in *Figure 11.8*.

Figure 11.8 – Servlet initialization parameters

As we can see, the rendered values correspond to the values we have set in each @WebInitParam annotation.

Now that we've seen how to initialize a servlet, we'll shift our attention to intercepting HTTP requests via servlet filters.

Servlet filters

A **servlet filter** is an object that can dynamically intercept a request and manipulate its data before the request is handled by the servlet. Filters can also manipulate a response after a servlet's doGet() or doPost() method finishes, but before the output is sent to the browser.

The only way to configure a filter in earlier servlet specifications was to use the <filter-mapping> tag in web.xml. **Servlet 3.0** introduced the ability to configure servlets via the @WebFilter annotation.

The following example illustrates how to do this:

```
package com.ensode.jakartaeebook.servletfilter;
//imports omitted

@WebFilter(initParams = {
  @WebInitParam(name = "filterparam1", value = "filtervalue1")},
        urlPatterns = {"/InitParamsServlet"})
public class SimpleFilter implements Filter {
  private static final Logger LOG
    = Logger.getLogger(SimpleFilter.class.getName());
  private FilterConfig filterConfig;

  @Override
  public void init(FilterConfig filterConfig) throws
    ServletException {
    this.filterConfig = filterConfig;
  }

  @Override
  public void doFilter(ServletRequest servletRequest,
    ServletResponse servletResponse, FilterChain filterChain)
    throws IOException, ServletException {
    LOG.log(Level.INFO, "Entering doFilter()");
    LOG.log(Level.INFO, "initialization parameters: ");
    Enumeration<String> initParameterNames = filterConfig.
      getInitParameterNames();
    String parameterName;
    String parameterValue;
```

```
    while (initParameterNames.hasMoreElements()) {
      parameterName = initParameterNames.nextElement();
      parameterValue =
        filterConfig.getInitParameter(parameterName);
      LOG.log(Level.INFO, "{0} = {1}",
        new Object[]{parameterName,
        parameterValue});
    }

    LOG.log(Level.INFO, "Invoking servlet...");
    filterChain.doFilter(servletRequest, servletResponse);
    LOG.log(Level.INFO, "Back from servlet invocation");

  }

  @Override
  public void destroy() {
    filterConfig = null;
  }
}
```

As we can see in the example, the @WebFilter annotation has several attributes we can use to configure the filter. Of special importance is the urlPatterns attribute. This attribute takes an array of String objects as its value. Each element in the array corresponds to a URL that our filter will intercept. In our example, we are intercepting a single URL pattern, which corresponds to the servlet we wrote in the previous section.

Other attributes in the @WebFilter annotation include the optional filterName attribute, which we can use to give our filter a name. If we don't specify a name for our filter, then the filter name defaults to the filter's class name.

As we can see in our example servlet filter, we can send initialization parameters to a filter. This is done just like we send initialization parameters to a servlet. The @WebFilter annotation has an initParams attribute that takes an array of @WebInitParam annotations as its value. We can obtain the values of said parameters by invoking the getInitParameter() method on jakarta.servlet.FilterConfig, as illustrated in the example.

Our filter is fairly simple; it simply sends some output to the server log before and after the servlet is invoked. Inspecting the server log after deploying our application and pointing the browser to the servlet's URL should reveal our filter's output:

```
Loading application [servletfilter] at [/servletfilter]|#]
servletfilter was successfully deployed in 69 milliseconds.|#]
Entering doFilter()|#]
```

```
initialization parameters: |#]
filterparam1 = filtervalue1|#]
Invoking servlet…|#]
Back from servlet invocation|#]
```

Some common uses of servlet filters include profiling web applications, applying security, and compressing data, among others.

Servlet listeners

During the lifetime of a typical web application, a number of events take place, such as HTTP requests being created or destroyed, request or session attributes being added, removed, or modified, and so on and so forth.

The servlet API provides a number of listener interfaces we can implement in order to react to these events. All of these interfaces are in the `jakarta.servlet` package. The following table summarizes them.

Listener Interface	Description
ServletContextListener	Contains methods for handling context initialization and destruction events.
ServletContextAttributeListener	Contains methods for reacting to any attributes added, removed, or replaced in the servlet context (application scope).
ServletRequestListener	Contains methods for handling request initialization and destruction events.
ServletRequestAttributeListener	Contains methods for reacting to any attributes added, removed, or replaced in the request.
HttpSessionListener	Contains methods for handling HTTP session initialization and destruction events.
HttpSessionAttributeListener	Contains methods for reacting to any attributes added, removed, or replaced in the HTTP session.

Table 11.2 – Servlet listener interfaces

All we need to do to handle any of the events handled by the interfaces described in the preceding table is to implement one of the interfaces and annotate it with the `@WebListener` interface or declare it in the `web.xml` deployment descriptor via the `<listener>` tag.

The API for all of the preceding interfaces is fairly straightforward and intuitive. We will show an example for one of the interfaces. Others will be very similar.

> **Note**
>
> The JavaDoc for all of the preceding interfaces can be found at `https://jakarta.ee/specifications/platform/10/apidocs/jakarta/servlet/package-summary`

The following example illustrates how to implement the `ServletRequestListener` interface, which can be used to perform some action whenever an HTTP request is created or destroyed:

```
package com.ensode.jakartaeebook.listener;
//imports omitted


@WebListener
public class HttpRequestListener implements ServletRequestListener {

  @Override
  public void requestInitialized(
   ServletRequestEvent servletRequestEvent) {
    ServletContext servletContext = servletRequestEvent.
    getServletContext();
    servletContext.log("New request initialized");
  }

  @Override
  public void requestDestroyed(
   ServletRequestEvent servletRequestEvent) {
    ServletContext servletContext = servletRequestEvent.
    getServletContext();
    servletContext.log("Request destroyed");
  }
}
```

As we can see, all we need to do to activate our listener class is to annotate it with the `@WebListener` annotation. Our listener must also implement one of the listener interfaces we listed. In our example, we chose to implement `jakarta.servlet.ServletRequestListener`. This interface has methods that are automatically invoked whenever an HTTP request is initialized or destroyed.

The `ServletRequestListener` interface has two methods, `requestInitialized()` and `requestDestroyed()`. In the preceding simple implementation, we simply sent some output to the log, but of course, we can do anything we need to do in our implementations.

Using our listener to listen to requests handled by the simple servlet we developed earlier in the chapter results in the following output in the Jakarta EE runtime log:

```
Loading application [servletlistener] at [/servletlistener]|#]
   servletlistener was successfully deployed in 142 milliseconds.|#]
   New request initialized|#]
   Request destroyed|#]
```

Implementing the other listener interfaces is just as simple and straightforward.

Pluggability

When the original servlet API was released back in the late 1990s, writing servlets was the only way of writing server-side web applications in Java. Since then, several Jakarta EE and third-party frameworks have been built on top of the Servlet API. Examples of such frameworks include JSP and JSF, Apache Struts, Apache Wicket, Spring Web MVC, and several others.

Nowadays, very few (if any) Java web applications are built using the Servlet API directly. Instead, the vast majority of projects utilize one of the available Java web application frameworks. All of these frameworks use the servlet API "under the covers," therefore setting up an application to use one of these frameworks has always involved making some configuration in the application's web.xml deployment descriptor. In some cases, some applications use more than one framework. This tends to make the web.xml deployment descriptor fairly large and hard to maintain.

Servlet 3.0 introduced the concept of pluggability. Web application framework developers now have not one, but two ways to avoid having application developers have to modify the web.xml deployment descriptor in order to use their framework. Framework developers can choose to use annotations instead of web.xml to configure their servlets. After doing this, all that is needed to use the framework is to include the library jar file(s) provided by the framework developers in the application's WAR file. Alternatively, framework developers may choose to include web-fragment.xml as part of the JAR file to be included in web applications that use their framework.

web-fragment.xml is almost identical to web.xml. The main difference is that the root element of web-fragment.xml is <web-fragment> as opposed to <web-app>. The following example illustrates a sample web-fragment.xml:

```xml
<?xml version="1.0" encoding="UTF-8"?>
<web-fragment xmlns="https://jakarta.ee/xml/ns/jakartaee"
   xmlns:xsi="http://www.w3.org/2001/XMLSchema-instance"
   xsi:schemaLocation="https://jakarta.ee/xml/ns/jakartaee
   https://jakarta.ee/xml/ns/jakartaee/web-fragment_5_0.xsd"
   version="5.0" metadata-complete="true">
   <servlet>
     <servlet-name>WebFragment</servlet-name>
     <servlet-class>
       com.ensode.jakartaeebook.webfragment.WebFragmentServlet
```

```
      </servlet-class>
    </servlet>
    <servlet-mapping>
      <servlet-name>WebFragment</servlet-name>
      <url-pattern>/WebFragment</url-pattern>
    </servlet-mapping>
  </web-fragment>
```

As we can see, web-fragment.xml is almost identical to typical web.xml. In this simple example, we only use the <servlet> and <servlet-mapping> elements, but all other usual web.xml elements such as <filter>, <filter-mapping>, and <listener> are available as well.

As specified in web-fragment.xml, our servlet can be invoked via its URL pattern, /WebFragment, therefore the URL to execute our servlet once deployed as part of a web application would be http://localhost:8080/webfragmentapp/WebFragment. Of course, the hostname, port, and context root must be adjusted as appropriate.

All we need to do for any Jakarta EE-compliant application server to pick up the settings in web-fragment.xml is to place the file in the META-INF folder of the library where we pack our servlet, filter, and/or listener, then place our library's jar file in the lib directory of the WAR file containing our application.

Configuring web applications programmatically

In addition to allowing us to configure web applications through annotations and web-fragment.xml, Servlet 3.0 also allows us to configure our web applications programmatically at runtime.

The ServletContext class has new methods to configure servlets, filters, and listeners programmatically. The following example illustrates how to configure a servlet programmatically at runtime, without resorting to the @WebServlet annotation or to XML:

```
package com.ensode.jakartaeebook.servlet;
//imports omitted

@WebListener()
public class ServletContextListenerImpl implements
  ServletContextListener {

  @Override
  public void contextInitialized(
    ServletContextEvent servletContextEvent) {
    ServletContext servletContext = servletContextEvent.
      getServletContext();
    try {
      ProgrammaticallyConfiguredServlet servlet = servletContext.
```

```
        createServlet(
          ProgrammaticallyConfiguredServlet.class);
      servletContext.addServlet(
        "ProgrammaticallyConfiguredServlet", servlet);
      ServletRegistration servletRegistration = servletContext.
        getServletRegistration(
          "ProgrammaticallyConfiguredServlet");
      servletRegistration.addMapping(
        "/ProgrammaticallyConfiguredServlet");
    } catch (ServletException servletException) {
      servletContext.log(servletException.getMessage());
    }
  }
  //additional methods omitted for brevity
}
```

In this example, we invoke the `createServlet()` method of `ServletContext` to create the servlet that we are about to configure. This method takes an instance of `java.lang.Class` corresponding to our servlet's class. This method returns a class implementing `jakarta.servlet.Servlet` or any of its child interfaces.

Once we create our servlet, we need to invoke `addServlet()` on our `ServletContext` instance to register our servlet with the servlet container. This method takes two parameters, the first being `String` corresponding to the servlet name and the second being the servlet instance returned by the call to `createServlet()`.

Once we have registered our servlet, we need to add a URL mapping to it. In order to do this, we need to invoke the `getServletRegistration()` method on our `ServletContext` instance, passing the servlet name as a parameter. This method returns the servlet container's implementation of `jakarta.servlet.ServletRegistration`. From this object, we need to invoke its `addMapping()` method, passing the URL mapping we wish our servlet to handle.

Our example servlet is very simple. It simply displays a text message in the browser. Its `doGet()` method looks as follows:

```
@Override
protected void doGet(HttpServletRequest request,
  HttpServletResponse response)
  throws ServletException, IOException {
  ServletOutputStream outputStream = response.getOutputStream();

  outputStream.println(
    "This message was generated from a servlet that was "
    + "configured programmatically.");
  }
```

After packing our code in a WAR file and deploying it to a Jakarta EE runtime, then pointing the browser to the appropriate URL (i.e `http://localhost:8080/programmaticservletwebapp/ProgrammaticallyConfiguredServlet`), we should see the following message in the browser:

This message was generated from a servlet that was configured programmatically.

The `ServletContext` interface has methods to create and add servlet filters and listeners. They work very similarly to the way the `addServlet()` and `createServlet()` methods work, therefore we won't be discussing them in detail. Refer to the Jakarta EE API documentation at `https://jakarta.ee/specifications/platform/10/apidocs/` for details.

Asynchronous processing

Traditionally, servlets have created a single thread per request in Java web applications. After a request is processed, the thread is made available for other requests to use. This model works fairly well for traditional web applications, in which HTTP requests are relatively few and far between. However, most modern web applications take advantage of **Ajax** (short for **Asynchronous JavaScript and XML**), a technique that makes web applications behave much more responsively than traditional web applications.

Ajax has the side effect of generating a lot more HTTP requests than traditional web applications. If some of these threads block for a long time waiting, for a resource to be ready or doing anything that takes a long time to process, it is possible our application may suffer from thread starvation.

To alleviate the situation described in the previous paragraph, the Servlet 3.0 specification introduced asynchronous processing. Using this new capability, we are no longer limited to a single thread per request. We can now spawn a separate thread and return the original thread back to the pool, to be reused by other clients.

The following example illustrates how to implement asynchronous processing using the new capabilities introduced in Servlet 3.0:

```
package com.ensode.jakartaeebook.asynchronousservlet;
//imports omitted for brevity
@WebServlet(name = "AsynchronousServlet", urlPatterns = {
  "/AsynchronousServlet"}, asyncSupported = true)
public class AsynchronousServlet extends HttpServlet {
  @Override
  protected void doGet(HttpServletRequest request,
    HttpServletResponse response) throws Exception {
    final AsyncContext ac = request.startAsync();
    ac.start(new Runnable() {
      @Override
      public void run() {
        try {
```

```
        Thread.sleep(10000);
        ac.getResponse().getWriter().
          println("You should see this after a brief wait");
        ac.complete();
      } catch (Exception ex) {
        //handle the exception
      }
    }
  });
  }
}
```

The first thing we need to do to make sure our asynchronous processing code works as expected is to set the `asyncSupported` attribute of the `@WebServlet` annotation to `true`.

To actually spawn an asynchronous process, we need to invoke the `startAsync()` method on the instance of `HttpServletRequest` that we receive as a parameter in the `doGet()` or `doPost()` method in our servlet. This method returns an instance of `jakarta.servlet.AsyncContext`. This class has a `start()` method that takes an instance of a class implementing `java.lang.Runnable` as its sole parameter. In our example, we used an anonymous inner class to implement `Runnable` in line. Of course, a standard Java class implementing `Runnable` can be used as well, or a lambda expression.

When we invoke the `start()` method of `AsyncContext`, a new thread is spawned and the `run()` method of the `Runnable` instance is executed. This thread runs in the background, the `doGet()` method returns immediately, and the request thread is immediately available to service other clients. It is important to notice that, even though the `doGet()` method returns immediately, the response is not committed until after the thread spawned finishes. It can signal it is done processing by invoking the `complete()` method on `AsyncContext`.

In our example, the message **You should see this after a brief wait** is displayed in the browser after 10 seconds, which is how long our spawned thread takes to complete.

Now that we've seen how to perform asynchronous processing in servlets, we'll focus our attention on how to implement HTTP/2 server push support.

HTTP/2 server push support

HTTP/2 is the newest version of the HTTP protocol. It offers several advantages over HTTP 1.1. For example, with HTTP/2 there is a single connection between the browser and the server, and this connection remains open until the user navigates to another page. HTTP/2 also offers multiplexing, meaning that several concurrent requests from the browser to the server are allowed. Additionally, HTTP/2 features server push, meaning that the server can send resources to the browser without the browser specifically having to request them.

HTTP/2 server push support was added to the servlet specification in version 4.0, released as part of Java EE 8. In this section, we'll see how we can write code to take advantage of HTTP/2's server push functionality. The following example illustrates how this can be done:

```
package com.ensode.jakartaeebook.servlet;
//imports omitted
@WebServlet(name = "ServletPushDemoServlet", urlPatterns = {"/
ServletPushDemoServlet"})
public class ServletPushDemoServlet extends HttpServlet {
  @Override
  protected void doPost(HttpServletRequest request,
      HttpServletResponse response) throws Exception {
    PushBuilder pushBuilder = request.newPushBuilder();
    if (pushBuilder != null) {
      pushBuilder.path("images/david_heffelfinger.png").
        addHeader("content-type", "image/png").push();
      response.sendRedirect("response.html");
    } else {
      //handle the case when the browser does not support HTTP/2.
    }
  }
}
```

We can push resources to the browser via the PushBuilder interface, introduced in version 4 of the servlet specification. We can obtain an instance of a class implementing PushBuilder by invoking the new PushBuilder() method on the instance of HttpServletRequest we get as a parameter in our doPost() method.

As its name implies, the PushBuilder interface implements the Builder pattern, meaning that most of its methods return a new instance of PushBuilder we can use, allowing us to conveniently chain together method invocations.

We indicate the path of the resource we'd like to push to the browser by invoking PushBuilder's appropriately named path() method. This method takes a single String argument indicating the path of the resource to push. Paths beginning with a forward slash ("/") indicate an absolute path; all other paths indicate a path relative to our application's context root.

Once we have specified the path of our resource, we can optionally set some HTTP headers. In our case, we are pushing an image in PNG format, therefore we set the content type as appropriate.

Finally, we invoke the push() method on our PushBuilder instance to actually push our resource to the browser.

What we accomplished with our example was pushing a resource to the browser before the browser submitted a request for it. This task was impossible before the HTTP/2 protocol was released.

Summary

This chapter covered how to develop, configure, package, and deploy servlets. The following topics were covered in this chapter:

- How to process HTML form information by accessing the HTTP request object

- Forwarding HTTP requests from one servlet to another was covered, as well as redirecting the HTTP response to a different server

- Persisting objects in memory across requests by attaching them to the servlet context and the HTTP session

- Configuring web applications via annotations

- Pluggability through `web-fragment.xml`

- Programmatic servlet configuration

- Asynchronous processing

- HTTP/2 server push

Armed with the knowledge from this chapter, we can now implement server-side web application logic using Jakarta servlets.

12

Jakarta Enterprise Beans

Jakarta Enterprise Beans are server-side components that encapsulate the business logic of an application. Enterprise beans simplify application development by automatically taking care of transaction management and security. There are two types of enterprise beans: **session beans**, which perform business logic, and **message-driven beans**, which act as a message listener.

The following topics will be covered in this chapter:

- Session beans
- Message-driven beans
- Transactions in enterprise beans
- Enterprise bean life cycles
- Enterprise bean timer service
- Enterprise bean security

> **Note**
> Example source code for this chapter can be found on GitHub at `https://github.com/PacktPublishing/Jakarta-EE-Application-Development/tree/main/ch12_src`.

Session beans

As we previously mentioned, session beans typically encapsulate business logic. One or two artifacts need to be created in order to create a session bean, including the bean itself, and an optional business interface. These artifacts need to be annotated adequately to let the Jakarta EE runtime know they are session beans.

A simple session bean

The following example illustrates a very simple session bean:

```
package com.ensode.jakartaeebook;
import jakarta.ejb.Stateless;
@Stateless
public class SimpleSessionBean implements SimpleSession{
  private final String message =
    "If you don't see this, it didn't work!";

  @Override
  public String getMessage() {
    return message;
  }
}
```

The `@Stateless` annotation lets the Jakarta EE runtime know that this class is a **stateless session bean**. There are three types of session beans: stateless, stateful, and singleton. Before we explain the difference between these types of session beans, we need to clarify how an instance of an enterprise bean is provided to a client application.

When a stateless or stateful session bean is deployed, the Jakarta EE container creates a series of instances of each session bean. This is what is typically referred to as the **enterprise bean pool**. When a client application obtains an instance of an enterprise bean, one of the instances in the pool is provided to this client application.

The difference between stateful and stateless session beans is that stateful session beans maintain a **conversational state** with the client, whereas stateless session beans do not. In simple terms, what this means is that when a client application obtains an instance of a stateful session bean, we are guaranteed that the value of any instance variables in the bean will be consistent across method calls. Therefore, it is safe to modify any instance variables on a stateful session bean, since they will retain their value for the next method call. The Jakarta EE runtime saves conversational state by passivating stateful session beans, and retrieves said state when the bean is activated. The conversational state is the reason why the life cycle of stateful session beans is a bit more complex than the life cycle of stateless session beans or message-driven beans (the enterprise bean life cycle is discussed later in this chapter).

The Jakarta EE runtime may provide any instance of an enterprise bean in the pool when a client application requests an instance of a stateless session bean. Since we are not guaranteed the same instance for every method call, values set to any instance variables in a stateless session bean may be "lost" (they are not really lost; the modification is in another instance of the enterprise bean in the pool).

Other than being decorated with the @Stateless annotation, there is nothing special about our example class. Notice that it implements an interface called SimpleSession. This interface is the bean's business interface. The SimpleSession interface is shown next:

```
package com.ensode.jakartaeebook;
import jakarta.ejb.Remote;
@Remote
public interface SimpleSession {
  public String getMessage();
}
```

The only peculiar thing about this interface is that it is decorated with the @Remote annotation. This annotation indicates that this is a **remote business interface**. What this means is that the interface may be in a different JVM than the client application invoking it. Remote business interfaces may even be invoked across the network.

Business interfaces may also be decorated with the @Local interface. This annotation indicates that the business interface is a **local business interface**. Local business interface implementations must be in the same JVM as the client application invoking its methods.

Once we have compiled the session bean and its corresponding business interface, we need to place them in a JAR file and deploy them. How to deploy an enterprise bean JAR file depends on what application server we are using. Most modern application servers have an autodeploy directory. We can simply copy our JAR file to this directory in most cases. Consult your application server documentation to find the exact location of its autodeploy directory.

Now that we have seen the session bean and its corresponding business interface, let's take a look at a client sample application:

```
package com.ensode.jakartaeebook;
import jakarta.ejb.EJB;
import javax.naming.NamingException;
public class SessionBeanClient {
  @EJB
  private static SimpleSession simpleSession;
  private void invokeSessionBeanMethods() throws
    NamingException {
    System.out.println(simpleSession.getMessage());
    System.out.println("\nSimpleSession is of type: "
        + simpleSession.getClass().getName());
  }
  public static void main(String[] args)
    throws NamingException {
    new SessionBeanClient().invokeSessionBeanMethods();
  }
}
```

The preceding code simply declares an instance variable of the `com.ensode.jakartaeebook.SimpleSession` type, which is the business interface for our session bean. The instance variable is annotated with @EJB. This annotation lets the Jakarta EE runtime know that this variable is a business interface for a session bean. The Jakarta EE runtime then injects an implementation of the business interface for the client code to use.

Since our client is a standalone application (as opposed to a Jakarta EE artifact such as a WAR file or a deployable JAR file), we don't need to deploy to the Jakarta EE runtime. In order for it to be able to access code deployed to the server, it must have access to the application server's client libraries. The procedure on how to accomplish this varies from application server to application server. When using GlassFish, our client code must be placed in a JAR file and executed through the **appclient** utility. This utility can be found at [glassfish installation directory]/glassfish/bin/. Assuming this directory is in the PATH environment variable, and assuming we placed our client code in a JAR file called `simplesessionbeanclient.jar`, we would execute the preceding client code by typing the following command in the command line:

```
appclient -client simplesessionbeanclient.jar
```

Executing this command results in the following console output:

```
If you don't see this, it didn't work!

SimpleSession is of type: com.ensode.jakartaeebook._SimpleSession_
Wrapper
```

This is the expected output upon executing the `SessionBeanClient` class.

> **Note**
>
> We are using Maven to build our code. For this example, we have used the Maven Assembly Plugin (http://maven.apache.org/plugins/maven-assembly-plugin/) to build a client JAR file that includes all dependencies. This frees us from having to specify all the dependent JAR files in the -classpath command-line option of appclient. To build this JAR file, simply invoke mvn assembly:assembly from the command line.

The first line of output is simply the return value of the getMessage() method we implemented in the session bean. The second line of output displays the fully qualified class name of the class implementing the business interface. Notice that the class name is not the fully qualified name of the session bean we wrote; instead, what is actually provided is an implementation of the business interface created behind the scenes by the Jakarta EE runtime.

A more realistic example

In the previous section, we saw a very simple "Hello World" type of example. In this section, we will show a more realistic example. Session beans are frequently used as **Data Access Objects** (**DAOs**). Sometimes they are used as a wrapper for JDBC calls; other times they are used to wrap calls to obtain or modify Jakarta Persistence entities. In this section, we will take the latter approach.

The following example illustrates how to implement the DAO design pattern in a session bean.

Let's now take a look at the session bean implementing our example business interface. As we are about to see, there are some differences between the way Jakarta Persistence code is implemented in a session bean versus in a plain old Java object:

```
package com.ensode.jakartaeebook;
//imports omitted for brevity
@Stateful
public class CustomerDaoBean implements CustomerDao {
  @PersistenceContext
  private EntityManager entityManager;

  @Override
  public void saveCustomer(Customer customer) {
    if (customer.getCustomerId() == null) {
      entityManager.persist(customer);
    } else {
      entityManager.merge(customer);
    }
  }

  @Override
  public Customer getCustomer(Long customerId) {
    Customer customer;
    customer = entityManager.find(Customer.class,
      customerId);
    return customer;
  }
  @Override
  public void deleteCustomer(Customer customer) {
    entityManager.remove(customer);
  }
}
```

It is worth pointing out that since we don't intend for our session bean to be invoked remotely, there is no need for a remote business interface in this case. Our client applications can simply inject an instance of the session bean via the @EJB annotation.

As we can see, our session bean implements three methods. The `saveCustomer()` method saves customer data to the database, the `getCustomer()` method obtains data for a customer from the database, and the `deleteCustomer()` method deletes customer data from the database. All of these methods take an instance of a Jakarta Persistence entity bean or type `Customer`.

Normally, when making Jakarta Persistence calls, we need to start and commit transactions via `UserTransaction.begin()` and `UserTransaction.commit()`. The reason we need to do this is that Jakarta Persistence calls are required to be wrapped in a transaction. If they are not in a transaction, most Jakarta Persistence calls will throw `TransactionRequiredException`. Session bean methods are implicitly transactional. There is nothing we need to do to make them that way. For this reason, we don't need to manually start and commit transactions when invoking Jakarta Persistence calls from a session bean. This default behavior is what is known as **container-managed transactions**. Container-managed transactions are discussed in detail later in this chapter.

Invoking session beans from web applications

Frequently, Jakarta EE applications consist of web applications acting as clients for enterprise beans. In this section, we will develop a Jakarta Faces web application with a CDI named bean acting as a client for the DAO session bean we just discussed in the previous section.

In order to make this application act as an enterprise bean client, we will develop a `CustomerController` named bean so that it delegates the logic to save a new customer to the database to the `CustomerDaoBean` session bean we developed in the previous section, as shown in the following example:

```
package com.ensode.jakartaeebook.facesjpa;
//imports omitted for brevity
@Named
@RequestScoped
public class CustomerController implements Serializable {
  @EJB
  private CustomerDaoBean customerDaoBean;
 //variable declarations omitted for brevity
  public CustomerController() {
    customer = new Customer();
  }
  public String saveCustomer() {
    String returnValue = "customer_saved";
    try {
      populateCustomer();
      customerDaoBean.saveCustomer(customer);
    } catch (Exception e) {
      e.printStackTrace();
      returnValue = "error_saving_customer";
```

```
    }

    return returnValue;
  }
  private void populateCustomer() {
    //method implementation omitted for brevity
  }
  //getters and setters omitted for brevity
}
```

As we can see, all we had to do was to obtain an instance of the `CustomerDaoBean` session bean and annotate it with the `@EJB` annotation, then invoke the bean's `saveCustomer()` method.

Notice that we injected an instance of the session bean directly into our client code. Since the client code is running on the same JVM as the enterprise bean, there is no need for remote interfaces.

Now that we have developed our web application client for our session bean, we need to package it in a WAR (web archive) file and deploy it in order to use it.

Singleton session beans

Another type of session bean is the **singleton session bean**. A single instance of each singleton session bean exists in the Jakarta EE runtime.

Singleton session beans are useful to cache database data. Caching frequently used data in a singleton session bean increases performance since it greatly minimizes trips to the database. The common pattern is to have a method in our bean decorated with the `@PostConstruct` annotation. In this method, we retrieve the data we want to cache. Then, we provide a setter method for the bean's clients to call. The following example illustrates this technique:

```
package com.ensode.jakartaeebook.singletonsession;
//imports omiktted for brevity
@Singleton
public class SingletonSessionBean implements
  SingletonSessionBeanRemote {
  @PersistenceContext
  private EntityManager entityManager;
  private List<UsStates> stateList;

  @PostConstruct
  public void init() {
    Query query = entityManager.createQuery(
      "Select us from UsStates us");
    stateList = query.getResultList();
  }
```

```
  @Override
  public List<UsStates> getStateList() {
    return stateList;
  }
}
```

The @Singleton annotation denotes our class as a singleton session bean. Since our bean is a singleton, all of its clients would access the same instance, avoiding having duplicate data in memory. Additionally, since it is a singleton, it is safe to have an instance variable, since all clients access the same instance of the bean.

Asynchronous method calls

Sometimes it is useful to have some processing done asynchronously, that is, invoke a method call and return control immediately to the client, without having the client wait for the method to finish.

The @Asynchronous annotation can be used to mark a method in a session bean as asynchronous. When an enterprise bean client invokes an asynchronous method, control immediately goes back to the client, without waiting for the method to finish.

Asynchronous methods can only return void or an implementation of the java.util.concurrent. Future interface. The following example illustrates both scenarios:

```
package com.ensode.jakartaeebook.asynchronousmethods;
//imports omitted for brevity
@Stateless
public class AsynchronousSessionBean implements
    AsynchronousSessionBeanRemote {
  private static Logger logger = Logger.getLogger(
    AsynchronousSessionBean.class.getName());
  @Asynchronous
  @Override
  public void slowMethod() throws InterruptedException{
    long startTime = System.currentTimeMillis();
    logger.log(Level.INFO, "entering slowMethod()");
    Thread.sleep(10000); //simulate processing for 10 seconds
    logger.log(Level.INFO, "leaving slowMethod()");
    long endTime = System.currentTimeMillis();
    logger.log(Level.INFO, "execution took {0} milliseconds",
      endTime - startTime)
  }
  @Asynchronous
  @Override
  public Future<Long> slowMethodWithReturnValue() throws
```

```
    InterruptedException{
    Thread.sleep(15000); //simulate processing for 15 seconds
    return new AsyncResult<>(42L);
  }
}
```

When our asynchronous method returns `void`, the only thing we need to do is decorate the method with the `@Asynchronous` annotation, and then call it as usual from the client code.

If we need a return value, this value needs to be wrapped in an implementation of the `jav.util.concurrent.Future` interface. Jakarta EE provides a convenient implementation in the form of the `jakarta.ejb.AsyncResult` class. Both the `Future` interface and the `AsyncResult` class use generics. We need to specify our return type as the type parameter of these artifacts.

The `Future` interface has several methods we can use to cancel the execution of an asynchronous method, check to see whether the method has been carried out, get the return value of the method, or check to see whether the method has been canceled. *Table 12.1* lists these methods:

Method	Description
`cancel(boolean mayInterruptIfRunning)`	Cancels method execution. If the Boolean parameter is `true`, then this method will attempt to cancel the method execution even if it is already running.
`get()`	Will return the "unwrapped" return value of the method. The return value will be of the type parameter of the `Future` interface implementation returned by the method.
`get(long timeout, TimeUnit unit)`	Will attempt the "unwrapped" return value of the method. The return value will be of the type parameter of the `Future` interface implementation returned by the method. This method will block for the amount of time specified by the first parameter. The unit of time to wait is determined by the second parameter. The `TimeUnit` enum has constants for NANOSECONDS, MILLISECONDS, SECONDS, MINUTES, and so on. Refer to its Javadoc documentation for the complete list.
`isCancelled()`	Returns `true` if the method has been canceled, and `false` otherwise.
`isDone()`	Returns `true` if the method has finished executing, and `false` otherwise.

Table 12.1 – Canceling asynchronous method execution

As we can see, the @Asynchronous annotation makes it very easy to make asynchronous calls without having the overhead of having to set up message queues or topics.

The following example illustrates how to invoke asynchronous Jakarta Enterprise Bean methods:

```
package com.ensode.jakarteebook.asynchronousmethodsclient;
//imports omitted for brevity
public class App {
  @EJB
  private static AsynchronousSessionBeanRemote async;

  public void invokeEjbMethods() {
    async.slowMethod();

    Future<Long> retVal
        = async.slowMethodWithReturnValue();

    if (!retVal.isDone()) {
      System.out.println("Canceling second method call");
      retVal.cancel(true);
    } else {
      try {
        System.out.println("second method call done, "
            + "return value is: " + retVal.get());
      } catch (Exception ex) {
        Logger.getLogger(App.class.getName()).
            log(Level.SEVERE, null, ex);
      }
    }
  }
}
```

As we can see, invoking the asynchronous Jakarta Enterprise Beans method returning void is no different from invoking a regular method. Things get a bit more interesting when invoking a method that returns a value. The asynchronous invocation returns an instance of Future. We can then check to see whether the invocation is done by invoking isDone() on the future instance, cancel it if it's taking too long by invoking cancel(), or obtain the value from the asynchronous method by invoking get().

Now that we've discussed session beans at length, we'll focus our attention on the other type of enterprise bean, message-driven beans.

Message-driven beans

The purpose of a message-driven bean is to consume messages from a Jakarta messaging queue or a Jakarta messaging topic, depending on the messaging domain used (refer to *Chapter 13*). A message-driven bean must be annotated with the `@MessageDriven` annotation. The `mappedName` attribute of this annotation must contain the **Java Naming and Directory Interface (JNDI)** name of the message queue or message topic that the bean will be consuming messages from. The following example illustrates a simple message-driven bean:

```
package com.ensode.jakartaeebook;
//imports omitted for brevity
@JMSDestinationDefinition(
    name = "java:global/queue/JakartaEEBookQueue",
    interfaceName = "jakarta.jms.Queue",
    destinationName = "JakartaEEBookQueue"
)
@MessageDriven(activationConfig = {
  @ActivationConfigProperty(propertyName = "destinationLookup»,
      propertyValue = "java:global/queue/JakartaEEBookQueue"),
  @ActivationConfigProperty(propertyName = "destinationType",
      propertyValue = "jakarta.jms.Queue")
})
public class ExampleMessageDrivenBean implements MessageListener {
  private static final Logger LOG = Logger.getLogger(
    ExampleMessageDrivenBean.class.getName());
  public void onMessage(Message message) {
    TextMessage textMessage = (TextMessage) message;
    try {
      LOG.log(Level.INFO, "Received message: ");
      LOG.log(Level.INFO, textMessage.getText());
    } catch (JMSException e) {
      e.printStackTrace();
    }
  }
}
```

The `@JMSDestinationDefinition` annotation defines a Jakarta messaging destination that the message-driven bean will use to consume messages from. The destination can either be a queue or a topic; in our case, we are using a queue, therefore `jakarta.jms.Queue` is the value of the annotation's `interfaceName` attribute. The annotation's name attribute defines a JNDI name that the message-driven bean can use to refer to the queue.

Message-driven beans must be decorated with the `@MessageDriven` annotation; they listen for messages on the queue or topic defined in the `destinationLookup` property as defined by an `@ActivationConfigProperty` annotation. Notice that in our example, the value of the `destinationLookup` property matches the value of the `name` attribute in the corresponding `@JMSDestinationDefinition` annotation. The type of Jakarta messaging destination (`jakarta.jmsQueue` or `jakarta.jms.Topic`) must be specified in the `destinationType` property of `@MessageDriven`, as illustrated in our example.

It is recommended, but not required, for message-driven beans to implement the `jakarta.jms.MessageListener` interface. However, message-driven beans must have a method called `onMessage()` whose signature is identical to the preceding example.

Client applications never invoke a message-driven bean's methods directly. Instead, they put messages in the message queue or topic, and then the bean consumes those messages and acts as appropriate. Our example simply prints the message to the Jakarta EE runtime log.

Both session and message-driven beans support transaction management, this is discussed in the following sections.

Transactions in enterprise beans

As we mentioned earlier in this chapter, by default, all enterprise bean methods are automatically wrapped in a transaction. This default behavior is known as **container-managed transactions**, since transactions are managed by the Jakarta EE runtime. Application developers may also choose to manage transactions themselves. This can be accomplished by using **bean-managed transactions**. Both of these approaches are discussed in the following sections.

Container-managed transactions

Because enterprise bean methods are transactional by default, we run into an interesting dilemma when an enterprise bean method is invoked from client code that is already in a transaction. How should the Jakarta EE runtime behave? Should it suspend the client transaction, execute its method in a new transaction, and then resume the client transaction? Should it not create a new transaction and execute its method as part of the client transaction? Should it throw an exception?

By default, if an enterprise bean method is invoked by client code that is already in a transaction, the Jakarta EE runtime will simply execute the enterprise bean method as part of the client transaction. If this is not the behavior we need, we can change it by annotating the method with the `@TransactionAttribute` annotation. This annotation has a `value` attribute that determines how the Jakarta EE runtime will behave when the session bean method is invoked within an existing transaction and when it is invoked outside any transactions. The value of the `value` attribute is typically a constant defined in the `jakarta.ejb.TransactionAttributeType` enum. *Table 12.2* lists the possible values for the `@TransactionAttribute` annotation:

@TransactionAttribute Value	Description
TransactionAttributeType. MANDATORY	Forces the method to be invoked as part of a client transaction. If the method is called outside any transactions, it will throw `TransactionRequiredException`.
TransactionAttributeType. NEVER	The method is never executed in a transaction. If the method is invoked as part of a client transaction, it will throw `RemoteException`. No transaction is created if the method is not invoked inside a client transaction.
TransactionAttributeType.NOT_ SUPPORTED	If the method is invoked as part of a client transaction, the client transaction is suspended. The method is executed outside any transaction. After the method completes, the client transaction is resumed. No transaction is created if the method is not invoked inside a client transaction.
TransactionAttributeType. REQUIRED	If the method is invoked as part of a client transaction, the method is executed as part of said transaction. If the method is invoked outside any transaction, a new transaction is created for the method. This is the default behavior.
TransactionAttributeType. REQUIRES_NEW	If the method is invoked as part of a client transaction, said transaction is suspended, and a new transaction is created for the method. Once the method completes, the client transaction is resumed. If the method is called outside any transactions, a new transaction is created for the method.
TransactionAttributeType. SUPPORTS	If the method is invoked as part of a client transaction, it is executed as part of said transaction. If the method is invoked outside a transaction, no new transaction is created for the method.

Table 12.2 – Container-managed transactions transaction attributes

Although the default transaction attribute is reasonable in most cases, it is good to be able to override this default if necessary. For example, transactions have a performance impact, therefore being able to turn off transactions for a method that does not need them is beneficial. For a case like this, we would annotate our method as illustrated in the following code snippet:

```
@TransactionAttribute(value=TransactionAttributeType.NEVER)
public void doitAsFastAsPossible(){
  //performance critical code goes here.
}
```

Other transaction attribute types can be declared by annotating the methods with the corresponding constant in the `TransactionAttributeType` enum.

If we wish to override the default transaction attribute consistently across all methods in a session bean, we can decorate the session bean class with the `@TransactionAttribute` annotation. The value of its `value` attribute will be applied to every method in the session bean.

Container-managed transactions are automatically rolled back whenever an exception is thrown inside an enterprise bean method. Additionally, we can programmatically roll back a container-managed transaction by invoking the `setRollbackOnly()` method on an instance of `jakarta.ejb.EJBContext` corresponding to the session bean in question. The following example is a new version of the session bean we saw earlier in this chapter, modified to roll back transactions if necessary:

```
package com.ensode.jakartaeebook;
//imports omitted for brevity
@Stateless
public class CustomerDaoRollbackBean implements
  CustomerDaoRollback {
  @Resource
  private EJBContext ejbContext;
  @PersistenceContext
  private EntityManager entityManager;
  @Resource(name = "java:app/jdbc/customerdbDatasource")
  private DataSource dataSource;
  @Override
  public void saveNewCustomer(Customer customer) {
    if (customer == null ||
      customer.getCustomerId() != null) {
      ejbContext.setRollbackOnly();
    } else {
      customer.setCustomerId(getNewCustomerId());
      entityManager.persist(customer);
    }
  }
  //additional methods omitted for brevity
}
```

In this version of the DAO session bean, we made the `saveNewCustomer()` `updateCustomer()` method public. This method now checks to see whether the `customerId` field is null. If it is not null, this implies we are working with a customer that already exists in the database. Our method also checks to make sure the object to be persisted is not null. If any of the checks result in invalid data, the method simply rolls back the transaction by invoking the `setRollBackOnly()` method on the injected instance of `EJBContext` and does not update the database.

Bean-managed transactions

As we have seen, container-managed transactions make it ridiculously easy to write code that is wrapped in a transaction; after all, there is nothing special that we need to do to make them that way. As a matter of fact, some developers are sometimes not even aware that they are writing code that will be transactional in nature when they develop session beans. Container-managed transactions cover most of the typical cases that we will encounter. However, they do have a limitation. Each method can be wrapped in a single transaction or with no transaction. With container-managed transactions, it is not possible to implement a method that generates more than one transaction, but this can be accomplished by using **bean-managed transactions**:

```
package com.ensode.jakartaee;
//imports omitted
@Stateless
@TransactionManagement(value =
  TransactionManagementType.BEAN)
public class CustomerDaoBmtBean implements CustomerDaoBmt {
  @Resource private UserTransaction userTransaction;
  @PersistenceContext
  private EntityManager entityManager;
  @Resource(name = "java:app/jdbc/customerdbDatasource")
  private DataSource dataSource;

@Override
  public void saveMultipleNewCustomers(
    List<Customer> customerList)
    throws Exception {
      for (Customer customer : customerList) {
        userTransaction.begin();
        customer.setCustomerId(getNewCustomerId());
        entityManager.persist(customer);
        userTransaction.commit();
      }
    }
  //additional methods omitted for brevity
}
```

In this example, we implemented a method named `saveMultipleNewCustomers()`. This method takes a `List` of customers as its sole parameter. The intention of this method is to save as many elements in the `ArrayList` as possible. An exception saving one of the entities should not stop the method from attempting to save the remaining elements. This behavior is not possible using container-managed transactions, since an exception thrown when saving one of the entities would roll back the whole transaction. The only way to achieve this behavior is through bean-managed transactions.

As can be seen in the example, we declare that the session bean uses bean-managed transactions by decorating the class with the `@TransactionManagement` annotation and using `TransactionManagementType.BEAN` as the value for its `value` attribute (the only other valid value for this attribute is `TransactionManagementType.CONTAINER`, but since this is the default value, it is not necessary to specify it).

To be able to programmatically control transactions, we inject an instance of `jakarta.transaction.UserTransaction`, which is then used in the `for` loop inside the `saveMultipleNewCustomers()` method to begin and commit transactions in each iteration of the loop.

If we need to roll back a bean-managed transaction, we can do it by simply calling the `rollback()` method on the appropriate instance of `jakarta.transaction.UserTransaction`.

Before moving on, it is worth noting that even though all the examples in this section were session beans, the concepts explained apply to message-driven beans as well.

We will now focus our attention on enterprise bean life cycles.

Enterprise bean life cycles

Enterprise beans go through different states throughout their life cycle. Each type of enterprise bean has different states. States specific to each type of enterprise bean are discussed in the following sections.

Stateful session bean life cycle

We can annotate methods in session beans so that they are automatically invoked by the Jakarta EE runtime at certain points in the bean's life cycle. For example, we could have a method invoked right after the bean is created or right before it is destroyed.

Before explaining the annotations available to implement life cycle methods, a brief explanation of the session bean life cycle is in order. The life cycle of a stateful session bean is different from the life cycle of a stateless or singleton session bean.

A stateful session bean life cycle contains three states: **Does Not Exist**, **Ready**, and **Passive**, as illustrated in *Figure 12.1.*

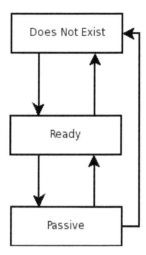

Figure 12.1 – Stateful session bean life cycle

Before a stateful session bean is deployed, it is in the **Does Not Exist** state. Upon successful deployment, the Jakarta EE runtime does any required dependency injection on the bean and it goes into the **Ready** state. At this point, the bean is ready to have its methods called by a client application.

When a stateful session bean is in the **Ready** state, the Jakarta EE runtime may decide to passivate it, that is, to move it from main memory to secondary storage. When this happens, the bean goes into the **Passive** state.

If an instance of a stateful session bean hasn't been accessed for a period of time, the Jakarta EE runtime will set the bean to the **Does Not Exist** state. How long a bean will stay in memory before being destroyed varies from application server to application server and is usually configurable.

Any methods in a stateful session bean annotated with @PostActivate will be invoked just after the stateful session bean has been activated. Similarly, any method annotated with @PrePassivate will be invoked just before the stateful session bean is passivated.

When a stateful session bean that is in the **Ready** state times out and is sent to the **Does Not Exist** state, any method decorated with the @PreDestroy annotation is executed. If the session bean is in the **Passive** state and it times out, methods decorated with the @PreDestroy annotation are not executed. Additionally, if a client of the stateful session bean executes any method decorated with the @Remove annotation, any methods decorated with the @PreDestroy annotation are executed and the bean is marked for garbage collection.

The @PostActivate, @PrePassivate, and @Remove annotations are valid only for stateful session beans. The @PreDestroy and @PostConstruct annotations are valid for stateful session beans, stateless session beans, and message-driven beans.

Stateless and singleton session bean life cycle

A stateless or singleton session bean life cycle contains only the **Does Not Exist** and **Ready** states, as illustrated in *Figure 12.2*.

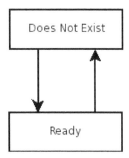

Figure 12.2 – Stateless and singleton session beans life cycle

Stateless and singleton session beans are never passivated. A stateless or singleton session bean's methods can be decorated with the @PostConstruct and @PreDestroy annotations. Just like in stateful session beans, any methods decorated with the @PostConstruct annotation will be executed when the session bean goes from the **Does Not Exist** state to the **Ready** state, and any methods decorated with the @PreDestroy annotation will be executed when a stateless session bean goes from the **Ready** state to the **Does Not Exist** state. Stateless and singleton session beans are never passivated, therefore any @PrePassivate and @PostActivate annotations in a stateless session bean are simply ignored by the Jakarta EE runtime.

Most Jakarta EE runtimes allow us to configure how long to wait before an idle stateless or singleton session bean is destroyed.

Message-driven bean life cycle

Just like stateless session beans, message-driven beans contain only the **Does Not Exist** and **Ready** states, as illustrated in *Figure 12.3*.

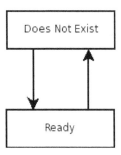

Figure 12.3 – Message-driven bean life cycle

A message-driven bean can have methods decorated with the @PostConstruct and @PreDestroy methods. Methods decorated with @PostConstruct are executed just before the bean goes to the **Ready** state. Methods decorated with the @PreDestroy annotation are executed just before the bean goes to the **Does Not Exist** state.

Now that we've covered enterprise bean life cycles, we'll focus our attention on another enterprise bean feature, namely the enterprise bean timer service.

Enterprise bean timer service

Stateless session beans and message-driven beans can have a method that is executed periodically at regular intervals of time. This can be accomplished by using the **enterprise bean timer service**. The following example illustrates how to take advantage of this feature:

```
package com.ensode.jakartaeebook;
//imports omitted
@Stateless
public class JebTimerExampleBean implements
  JebTimerExample

  private static final Logger LOG =
    Logger.getLogger(JebTimerExampleBean.class.getName());
  @Resource
  TimerService timerService;
  @Override
  public void startTimer(Serializable info) {
    timerService.createTimer(new Date(), 5000, info);
  }
  @Override
  public void stopTimer(Serializable info) {
    Collection<Timer> timers = timerService.getTimers();
    timers.stream().filter(t -> t.getInfo().equals(info)).
      forEach(t -> t.cancel());
  }
  @Timeout
  @Override
  public void logMessage(Timer timer) {
    LOG.log(Level.INFO, "Message triggered by :{0} at {1}",
      new Object[]{timer.getInfo(),
        System.currentTimeMillis()});
  }
}
```

In this example, we inject an implementation of the `jakarta.ejb.TimerService` interface by annotating an instance variable of this type with the `@Resource` annotation. We can then create a timer by invoking the `createTimer()` method of this `TimerService` instance.

There are several overloaded versions of the `createTimer()` method. The one we chose to use takes an instance of `java.util.Date` as its first parameter. This parameter is used to indicate the first time the timer should expire ("go off"). In the example, we chose to use a brand-new instance of the `Date` class, which in effect makes the timer expire immediately. The second parameter of the `createTimer()` method is the amount of time to wait, in milliseconds, before the timer expires again. In our example, the timer will expire every five seconds. The third parameter of the `createTimer()` method can be an instance of any class implementing the `java.io.Serializable` interface. Since a single enterprise bean can have several timers executing concurrently, this third parameter is used to uniquely identify each of the timers. If we don't need to identify the timers, null can be passed as a value for this parameter.

We can stop a timer by invoking its `cancel()` method. There is no way to directly obtain a single timer associated with an enterprise bean. What we need to do is invoke the `getTimers()` method on the instance of `TimerService` that is linked to the enterprise bean. This method will return a collection containing all the timers associated with the enterprise bean. We can then obtain a stream from the collection, filter it so that it only contains elements with the desired value for `getInfo()`, and then invoke `cancel()` on the matching timers.

Finally, any enterprise bean method decorated with the `@Timeout` annotation will be executed when a timer expires. Methods decorated with this annotation must return `void` and take a single parameter of type `jakarta.ejb.Timer`. In our example, the method simply writes a message to the server log.

The following class is a standalone client for our example enterprise bean:

```
package com.ensode.jakartaeebook;
import jakarta.ejb.EJB;
public class Client {
  @EJB
  private static JebTimerExample jebTimerExample;
  public static void main(String[] args) {
    try {
      jebTimerExample.startTimer("Timer 1");
      Thread.sleep(2000);
      jebTimerExample.startTimer("Timer 2");
      Thread.sleep(30000);
      jebTimerExample.stopTimer("Timer 1");
      jebTimerExample.stopTimer("Timer 2");
    } catch (InterruptedException e) {
      e.printStackTrace();
    }
  }
}
```

The example simply starts a timer, waits for a couple of seconds, and then starts a second timer. It then sleeps for 30 seconds and then stops both timers. After deploying the enterprise bean and executing the client, we should see some entries like this in the server log:

```
This message was triggered by :Timer 1 at 1,699,468,776,716|#]
This message was triggered by :Timer 2 at 1,699,468,778,762|#]
This message was triggered by :Timer 1 at 1,699,468,781,716|#]
This message was triggered by :Timer 2 at 1,699,468,783,762|#]
This message was triggered by :Timer 1 at 1,699,468,786,716|#]
This message was triggered by :Timer 2 at 1,699,468,788,762|#]
```

These entries are created each time one of the timers expires.

In addition to starting a timer programmatically, as seen in the example in this section, we can schedule our timers via the @Schedule annotation, which uses calendar-based expressions for scheduling enterprise bean timers.

Calendar-based enterprise bean timer expressions

The example in the previous section has one disadvantage: the startTimer() method in the session bean must be invoked from a client in order to start the timer. This restriction makes it difficult to have the timer start as soon as the bean is deployed.

Java EE 6 introduced calendar-based enterprise bean timer expressions. Calendar-based expressions allow one or more methods in our session beans to be executed at a certain date and time. For example, we could configure one of our methods to be executed every night at 8:10 p.m., which is exactly what our next example does:

```
package com.ensode.javaee8book.calendarbasedtimer;
//imports omitted for brevity
@Stateless
public class CalendarBasedTimerJebExampleBean {
  private static Logger logger = Logger.getLogger(
    CalendarBasedTimerJebExampleBean.class.getName());
  @Schedule(hour = "20", minute = "10")
  public void logMessage() {
    logger.log(Level.INFO,
      "This message was triggered at:{0}",
      System.currentTimeMillis());
  }
}
```

As we can see in this example, we set up the time when the method will be executed via the jakarta. ejb.Schedule annotation. In this particular example, we set up our method to be executed at 8:10 p.m. by setting the hour attribute of the @Schedule annotation to "20", and its minute attribute to "10" (the value of the hour attribute is 24-hour based; hour 20 is equivalent to 8:00 p.m.).

The `@Schedule` annotation has several other attributes, which allows a lot of flexibility in specifying when the method should be executed. We could, for instance, have a method executed on the third Friday of every month, on the last day of the month, and so on and so forth.

The following table lists all the attributes in the `@Schedule` annotation that allow us to control when the annotated method will be executed:

Attribute	Description	Example Values	Default Value
dayOfMonth	The day of the month	"3": The third day of the month "Last": The last day of the month "-2": Two days before the end of the month "1st Tue": The first Tuesday of the month	"*"
dayOfWeek	The day of the week	"3": Every Wednesday "Thu": Every Thursday	"*"
hour	Hour of the day (24-hour based)	"14": 2:00 p.m.	"0"
minute	Minute of the hour	"10": 10 minutes after the hour	"0"
month	Month of the year	"2": February "March": March	"*"
second	Second of the minute	"5": Five seconds after the minute	"0"
timezone	Time zone ID	"America/New York"	""
year	Four-digit year	"2010"	"*"

Table 12.3 – @Schedule annotation attributes

In addition to single values, most attributes accept the asterisk ("*") as a wildcard, meaning that the annotated method will be executed every unit of time (every day, hour, etc.).

Additionally, we can specify more than one value by separating the values with commas. For example, if we needed a method to be executed every Tuesday and Thursday, we could annotate the method as `@Schedule(dayOfWeek="Tue, Thu")`.

We can also specify a range of values. The first value and last value are separated by a dash (-). To execute a method from Monday through Friday, we could use `@Schedule(dayOfWeek="Mon-Fri")`.

Additionally, we could specify that we need the method to be executed every *n* units of time (for example, every day, every 2 hours, or every 10 minutes). To do something like this, we could use `@Schedule(hour="*/12")`, which would execute the method every 12 hours.

As we can see, the @Schedule annotation provides a lot of flexibility regarding how to specify when we need our methods executed. Plus it provides the advantage of not needing a client call to activate the scheduling. Additionally, it also has the advantage of using cron-like syntax, therefore developers familiar with that Unix tool will feel right at home using this annotation.

The final topic we will cover in this chapter is enterprise bean security.

Enterprise bean security

Enterprise beans allow us to declaratively decide which users can access their methods. For example, some methods might only be available to users in certain roles. A typical scenario is that only users with the role of administrator can add, delete, or modify other users in the system.

The following example is a slightly modified version of the DAO session bean we saw earlier in this chapter. In this version, some methods that were previously private have been made public. Additionally, the session bean has been modified to allow only users in certain roles to access its methods:

```
package com.ensode.jakartaeebook;
//imports omitted for brevity
@Stateless
@RolesAllowed("admin")
public class SecureCustomerDaoBean {
  @PersistenceContext
  private EntityManager entityManager;
  public Long saveCustomer(Customer customer) {
    if (customer.getCustomerId() == null) {
      entityManager.persist(customer);
    } else {
      entityManager.merge(customer);
    }
    return customer.getCustomerId();
  }
  @RolesAllowed({"user", "admin"})
  public Customer getCustomer(Long customerId) {
    Customer customer;
    customer = entityManager.find(Customer.class,
      customerId);
    return customer;
  }
  public void deleteCustomer(Customer customer) {
    entityManager.remove(customer);
  }
}
```

As we can see, we declare what roles have access to the methods by using the `@RolesAllowed` annotation. This annotation can take either a single `String` or an array of `String` as a parameter. When a single String is used as a parameter for this annotation, only users with the role specified by the parameter can access the method. If an array of `String` is used as a parameter, users with any of the roles specified by the array's elements can access the method.

The `@RolesAllowed` annotation can be used at the class level, in which case its values apply to all the methods in the enterprise bean. It can also be used at the method level, in which case its values apply only to the method the annotation is decorating. If, like in our example, both the class and one or more of its methods are decorated with the `@RolesAllowed` annotation, the method-level annotation takes precedence.

In our example, only users with the role of "admin" can save or update customer data, both admins and users can retrieve customer data.

Clients invoking secured enterprise beans must be authenticated (refer to *Chapter 10*) and must have the appropriate role.

Summary

In this chapter, we covered how to implement business logic via stateless and stateful session beans. Additionally, we covered how to implement message-driven beans to consume Jakarta messaging messages.

The following topics were covered in this chapter:

- How to take advantage of the transactional nature of enterprise beans to simplify implementing the DAO pattern
- Container-managed transactions and how to control transactions by using the appropriate annotations
- Bean-managed transactions, for cases in which container-managed transactions are not enough to satisfy our requirements
- Life cycles for the different types of Enterprise Java beans, including an explanation of how to have enterprise bean methods automatically invoked by the Jakarta EE runtime at certain points in the life cycle
- How to have enterprise bean methods invoked periodically by the runtime by taking advantage of the timer service
- How to make sure enterprise bean methods are only invoked by authorized users by annotating enterprise bean classes and/or methods with the appropriate security annotations

As we have seen in this chapter, Jakarta Enterprise Beans take care of some enterprise requirements such as transactions and security, freeing us as application developers from having to implement them, and allowing us to focus on implementing business logic.

13
Jakarta Messaging

Jakarta Messaging provides a mechanism for Jakarta EE applications to send messages to each other. Jakarta Messaging applications do not communicate directly; instead, message producers send messages to a destination, and message consumers receive the message from the destination.

The message destination is a message queue when the **point-to-point** (**PTP**) messaging domain is used, or a message topic when the **publish/subscribe** (**pub/sub**) messaging domain is used.

In this chapter, we will cover the following topics:

- Working with message queues
- Working with message topics

> **Note**
>
> Example source code for this chapter can be found on GitHub at `https://github.com/PacktPublishing/Jakarta-EE-Application-Development/tree/main/ch13_src`.

Working with message queues

As we mentioned earlier, message queues are used when our Jakarta Messaging code uses the PTP messaging domain. For the PTP messaging domain, there is usually one message producer and one message consumer. The message producer and the message consumer don't need to be running concurrently in order to communicate. The messages placed in the message queue by the message producer will stay in the message queue until the message consumer executes and requests the messages from the queue.

Sending messages to a message queue

The following example illustrates how to add messages to a message queue:

```java
package com.ensode.jakartaeebook.ptpproducer;

//imports omitted for brevity

@JMSDestinationDefinition(
    name = "java:global/queue/JakartaEEBookQueue",
    interfaceName = "jakarta.jms.Queue"
)

@Named
@RequestScoped
public class MessageSender {
  @Resource
  private ConnectionFactory connectionFactory;

  @Resource(mappedName = "java:global/queue/JakartaEEBookQueue")
  private Queue queue;

  public void produceMessages() {
    JMSContext jmsContext = connectionFactory.createContext();
    JMSProducer jmsProducer = jmsContext.createProducer();

    String msg1 = "Testing, 1, 2, 3. Can you hear me?";
    String msg2 = "Do you copy?";
    String msg3 = "Good bye!";

    jmsProducer.send(queue, msg1);
    jmsProducer.send(queue, msg2);
    jmsProducer.send(queue, msg3);
  }
}
```

> **Note**
>
> Most examples in this chapter are implemented as **Contexts and Dependency Injection (CDI)** beans. Refer to *Chapter 2* for an explanation of CDI.

The class-level `@JMSDestinationDefinition` annotation defines a Jakarta Messaging destination where our messages will be placed. This annotation has two required attributes, `name` and `interfaceName`. The name attribute of `@JMSDestinationDefinition` defines a **Java Naming and Directory Interface (JNDI)** name for our Jakarta Messaging destination, which is used by the Jakarta EE runtime to look up the destination. Meanwhile, the `interfaceName` specifies the Jakarta Messaging destination interface; PTP messaging, this value must always be **jakarta.jms.Queue**. The `produceMessages()` method of the preceding class is invoked from a `commandButton` from a Jakarta Faces page implemented using Facelets. For brevity, we will not show the XHTML markup for this page. The code download bundle for this chapter contains the complete example.

The `produceMessages()` method in the `MessageSender` class performs all the necessary steps to send messages to a message queue.

The first thing this method does is create an instance of `jakarta.jms.JMSContext` by invoking the `createContext()` method on the injected instance of `jakarta.jms.ConnectionFactory`. Notice that the `mappedName` attribute of the `@Resource` annotation decorating the connection factory object matches the name attribute of the `@JMSDestinationDefinition` annotation. Behind the scenes, a JNDI lookup is made using this name to obtain the connection factory object.

Next, we create an instance of `jakarta.jms.JMSProducer` by invoking the `createProducer()` method on the `JMSContext` instance we just created.

After obtaining an instance of `JMSProducer`, the code sends a series of text messages by invoking its `send()` method. This method takes the message destination as its first parameter, and a `String` containing the message text as its second parameter.

There are several overloaded versions of the `send()` method in `JMSProducer`. The one we used in our example is a convenient method that creates an instance of `jakarta.jms.TextMessage` and sets its text to the `String` we provide as the second parameter in the method invocation.

Although the preceding example sends only text messages to the queue, we are not limited to this type of message. Jakarta Messaging provides several types of messages that can be sent and received by Jakarta Messaging applications. All message types are defined as interfaces in the `jakarta.jms` package. *Table 13.1* lists all of the available message types:

Message Type	Description
BytesMessage	Allows sending an array of bytes as a message. JMSProducer has a convenient send() method that takes an array of bytes as one of its parameters. This method creates an instance of jakarta.jms.BytesMessage on the fly as the message is being sent.
MapMessage	Allows sending an implementation of java.util.Map as a message. JMSProducer has a convenient send() method that takes a Map as one of its parameters. This method creates an instance of jakarta.jms.MapMessage on the fly as the message is being sent.
ObjectMessage	Allows sending any Java object implementing java.io.Serializable as a message. JMSProducer has a convenient send() method, which takes an instance of a class implementing java.io.Serializable as its second parameter. This method creates an instance of jakarta.jms.ObjectMessage on the fly as the message is being sent.
StreamMessage	Allows sending an array of bytes as a message. Differs from BytesMessage in that it stores the type of each primitive added to the stream
TextMessage	Allows sending java.lang.String as a message. As seen in the preceding example, JMSProducer has a convenient send() method that takes a String as its second parameter. This method creates an instance of jakarta.jms.TextMessage on the fly as the message is being sent.

Table 13.1 – Jakarta Messaging message types

> **Note**
>
> For more information on all of the preceding message types, consult the JavaDoc documentation at https://jakarta.ee/specifications/messaging/3.0/apidocs/jakarta/jms/package-summary.

Retrieving messages from a message queue

Of course, there is no point in sending messages from a queue if nothing is going to receive them. The following example illustrates how to retrieve messages from a message queue:

```
package com.ensode.jakartaeebook.ptpconsumer;
//imports omitted for brevity
@JMSDestinationDefinition(
  name = "java:global/queue/JakartaEEBookQueue",
  interfaceName = "jakarta.jms.Queue"
)
@Named
```

```
@RequestScoped
public class MessageReceiver implements Serializable {
  @Resource
  private ConnectionFactory connectionFactory;
  @Resource(mappedName =
    "java:global/queue/JakartaEEBookQueue")
  private Queue queue;
  private static final Logger LOG =
    Logger.getLogger(MessageReceiver.class.getName());

  public void receiveMessages() {
    String message;
    boolean goodByeReceived = false;
    JMSContext jmsContext = connectionFactory.
      createContext();
    JMSConsumer jMSConsumer =
      jmsContext.createConsumer(queue);
    while (!goodByeReceived) {
      message = jMSConsumer.receiveBody(String.class);
      LOG.log(Level.INFO, "Received message: {0}", message);
      if (message.equals("Good bye!")) {
        goodByeReceived = true;
      }
    }
  }
}
```

Just like in the previous example, we define a destination via the @JMSDestinationDefinition annotation, plus we inject instances of jakarta.jms.ConnectionFactory and jakarta.jms.Queue by using the @Resource annotation.

In our code, we get an instance of jakarta.jms.JMSContext by invoking the createContext() method of ConnectionFactory, just like in the previous example.

In this example, we obtain an instance of jakarta.jms.JMSConsumer by calling the createConsumer() method on our JMSContext instance.

Messages are received by invoking the receiveBody() method on our instance of JMSConsumer. This method takes the type of the message we are expecting as its sole parameter (String.class in our example). This method returns an object of the type specified in its parameter (an instance of java.lang.String in our example). Once the message is consumed by JMSConsumer.receiveBody(), it is removed from the queue.

In this particular example, we placed this method call in a `while` loop since we are expecting a message that will let us know no more messages are coming. Specifically, we are looking for a message containing the text "Good bye!". Once we receive said message, we break out of the loop and continue processing. In this particular case, there is no more processing to do, therefore execution ends after we break out of the loop.

After executing the code, we should see the following output in the server log:

```
Waiting for messages...
Received the following message: Testing, 1, 2, 3. Can you hear me?
Received the following message: Do you copy?
Received the following message: Good bye!
```

This of course assumes that the previous example was already executed and it placed messages in the message queue.

> **Note**
>
> A disadvantage of processing messages as discussed in this section is that message processing is synchronous. In Jakarta EE environments, we can process messages asynchronously by employing message-driven beans, as discussed in *Chapter 12*.

Browsing message queues

Jakarta Messaging provides a way to browse message queues without actually removing the messages from the queue. The following example illustrates how to do this:

```java
package com.ensode.jakartaeebook.queuebrowser;
//imports omitted for brevity
//Messaging destination definition annotation omitted
@Named
@RequestScoped
public class MessageQueueBrowser {
  @Resource
  private ConnectionFactory connectionFactory;
  @Resource(mappedName =
    "java:global/queue/JakartaEEBookQueue")
  private Queue queue;
  private static final Logger LOG =
    Logger.getLogger(MessageQueueBrowser.class.getName());
  public void browseMessages() throws JMSException {
    Enumeration messageEnumeration;
    TextMessage textMessage;
    JMSContext jmsContext =
```

```
      connectionFactory.createContext();
    QueueBrowser browser = jmsContext.createBrowser(queue);
    messageEnumeration = browser.getEnumeration();
    LOG.log(Level.INFO, "messages in the queue:");
    while (messageEnumeration.hasMoreElements()) {
      textMessage = (TextMessage) messageEnumeration.
        nextElement();
      LOG.log(Level.INFO, textMessage.getText());
    }
  }
}
```

As we can see, the procedure to browse messages in a message queue is straightforward. We obtain a connection factory, a queue, and a context the usual way, then invoke the createBrowser() method on the context object. This method returns an implementation of the jakarta.jms. QueueBrowser interface. This interface contains a getEnumeration() method, which we can invoke to obtain an Enumeration containing all messages in the queue. To examine the messages in the queue, we simply traverse this enumeration and obtain the messages one by one. In the example that we discussed, we simply invoke the getText() method of each message in the queue.

Now that we've seen how to send and receive messages to and from a queue with the PTP messaging domain, we'll focus our attention on sending and receiving messages to and from message topics with the pub/sub messaging domain.

Working with message topics

Message topics are used when our Jakarta Messaging code uses the pub/sub messaging domain. When using this messaging domain, the same message can be sent to all subscribers to the topic.

Sending messages to a message topic

The following example illustrates how to send messages to a message topic:

```
package com.ensode.jakartaeebook.pubsubproducer;
//imports omitted
@JMSDestinationDefinition(
    name = "java:global/topic/JakartaEEBookTopic",
    interfaceName = "jakarta.jms.Topic"
)
@Named
@RequestScoped
public class MessageSender {
  @Resource
  private ConnectionFactory connectionFactory;
```

```
  @Resource(mappedName =
    "java:global/topic/JakartaEEBookTopic")
  private Topic topic;
  public void produceMessages() {
    JMSContext jmsContext =
      connectionFactory.createContext();
    JMSProducer jmsProducer = jmsContext.createProducer();
    String msg1 = "Testing, 1, 2, 3. Can you hear me?";
    String msg2 = "Do you copy?";
    String msg3 = "Good bye!";
    jmsProducer.send(topic, msg1);
    jmsProducer.send(topic, msg2);
    jmsProducer.send(topic, msg3);
  }
}
```

As we can see, the preceding code is nearly identical to the MessageSender class we saw when we discussed PTP messaging. Jakarta Messaging was designed so that the same API can be used for both the PTP and pub/sub domains.

Since the code in this example is nearly identical to the corresponding example in the *Working with message queues* section, we will only explain the differences between the two examples. In this case, @JMSDestinationDefinition has a value of jakarta.jms.Topic for its name attribute, as required when using the pub/sub messaging domain. Additionally, instead of declaring an instance of a class implementing jakarta.jms.Queue, we declare an instance of a class implementing jakarta.jms.Topic. We then pass this instance of jakarta.jms.Topic as the first method of the send() method of our JMSProducer object, along with the message we wish to send.

Receiving messages from a message topic

Just as sending messages to a message topic is nearly identical to sending messages to a message queue, receiving messages from a message topic is nearly identical to receiving messages from a message queue:

```
package com.ensode.jakartaeebook.pubsubconsumer;
//imports omitted
@JMSDestinationDefinition(
    name = "java:global/topic/JakartaEEBookTopic",
    interfaceName = "jakarta.jms.Topic"
)
@Named
@RequestScoped
public class MessageReceiver {
  @Resource
  private ConnectionFactory connectionFactory;
```

```
@Resource(mappedName = "java:global/topic/JakartaEEBookTopic")
private Topic topic;
private static final Logger LOG =
  Logger.getLogger(MessageReceiver.class.getName());
public void receiveMessages() {
  String message;
  boolean goodByeReceived = false;
  JMSContext jmsContext = connectionFactory.createContext();
  JMSConsumer jMSConsumer = jmsContext.createConsumer(topic);
  while (!goodByeReceived) {
    message = jMSConsumer.receiveBody(String.class);
    LOG.log(Level.INFO, "Received message: {0}", message);
    if (message.equals("Good bye!")) {
      goodByeReceived = true;
    }
  }
}
}
```

Once again, the differences between this code and the corresponding code for PTP are trivial. Instead of declaring an instance of a class implementing jakarta.jms.Queue, we declare a class implementing jakarta.jms.Topic. We use the @Resource annotation to inject an instance of this class into our code, using the JNDI name we used when configuring our application server. We then obtain an instance of JMSContext and JMSConsumer like before, then it receives the messages from the topic by invoking the receiveBody() method on JMSConsumer.

Using the pub/sub messaging domain as illustrated in this section has the advantage that messages can be sent to several message consumers. This can be easily tested by concurrently executing two instances of the MessageReceiver class we developed in this section, and then executing the MessageSender class we developed in the previous section. We should see console output for each instance, indicating that both instances received all messages.

Creating durable subscribers

The disadvantage of using the pub/sub messaging domain is that message consumers must be executing when the messages are sent to the topic. If the message consumer is not executing at the time, it will not receive the messages, whereas in PTP, messages are kept in the queue until the message consumer executes. Fortunately, Jakarta Messaging provides a way to use the pub/sub messaging domain and keep messages in the topic until all subscribed message consumers execute and receive the message. This can be accomplished by creating durable subscribers to a message topic.

In order to be able to service durable subscribers, we need to set the clientId property of our Jakarta Messaging connection factory. Each durable subscriber must have a unique client ID, therefore a unique connection factory must be declared for each potential durable subscriber.

We can set the `clientId` property of our connection factory using the
`@JMSConnectionFactoryDefinition` annotation, as illustrated in the following example:

```
package com.ensode.jakartaeebook.pubsubdurablesubscriber;
//imports omitted for brevity
@JMSConnectionFactoryDefinition(
    name = "java:global/messaging/DurableConnectionFactory",
    clientId = "DurableConnectionFactoryClientId"
)
//Messaging destination definition annotation omitted
@Named
@ApplicationScoped
public class MessageReceiver {
  @Resource(mappedName =
   "java:global/messaging/DurableConnectionFactory")
  private ConnectionFactory connectionFactory;
  @Resource(mappedName =
    "java:global/topic/JakartaEEBookTopic")
  private Topic topic;
  private static final Logger LOG =
   Logger.getLogger(MessageReceiver.class.getName());
  public void receiveMessages() {
    String message;
    boolean goodByeReceived = false;
    JMSContext jmsContext =
      connectionFactory.createContext();
    JMSConsumer jMSConsumer =
      jmsContext.createDurableConsumer(topic,"Subscriber1");
    while (!goodByeReceived) {
      message = jMSConsumer.receiveBody(String.class);
      LOG.log(Level.INFO, "Received message: {0}", message);
      if (message.equals("Good bye!")) {
        goodByeReceived = true;
      }
    }
  }
}
```

As we can see, the preceding code is not much different from previous examples whose purpose
was to retrieve messages. There are only a few differences from previous examples: the instance of
ConnectionFactory we are injecting is defined via @JMSConnectionFactoryDefinition
and given a client ID via its clientId attribute. Notice the @Resource annotation for our
connection factory has a mappedName attribute whose value matches the name attribute we defined
in @JMSConnectionFactoryDefinition.

Another difference is that instead of calling the `createConsumer()` method on `JMSContext`, we are calling `createDurableConsumer()`. The `createDurableConsumer()` method takes two arguments, a messaging `Topic` object to retrieve messages from and a `String` designating a name for this subscription. This second parameter must be unique between all subscribers to the durable topic.

Summary

In this chapter, we discussed at length how to send messages with Jakarta Messaging, using both the PTP and pub/sub messaging domains.

Topics we covered included the following:

- How to send messages to a message queue via the `jakarta.jms.JMSProducer` interface
- How to receive messages from a message queue via the `jakarta.jms.JMSConsumer` interface
- How to asynchronously receive messages from a message queue by implementing the `jakarta.jms.MessageListener` interface
- How to use the preceding interfaces to send and receive messages to and from a message topic
- How to browse messages in a message queue without removing the messages from the queue via the `jakarta.jms.QueueBrowser` interface
- How to set up and interact with durable subscriptions to messaging topics

Armed with the knowledge in this chapter, we can now implement asynchronous communication between processes with Jakarta Messaging.

14
Web Services with Jakarta XML Web Services

Web services are application programming interfaces that can be invoked remotely. Web services can be invoked from clients written in any language.

Jakarta EE includes the XML Web Services API as one of its technologies. We can use **XML Web Services** to develop **SOAP (Simple Object Access Protocol)** web services in the Java platform. Jakarta XML Web Services is a high-level API; invoking web services via Jakarta XML Web Services is done via remote procedure calls.

SOAP-based web services are now a legacy technology. In most cases, RESTful web services are preferred to SOAP-based services for new development. Knowledge of SOAP-based web services is primarily useful for maintaining legacy applications.

In this chapter, we will cover the following topics:

- Developing web services with Jakarta XML Web Services
- Exposing Enterprise Beans as web services

> **Note**
> The example source code for this chapter can be found on GitHub at the following link: `https://github.com/PacktPublishing/Jakarta-EE-Application-Development/tree/main/ch14_src`.

Developing web services with Jakarta XML Web Services

Jakarta XML Web Services is a high-level API that simplifies the development of SOAP-based web services. Developing a web service with Jakarta XML Web Services consists of writing a class with public methods to be exposed as web services. The class needs to be annotated with `@WebService`.

All public methods in the class are automatically exposed as web services; they can optionally be annotated with @WebMethod. The following example illustrates this process:

```
package com.ensode.jakartaeebook.xmlws;
import jakarta.jws.WebMethod;
import jakarta.jws.WebService;


@WebService
public class Calculator {
  @WebMethod
  public int add(int first, int second) {
    return first + second;
  }

  @WebMethod
  public int subtract(int first, int second) {
    return first - second;
  }
}
```

The preceding class exposes its two methods as web services. The add() method simply adds the two int primitives it receives as parameters and returns the result, and the substract() method subtracts its two parameters and returns the result.

We indicate that the class implements a web service by decorating it with the @WebService annotation. Any methods that we would like to expose as web services can be decorated with the @WebMethod annotation, but this isn't necessary. Since all public methods are automatically exposed as web services, we can still use the @WebMethod annotation for clarity, but it isn't strictly necessary. To deploy our web service, we simply need to package it in a WAR file as usual.

Web service clients need a **WSDL (Web Services Definition Language)** file in order to generate executable code that they can use to invoke the web service. WSDL is an XML-based language that describes the functionality offered by a SOAP-based web service. WSDL files are typically placed in a web server and acccssed by the client via its URL.

When deploying web services developed using Jakarta XML Web Services, a WSDL is automatically generated for us. The exact URL for the generated WSDL varies depending on the Jakarta EE runtime we are using. When using GlassFish, URLs for the generated WSDLs follow the following format:

```
[http|https]://[server]:[port]/[context root]/[service name]?wsdl
```

In our example, the URL for our web service's WSDL (when deployed to GlassFish) would be http://localhost:8080/calculatorservice/CalculatorService?wsdl (assuming GlassFish is running on our local workstation, and GlassFish is listening for HTTP connections in its default 8080 port).

We can see the generated WSDL by pointing the browser to its URL, as illustrated in *Figure 14.1*.

Figure 14.1 – Automatically generated WSDL

The specifics of the WSDL aren't really relevant to the discussion. It can be considered as "behind-the-scenes plumbing," which is necessary for SOAP-based web services to work correctly. The WSDL URL though, is needed when developing web service clients.

Developing a web service client

As we mentioned earlier, web service clients need to generate executable code from a web service's WSDL. A web service client will then invoke this executable code to access the web service.

In order to generate Java code from a WSDL, we need to use a tool called `wsimport`.

The `wsimport` tool can be obtained by downloading Eclipse Metro, at `https://eclipse-ee4j.github.io/metro-wsit/`.

The only required argument for `wsimport` is the URL of the WSDL corresponding to the web service, which is as follows:

```
wsimport http://localhost:8080/calculatorservice/
CalculatorService?wsdl
```

This command will generate a number of compiled Java classes that allow client applications to access our web service:

- `Add.class`
- `AddResponse.class`

- `Calculator.class`

- `CalculatorService.class`

- `ObjectFactory.class`

- `package-info.class`

- `Subtract.class`

- `SubtractResponse.class`

Note

By default, the source code for the generated class files is automatically deleted. It can be kept by passing the `-keep` parameter to `wsimport`.

These classes need to be added to the client's `CLASSPATH` in order for them to be accessible to the client's code.

If we are using Apache Maven to build our code, we can take advantage of the JAX-WS Maven plugin to automatically invoke `wsimport` when building our client code. This approach is illustrated in the following `pom.xml` file:

```xml
<?xml version="1.0" encoding="UTF-8"?>
<project xmlns="http://maven.apache.org/POM/4.0.0" xmlns:xsi="http://
www.w3.org/2001/XMLSchema-instance" xsi:schemaLocation="http://maven.
apache.org/POM/4.0.0 http://maven.apache.org/xsd/maven-4.0.0.xsd">
  <modelVersion>4.0.0</modelVersion>
  <!-- Irrelevant markup omitted for brevity -->
  <build>
    <finalName>calculatorserviceclient</finalName>
    <plugins>
      <plugin>
        <groupId>com.sun.xml.ws</groupId>
        <artifactId>jaxws-maven-plugin</artifactId>
        <version>4.0.2</version>
        <executions>
          <execution>
            <goals>
              <goal>wsimport</goal>
            </goals>
            <configuration>
              <vmArgs>
                <vmArg>-Djavax.xml.accessExternalSchema=all</vmArg>
              </vmArgs>
              <wsdlUrls>
```

```
                 <wsdlUrl>
        http://localhost:8080/calculatorservice/CalculatorService?wsdl
                 </wsdlUrl>
               </wsdlUrls>
               <keep>true</keep>
             </configuration>
           </execution>
         </executions>
       </plugin>
     </plugins>
   </build>
 </project>
```

The preceding pom.xml Maven build file will automatically invoke the wsimport utility whenever we build our code via the mvn package or mvn install commands.

At this point, we are ready to develop a simple client to access our web service. We will implement our client as a Jakarta Faces application; the most relevant parts of our client application source are shown here:

```
package com.ensode.jakartaeebook.calculatorserviceclient;
//imports omitted for brevity
@Named
@RequestScoped
public class CalculatorClientController {
  @WebServiceRef(wsdlLocation =
    "http://localhost:8080/calculatorservice/CalculatorService?wsdl")
  private CalculatorService calculatorService;

  @Inject
  private CalculatorServiceClientModel calculatorServiceClientModel;

  private Integer sum;
  private Integer difference;

  public void add(ActionEvent actionEvent) {
    Calculator calculator = calculatorService.getCalculatorPort();
    sum = calculator.add(calculatorServiceClientModel.getAddend1(),
      calculatorServiceClientModel.getAddend2());
  }

  public void subtract(ActionEvent actionEvent) {
    Calculator calculator = calculatorService.getCalculatorPort();
    difference =
```

```
        calculator.subtract(calculatorServiceClientModel.getMinuend(),
        calculatorServiceClientModel.getSubtrahend());
    }
    //getters and setters omitted for brevity
}
```

The @WebServiceRef annotation injects an instance of the web service into our client application. Its wsdlLocation attribute contains the URL of the WSDL corresponding to the web service we are invoking.

Notice that the web service class is an instance of a class called CalculatorService. This class was created when we invoked the wsimport utility, as wsimport always generates a class whose name is the name of the class we implemented plus the "Service" suffix. We use this service class to obtain an instance of the web service class we developed. In our example, we do this by invoking the getCalculatorPort() method on the CalculatorService instance. In general, the method to invoke an instance of our web service class follows the pattern of getNamePort(), where Name is the name of the class we wrote to implement the web service. Once we get an instance of our web service class, we can simply invoke its methods like with any regular Java object.

> **Note**
>
> Strictly speaking, the getNamePort() method of the service class returns an instance of a class implementing an interface generated by wsimport. This interface is given the name of our web service class and declares all of the methods we declared to be web services. For all practical purposes, the object returned is equivalent to our web service class.

The user interface for our simple client application is developed using Facelets, as customary when developing Jakarta Faces applications. The following code snippet shows the most relevant markup for our Jakarta Faces Facelets client:

```
<h:form>
  <h:panelGrid columns="4">
    <h:inputText id="addend1"
      value="#{calculatorServiceClientModel.addend1}"/>
    <h:inputText id="addend2"
      value="#{calculatorServiceClientModel.addend2}"/>
    <h:commandButton value="Add"
      actionListener="#{calculatorClientController.add}">
      <f:ajax execute="addend1 addend2" render="sum"/>
    </h:commandButton>
    <h:panelGroup>
      Total: <h:outputText id="sum"
        value="#{calculatorClientController.sum}"/>
    </h:panelGroup>
```

```
    </h:panelGrid>
    <br/>
    <h:panelGrid columns="4">
      <h:inputText id="minuend"
        value="#{calculatorServiceClientModel.minuend}"/>
      <h:inputText id="subtrahend"
        value="#{calculatorServiceClientModel.subtrahend}"/>
      <h:commandButton value="Subtract"
        actionListener="#{calculatorClientController.subtract}">
        <f:ajax execute="minuend subtrahend" render="difference"/>
      </h:commandButton>
      <h:panelGroup>
        Difference: <h:outputText id="difference"
          value="#{calculatorClientController.difference}"/>
      </h:panelGroup>
    </h:panelGrid>
  </h:form>
```

The user interface uses Ajax to invoke the relevant methods on the `CalculatorClientController` CDI named bean (refer to *Chapter 6* for details).

After deploying our code, our browser should render our page as shown in *Figure 14.2* (this is shown after entering some data and clicking the corresponding buttons).

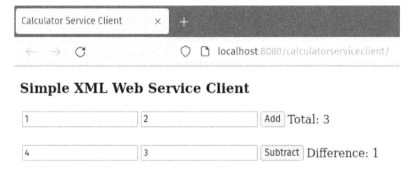

Figure 14.2 – XML Web Service Client in action

In this example, we passed the `Integer` objects as parameters and return values. Of course, it is also possible to pass primitive types both as parameters and as return values. Unfortunately, not all standard Java classes or primitive types can be used as method parameters or return values when invoking SOAP-based web services implemented with Jakarta XML Web Services. The reason for this is that behind the scenes, method parameters and return types get mapped to XML definitions, and not all types can be properly mapped.

Valid types that can be used in Jakarta XML Web Service calls are listed here:

- `java.awt.Image`
- `java.lang.Object`
- `Java.lang.String`
- `java.math.BigDecimal`
- `java.math.BigInteger`
- `java.net.URI`
- `java.util.Calendar`
- `java.util.Date`
- `java.util.UUID`
- `jakarta.activation.DataHandler`
- `javax.xml.datatype.Duration`
- `javax.xml.datatype.XMLGregorianCalendar`
- `javax.xml.namespace.QName`
- `javax.xml.transform.Source`

Additionally, the following primitive types can be used:

- `boolean`
- `byte`
- `byte[]`
- `double`
- `float`
- `int`
- `long`
- `short`

We can also use our own custom classes as method parameters and/or return values for web service methods, but member variables of our classes must be one of the listed types.

Additionally, it is legal to use arrays both as method parameters or return values. However, when executing `wsimport`, these arrays get converted to Lists, generating a mismatch between the method signature in the web service and the method call invoked in the client. For this reason, it is preferred to use Lists as method parameters and/or return values, since this is also legal and does not create a mismatch between the client and the server.

> **Note**
>
> Jakarta XML Web Services internally uses the **Jakarta XML Binding API** to create SOAP
> messages from method calls. The types we are allowed to use for method calls and return
> values are the ones that Jakarta XML Binding supports. For more information, see `https://`
> `jakarta.ee/specifications/xml-binding/`.

Sending attachments to web services

In addition to sending and accepting the data types discussed in the previous sections, web service
methods can send and accept file attachments. The following example illustrates how to do this:

```java
package com.ensode.jakartaeebook.xmlws;
//imports omitted for brevity

@WebService
public class FileAttachment {

  @WebMethod
  public void attachFile(DataHandler dataHandler) {
    FileOutputStream fileOutputStream;
    try {
      fileOutputStream = new FileOutputStream("/tmp/logo.png");
      dataHandler.writeTo(fileOutputStream);
      fileOutputStream.flush();
      fileOutputStream.close();
    } catch (IOException e) {
      e.printStackTrace();
    }

  }
}
```

In order to write a web service method that receives one or more attachments, all we need to do is
add a parameter of the `jakarta.activation.DataHandler` type for each attachment the
method will receive. In our example, the `attachFile()` method takes a single parameter of this
type and simply writes it to the file system.

Just like with any standard web service, the web service code needs to be packaged in a WAR file and
deployed. Once deployed, a WSDL will automatically be generated. We then need to execute the
`wsimport` utility to generate the code that our web service client can use to access the web service.
As previously discussed, the `wsimport` can be invoked from the command line or via an Apache
Maven plugin.

Once we have executed `wsimport` to generate code to access the web service, we can write and compile our client code:

```
package com.ensode.jakartaeebook.fileattachmentserviceclient;
//imports omitted for brevity

@Named
@RequestScoped
public class FileAttachmentServiceClientController {

  @WebServiceRef(wsdlLocation =
    "http://localhost:8080/fileattachmentservice/"
    + "FileAttachmentService?wsdl")
  private FileAttachmentService fileAttachmentService;

  public void invokeWebService() {
    try {
      URL attachmentUrl = new URL(
        "http://localhost:8080/fileattachmentserviceclient/" +
        "resources/img/logo.png");

      FileAttachment fileAttachment = fileAttachmentService.
          getFileAttachmentPort();

      InputStream inputStream = attachmentUrl.openStream();
      byte[] fileBytes = inputStreamToByteArray(inputStream);
      fileAttachment.attachFile(fileBytes);
    } catch (IOException ioe) {
      ioe.printStackTrace();
    }
  }
  private byte[] inputStreamToByteArray(InputStream inputStream)
    throws IOException {
    //method body omitted for brevity
  }
}
```

Web service attachments need to be sent as a byte array to the web service; therefore, web service clients need to convert the file to attach to this type. In our example, we send an image as an attachment, we load the image into memory by creating an instance of `java.net.URL`, passing the URL of the image in question as a parameter to its constructor. We then obtain an `InputStream` instance corresponding to the image by invoking the `openStream()` method on our URL instance, convert our `InputStream` instance to a byte array, and then pass this byte array to the web service method that expects an attachment.

Notice that, unlike when passing standard parameters, the parameter type used when the client invokes a method expecting an attachment is different from the parameter type of the method in the web server code. The method in the web server code expects an instance of `jakarta.activation.DataHandler` for each attachment; however, the code generated by `wsimport` expects an array of bytes for each attachment. These arrays of bytes are converted to the right type (`jakarta.activation.DataHandler`) behind the scenes by the `wsimport` generated code. We as application developers don't need to concern ourselves with the details of why this happens, we just need to keep in mind that when sending attachments to a web service method, the parameter types will be different in the web service code and in the client invocation.

Exposing Enterprise Beans as web services

In addition to creating web services as described in the previous section, public methods of stateless session beans can easily be exposed as web services by simply adding an annotation to the Enterprise Bean class. The following example illustrates how to do this:

```
package com.ensode.jakartaeebook.jebws;

import jakarta.ejb.Stateless;
import jakarta.jws.WebService;

@Stateless
@WebService
public class DecToHexBean {

  public String convertDecToHex(Integer i) {
    return Integer.toHexString(i);
  }
}
```

As we can see, the only thing we need to do to expose a stateless session bean's public methods as web services is to decorate its class declaration with the `@WebService` annotation. Needless to say, since the class is a session bean, it also needs to be decorated with the `@Stateless` annotation.

Just like regular stateless session beans, the ones whose methods are exposed as web services need to be deployed in a JAR file.

Just like standard web services, WSDL URLs for Enterprise Beans web services depend on the application server being used. You can consult your application server documentation for details.

Enterprise Beans web service clients

The following class illustrates the procedure to be followed to access an Enterprise Beans web service from a client application:

```
package com.ensode.jakartaeebook.jebwsclient;
//imports omitted for brevity

@Named
@RequestScoped
public class JebClientController {
  @WebServiceRef(wsdlLocation =
    "http://localhost:8080/DecToHexBeanService/DecToHexBean?wsdl")
  private DecToHexBeanService decToHexBeanService;

  @Inject
  private JebClientModel jebClientModel;

  private String hexVal;

  public void convertIntToHex() {
    hexVal = decToHexBeanService.getDecToHexBeanPort().
        convertDecToHex(jebClientModel.getIntVal());
  }
  //getters and setters omitted for brevity
}
```

As we can see, nothing special needs to be done when accessing an Enterprise Beans web service from a client. The procedure is the same as with standard web services.

The preceding class is a CDI named bean. *Figure 14.3* illustrates a simple Jakarta Faces user interface utilizing the preceding class to invoke our web service.

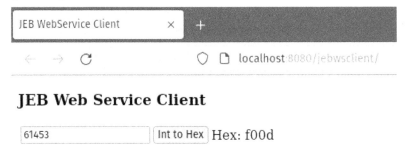

Figure 14.3 – Enterprise Bean Web Service Client

Clicking on the **Int to Hex** button generates a call to the web service, which returns a hexadecimal value equivalent to the decimal value the user entered in the text input field.

Summary

In this chapter, we covered how to develop web services and web service clients via the Jakarta XML Web Service API.

This chapter covered the following topics:

- How to develop SOAP-based web services using Jakarta XML Web Services
- How to incorporate web service code generation for web service clients when using Maven as a build tool
- Valid data types that can be used for remote method calls via Jakarta XML Web Services
- How to send attachments to a web service
- How to expose Enterprise Beans methods as web services

Armed with the knowledge in this chapter, we can now develop SOAP-based web services, as well as maintain existing SOAP-based applications.

15

Putting it All Together

In previous chapters, we've been covering Jakarta EE APIs and specifications individually. In this chapter, however, we will develop an application using popular Jakarta EE APIs, illustrating how to use them together.

In this chapter, we will cover the following topics:

- The sample application
- Creating customer data
- Viewing customer data
- Updating customer data
- Deleting customer data
- Implementing pagination

By the end of this chapter, you will have learned how to develop a complete application combining several popular Jakarta EE APIs.

> **Note**
>
> Example source code for this chapter can be found on GitHub at `https://github.com/PacktPublishing/Jakarta-EE-Application-Development/tree/main/ch15_src`

The sample application

The sample application that we will develop in this chapter is a typical CRUD (Create, Read, Update and Delete) application. We will be using CDI to develop our controllers, Jakarta Persistence as our Object-Relational Mapping tool, leveraging Jakarta Enterprise Beans to handle transactions, plus Jakarta Faces to develop the user interface. We'll cover some advanced Jakarta Faces features such as developing custom converters and implementing custom **Expression Language** (**EL**) Resolvers.

The application is a web-based application used to maintain customers in a database. It provides functionality to view all customers, views details for a single customer, and updates and deletes new customers.

The landing page

Our application's landing page is a very simple Facelets page, that has a simple command link that invokes a method on the main controller, as shown in the following snippet.

```
<h:body>
  <h:form>
    <h:commandLink action="#{customerController.listSetup}"
      value="View all customers"/>
  </h:form>
</h:body>
```

The main controller for our application is a class called `CustomerController`. It is implemented as a session-scoped CDI named bean. When the user clicks on the link on the page, our Facelets page invokes a method called `listSetup()` on our controller. This method does some initialization and then directs the user to a page displaying all existing customers, as illustrated in the following code segment.

```
package com.ensode.jakartaeealltogether.faces.controller;
//imports omitted for brevity
@Named
@SessionScoped
public class CustomerController implements Serializable {
  //variable declarations omitted
  public String listSetup() {
    reset(true);
    return "/customer/List";
  }
  private void reset(boolean resetFirstItem) {
    customer = null;
    customerItems = null;
    pagingInfo.setItemCount(-1);
    if (resetFirstItem) {
      pagingInfo.setFirstItem(0);
    }
  }
  //additional methods omitted
}
```

The `listSetup()` method in our controller invokes a `reset()` method which is used for pagination (more on that later), then returns a string matching the path of the page that displays the list of existing customers.

The first time we navigate to the page displaying the list of customers, we simply display a message stating that no customers have been found, as the CUSTOMERS table in the database is empty.

Figure 15.1 – Empty Customer List

Our Facelets page has an `<h:outputText>` tag that is rendered only if the list of customers is empty.

```
<h:form styleClass="jsfcrud_list_form">
  <h:outputText escape="false" value="(No customers found)"
    rendered=
      "#{customerController.pagingInfo.itemCount == 0}" />
  <!-- Additional markup omitted →
  <h:commandButton
    action="#{customerController.createSetup}"
    value="New Customer"/>
</form>
```

Our Facelets page also has a command button labeled **New Customer**, which invokes logic on our controller to insert Customer data into the database.

Creating customer data

The command button on the Facelets page displaying a list of customers invokes a method called `createSetup()` on our `CustomerController`, which does some initialization before displaying a form allowing the user to enter data for a new customer.

```
package com.ensode.jakartaeealltogether.faces.controller;
//imports omitted
@Named
@SessionScoped
public class CustomerController implements Serializable {
  private Customer customer = null;
```

```
    private PagingInfo pagingInfo = null;
    //additional variable declarations omitted

    public String createSetup() {
      reset(false);
      customer = new Customer();
      List<Address> addressList = new ArrayList<>(1);
      Address address = new Address();
      List<Telephone> telephoneList = new ArrayList<>(1);
      Telephone telephone = new Telephone();
      address.setCustomer(customer);
      addressList.add(address);
      telephone.setCustomer(customer);
      telephoneList.add(telephone);
      customer.setAddressList(addressList);
      customer.setTelephoneList(telephoneList);
      return "/customer/New";
    }
    private void reset(boolean resetFirstItem) {
      customer = null;
      customerItems = null;
      pagingInfo.setItemCount(-1);
      if (resetFirstItem) {
        pagingInfo.setFirstItem(0);
      }
    }
  }
```

As we can see, the `createSetup()` method invokes the `reset()` method, which simply clears
some data from memory and performs some logic for pagination, then creates a new `Customer`
object. The `Customer` class is a straightforward JPA Entity, it has one too many relationships with
two additional JPA Entities, `Address` and `Telephone`.

```
package com.ensode.jakartaeealltogether.entity;
//imports omitted
@Entity
@Table(name = "CUSTOMERS")
public class Customer implements Serializable {
  private static final long serialVersionUID = 1L;
  @Id
  @Basic(optional = false)
  @GeneratedValue(strategy = GenerationType.AUTO)
  @Column(name = "CUSTOMER_ID")
  private Integer customerId;
```

```
    @Column(name = "FIRST_NAME")
    private String firstName;
    @Column(name = "LAST_NAME")
    private String lastName;
    @Column(name = "EMAIL")
    private String email;
    @OneToMany(mappedBy = "customer",
        cascade = CascadeType.ALL)
    private List<Address> addressList;
    @OneToMany(mappedBy = "customer",
        cascade = CascadeType.ALL)
    private List<Telephone> telephoneList;
    //methods omitted
}
```

The `createSetup()` method initializes the lists of `Address` and `Telephone` on the new instance of `Customer` to instances of `ArrayList` containing a single element of the corresponding type, then navigates to the Facelets page where the user can enter data for the new customer. See *Figure 15.2*.

Figure 15.2 – Entering New Customer data

The markup for our page is a fairly standard Facelets page, it implements some custom logic to populate all drop-down menus on the page, for example, to obtain the options on the **Address Type** drop-down, the page invokes a method called addressTypeItemsAvailableSelectOne(), on a CDI bean named AddressTypeController.

```
 <h:selectOneMenu id="selectOneAddr" value=
   "#{customerController.customer.addressList[0].
      addressType}" required="true">
   <f:selectItems id="selectOneAddrOpts"
value="#{addressTypeController.addressTypeItemsAvailableSelectOne}"/>
 </h:selectOneMenu>
```

The AddressTypeController.getAddressTypeItemsAvailableSelectOne() method invokes a trivial method on a **Data Access Object (DAO)**, which returns a list of entities containing all address types in the database, then passes this list to a method called getSelectItems() on a utility class called JSFUtil.

```
package com.ensode.jakartaeealltogether.faces.controller;
//imports omitted
@Named
@SessionScoped
public class AddressTypeController implements Serializable {
  @EJB
  private AddressTypeDao dao;
  public SelectItem[]
       getAddressTypeItemsAvailableSelectOne() {
    return JsfUtil.getSelectItems(
       dao.findAddressTypeEntities(), true);
  }
}
```

The JSFUtil.getSelectItems() method iterates through the returned entities and returns an array of SelectItem, using the return value of the toString() method of each entities as the label, and the entity itself as the value.

```
package com.ensode.jakartaeealltogether.faces.util;
//imports omitted
public class JsfUtil {
  public static SelectItem[] getSelectItems(List<?> entities,
    boolean selectOne) {
    int size = selectOne ? entities.size() + 1 :
      entities.size();
    SelectItem[] items = new SelectItem[size];
    int i = 0;
    if (selectOne) {
```

```
    items[0] = new SelectItem("", "---");
    i++;
  }
  for (Object x : entities) {
    items[i++] = new SelectItem(x, x.toString());
  }
  return items;
  }
}
```

The logic to populate other drop-down menus on the page is very similar.

The **Save** button on the new customer page is implemented as a command button:

```
<h:commandButton action="#{customerController.create}"
  value="Save"/>
```

The command button invokes a method called `create()` on our `CustomerController` class.

```
package com.ensode.jakartaeealltogether.faces.controller;
//imports omitted
@Named
@SessionScoped
public class CustomerController implements Serializable {
  @EJB
  private CustomerDao dao;
  //additional methods and variable declarations omitted
  public String create() {
    try {
      dao.create(customer);
      JsfUtil.addSuccessMessage(
        "Customer was successfully created.");
    } catch (Exception e) {
      JsfUtil.ensureAddErrorMessage(e,
        "A persistence error occurred.");
      return null;
    }
    return listSetup();
  }
}
```

The `CustomerController.create()` method simply invokes a similarly named `create()` method on our data access object, the DAO method simply inserts a new row into the CUSTOMERS, ADDRESSES and TELEPHONES database tables, which correspond to the `Customer`, `Address` and `Telephone` Jakarta Persistence Entities.

The `CustomerrController.create()` method then displays a success message to the user if the operation was successful, or an error message if the operation failed. It then directs the user to the page listing all customer objects. See *Figure 15.3*.

Figure 15.3 – Populated Customer List

Now that we have created a customer, our **Customer List** page displays a data table listing the customer we just created. It contains command links for viewing, editing or deleting each customer. We will cover how to view existing customer data in the next section.

Viewing customer data

As mentioned in the previous section, each row on the data table on the **Customer List** page has a **View** command link. The markup for the command link looks like the following:

```
<h:commandLink value="View" action="#{customerController.
detailSetup}">
  <f:param name="jsfcrud.currentCustomer" value="#{jsfcrud_
class['com.ensode.jakartaeealltogether.faces.util.JsfUtil'].jsfcrud_
method['getAsConvertedString'][item1][customerController.converter].
jsfcrud_invoke}"/>
</h:commandLink>
```

Notice the `<f:param>` tag inside the command link. This tag adds a request parameter to the HTTP request created when the user clicks the button.

We are using an advanced Jakarta Faces technique to dynamically generate the value of the request parameter. We are using a custom Expression Language resolver, so that we can implement custom logic to our Jakarta Faces expression language.

In order to use a custom Expression Language resolver, we need to declare it in our application's `faces-config.xml` configuration file.

```xml
<?xml version='1.0' encoding='UTF-8'?>
<faces-config version="4.0"
  xmlns="https://jakarta.ee/xml/ns/jakartaee"
  xmlns:xsi="http://www.w3.org/2001/XMLSchema-instance"
    xsi:schemaLocation="https://jakarta.ee/xml/ns/jakartaee https://
      jakarta.ee/xml/ns/jakartaee/web-facesconfig_4_0.xsd">
  <application>
  <el-resolver>
    com.ensode.jakartaeealltogether.faces.util.JsfCrudELResolver
  </el-resolver>
  </application>
</faces-config>
```

As we can see, we register our custom Expression Language resolver by placing its fully qualified name inside the `<el-resolver>` tag in faces-config.xml.

The details of our Expression Language resolver are out of scope, suffice to say that its `getValue()` method is invoked automatically when resolving the value attribute of `<f:param>`, it uses Java's reflection API to determine which method to call. In our specific example, it calls a method call `getConvertedAsString()` in a class called `JsfUtil`, passing an instance of a custom converter called `CustomerConverter` as a parameter.

The following code snippet shows the signature of the `getValue()` method of our custom `ELResolver`, the GitHub repository for this book contains the complete source code.

```java
package com.ensode.jakartaeealltogether.faces.util;
//imports omitted
public class JsfCrudELResolver extends ELResolver {
  //variable declarations omitted
  @Override
  public Object getValue(ELContext context, Object base,
    Object property) {
    //use reflection to determine which method to invoke
  }
  //additional methods omitted
}
```

After all is said and done, our `ELResolver` returns the value of the primary key for the corresponding `Customer` object.

When the user clicks on the **View** link, a method called `CustomerController.detailSetup()` is invoked, which performs some initialization before displaying customer information on the browser.

```
package com.ensode.jakartaeealltogether.faces.controller;
//imports omitted
@Named
@SessionScoped
public class CustomerController implements Serializable {
  @PostConstruct
  public void init() {
    converter = new CustomerConverter();
  }
  private Customer customer = null;
  private CustomerConverter converter = null;
  //additional variable declarations omitted
  public String detailSetup() {
    return scalarSetup("/customer/Detail");
  }
  private String scalarSetup(String destination) {
    reset(false);
    customer = (Customer) JsfUtil.
      getObjectFromRequestParameter(
        "jsfcrud.currentCustomer", converter, null);
    if (customer == null) {
     //error handling code omitted
    }
    return destination;
  }
  //additional methods omitted
}
```

The `CustomerController.detailSetup()` method simply delegates most of its logic to the `scalarSetup()` method, which is used every time we need to display information about a single customer.

`CustomerController.scalarSetup()` invokes `JsfUtil.getObjectFromRequestParameter()`, passing the request parameter name, and our custom Jakarta Faces converter.

`JSFUtil.getObjectFromRequestParameter()`, in turn, uses our custom converter to obtain an instance of our `Customer` object.

```
package com.ensode.jakartaeealltogether.faces.util;
//imports omitted
public class JsfUtil {
```

```
  public static String getRequestParameter(String key) {
    return FacesContext.getCurrentInstance().getExternalContext().
    getRequestParameterMap().get(key);
  }
  public static Object getObjectFromRequestParameter(String
requestParameterName, Converter converter, UIComponent component) {
    String theId =
    JsfUtil.getRequestParameter(requestParameterName);
    return converter.getAsObject(
      FacesContext.getCurrentInstance(), component, theId);
  }
  //additional methods omitted
}
```

As we can see, `JSFUtil` invokes the `getAsObject()` method of our custom Faces converter. Our converter, in turn, obtains our session-scoped `CustomerController` instance via the Jakarta Faces API, then invokes its `findCustomer()` method to obtain the corresponding instance of the `Customer` Jakarta Persistence entity, as shown in the following example.

```
package com.ensode.jakartaeealltogether.faces.converter;
//imports omitted
@FacesConverter(forClass = Customer.class)
public class CustomerConverter implements Converter {
  @Override
  public Object getAsObject(FacesContext facesContext, UIComponent
component, String string) {
    if (string == null || string.length() == 0) {
      return null;
    }
    Integer id = Integer.valueOf(string);
    CustomerController controller =
      (CustomerController) facesContext.getApplication().
    getELResolver().getValue(
    facesContext.getELContext(), null,
    "customerController");
    return controller.findCustomer(id);
  }
  //additional methods omitted
}
```

Once we obtain the `Customer` instance, control is passed to the **Customer Detail** page, which is a basic Facelets page that displays customer information. See *Figure 15.4*.

Customer Detail

FirstName: John
LastName: Doe
Email: jdoe@example.com
Address Type   Home
Line 1   Home Line 1
Line 2   Home Line 2
City   City
State   Alabama
Zip Code   12345
Telephone Type   Home
Telephone Number 123-123-1234

Edit | Delete | Back

Figure 15.4 – The Customer Detail page

Now that we've seen how we can display customer information, we'll focus our attention on updating existing customer data.

Updating customer data

There isn't much we haven't already discussed when it comes to updating customer data. The command link labeled **Edit** on each row navigates to the **Edit Customer** page. The markup for the command link looks as follows:

```
<h:commandLink value="Edit" action="#{customerController.editSetup}">
  <f:param name="jsfcrud.currentCustomer" value=
"#{jsfcrud_class['com.ensode.jakartaeealltogether.faces.
util.JsfUtil'].jsfcrud_method['getAsConvertedString'][item1]
[customerController.converter].jsfcrud_invoke}"/>
</h:commandLink>
```

The command link uses the same technique to pass involving a custom Expression Language resolver we discussed in the previous section to pass the id of the customer to update as a request parameter, then invokes the `CustomerController.editSetup()` method which performs some initialization before directing the user to the **Edit Customer** page. Relevant methods in our `CustomerController` CDI bean are shown in the following code snippet.

```
package com.ensode.jakartaeealltogether.faces.controller;
//imports omitted
@Named
@SessionScoped
public class CustomerController implements Serializable {
  private Customer customer = null;
  //additional variable declarations omitted
  public String editSetup() {
    return scalarSetup("/customer/Edit");
  }

  private String scalarSetup(String destination) {
    reset(false);
    customer = (Customer) JsfUtil.
      getObjectFromRequestParameter(
      "jsfcrud.currentCustomer", converter, null);
    if (customer == null) {
      //error handling code omitted
    }
    return destination;
  }
  //additional methods omitted
}
```

As we can see, the `editSetup()` method follows the same pattern we discussed when we covered how to navigate to the read-only **Customer Detail** page, it invokes the previously discussed `scalarSetup()` method to obtain the appropriate instance of the Customer entity, then directs the user to the **Edit Customer** page.

The markup for the **Edit Customer** page is fairly trivial. It includes a number of input fields using binding expressions mapping to different fields on the Customer entity. It uses the same technique we discussed in the Creating Customer Data section to populate all drop-downs on the page. Upon successful navigation, the **Edit Customer** page is rendered as illustrated in *Figure 15.5*.

Edit Customer

First Name: John
Last Name: Doe
Email: jdoe@example.com

Address

Address Type   Home
Line 1   Home Line 1
Line 2   Home Line 2
City   City
State   Alabama
Zip Code   12345

Telephone

Telephone Type   Home
Telephone Number   123-123-1234
                   Save Cancel

Figure 15.5 – Edit Customer page

The **Save** button at the bottom of the form invokes the edit() method on our CustomerController class. The markup Our DAO retrieves the customer:

```
<h:commandButton action="#{customerController.edit}"
  value="Save">
  <f:param name="jsfcrud.currentCustomer"
  value=
"#{jsfcrud_class['com.ensode.jakartaeealltogether.faces.util.
JsfUtil'].jsfcrud_method['getAsConvertedString'][customerController.
customer][customerController.converter].jsfcrud_invoke}"/>
</h:commandButton>
```

The **Save** button uses the previously discussed technique to send the ID of the customer being edited as a request parameter, then invokes the `edit()` method on `CustomerController`, which looks as follows:

```
package com.ensode.jakartaeealltogether.faces.controller;
//imports omitted
@Named
@SessionScoped
public class CustomerController implements Serializable {
  private Customer customer = null;
  private CustomerConverter converter = null;
  //additional variable declarations omitted
  @EJB
  private CustomerDao dao;
  public String edit() {
    String customerString = converter.getAsString(
      FacesContext.getCurrentInstance(), null, customer);
    String currentCustomerString =
      JsfUtil.getRequestParameter(
      "jsfcrud.currentCustomer");
    if (customerString == null ||
        customerString.length() == 0 ||
        !customerString.equals(currentCustomerString)) {
      String outcome = editSetup();
      if ("customer_edit".equals(outcome)) {
        JsfUtil.addErrorMessage(
          "Could not edit customer. Try again.");
      }
      return outcome;
    }
    try {
      dao.edit(customer);
      JsfUtil.addSuccessMessage(
        "Customer was successfully updated.");
    } catch (Exception e) {
      //exception handling code omitted
    }
    return detailSetup();
  }
  //additional methods omitted
}
```

The edit() method on CustomerController performs a sanity check to make sure the ID of the customer in memory matches the ID passed as a request parameter, and displays an error message if this is not the case. If the sanity check is successful, the method invokes the edit() method on the CustomerDao data access object, as illustrated in the following code snippet:

```
package com.ensode.jakartaeealltogether.dao;
//imports omitted
@Stateless
public class CustomerDao implements Serializable {
  @Resource
  private EJBContext ejbContext;
  @PersistenceContext
  private EntityManager em;
  public void edit(Customer customer) throws Exception {
    try {
      customer = em.merge(customer);
    } catch (Exception ex) {
      ejbContext.setRollbackOnly();
      String msg = ex.getLocalizedMessage();
      if (msg == null || msg.length() == 0) {
        Integer id = customer.getCustomerId();
        if (findCustomer(id) == null) {
          throw new NonexistentEntityException(
            "The customer with id " + id +
            " no longer exists.");
        }
      }
      throw ex;
    }
  }
}
```

The edit() method on our DAO invokes the merge() method on its injected EntityManager, which updates the corresponding customer data in the database. If there is an exception, the method rolls back the transaction and then attempts to retrieve the customer from the database. In case the edit() method can't find the customer in the database, it displays an error message stating that the customer doesn't exist anymore. The reason why this logic is necessary is because another user or process may have deleted our customer from the database while our user was updating it.

If the customer data is successfully updated, the user is directed to the **Customer Detail** page, displaying updated customer data. See *Figure 15.6*.

Figure 15.6 – Customer Detail page displaying updated customer data

In the next section, we will discuss how our sample application deletes customer data from the database.

Deleting customer data

The **Customer List** page has a link labeled Destroy for each element on the table.

Figure 15.7 – Customer List page

The markup for the **Delete** command link follows the previously discussed pattern of setting a request parameter with the ID of the customer to delete, as seen in the following example.

```
<h:commandLink value="Delete"
  action="#{customerController.destroy}">
  <f:param name="jsfcrud.currentCustomer" value=
"#{jsfcrud_class['com.ensode.jakartaeealltogether.faces.
util.JsfUtil'].jsfcrud_method['getAsConvertedString'][item1]
[customerController.converter].jsfcrud_invoke}"/>
</h:commandLink>
```

When clicked, the command link invokes the `destroy()` method on `CustomerController`, as shown in the following example.

```
package com.ensode.jakartaeealltogether.faces.controller;
//imports omitted

@Named
@SessionScoped
public class CustomerController implements Serializable {
  @EJB
  private CustomerDao dao;
  //additional variable declarations omitted
  public String destroy() {
    String idAsString =
     JsfUtil.getRequestParameter("jsfcrud.currentCustomer");
    Integer id = Integer.valueOf(idAsString);
    try {
      dao.destroy(id);
      JsfUtil.addSuccessMessage(
        "Customer was successfully deleted.");
    } catch (Exception e){
      //exception handling logic omitted
    }
    return relatedOrListOutcome();
  }
  //additional methods omitted
}
```

The `destroy()` method in `CustomerController` simply invokes the `destroy()` method on `CustomerDAO`, passing the customer ID as obtained from the request parameter. The controller then navigates back to the **Customer List** page and displays a success message upon successful deletion. If there are any exceptions when attempting to delete the customer, they are handled appropriately.

Our DAO retrieves the customer from the database, using the ID it receives as a parameter, performs a sanity check to make sure the data wasn't deleted by another process and then deletes the customer from the database by invoking the `remove()` method on the injected `EntityManager` instance, as illustrated below.

```
package com.ensode.jakartaeealltogether.dao;
//imports omitted
@Stateless
public class CustomerDao implements Serializable {
  @Resource
  private EJBContext ejbContext;
  @PersistenceContext
  private EntityManager em;
  public void destroy(Integer id) throws
    NonexistentEntityException, RollbackFailureException,
    Exception {
    try {
      Customer customer;
      try {
        customer = em.getReference(Customer.class, id);
        customer.getCustomerId();
      } catch (EntityNotFoundException enfe) {
        throw new NonexistentEntityException(
          "The customer with id " + id +
          " no longer exists.", enfe);
      }

      em.remove(customer);
    } catch (Exception ex) {
      try {
        ejbContext.setRollbackOnly();
      } catch (Exception re) {
        throw new RollbackFailureException("An error "
          + "occurred attempting to roll back", re);
      }
      throw ex;
    }
  }
  //additional methods omitted
}
```

After successfully deleting a customer from the database, the **Customer List** is displayed, containing a success message indicating the deletion was successful.

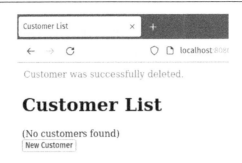

Figure 15.8 – Successful deletion

We have now seen how our sample application creates, updates, displays and deletes data, including some advanced techniques it uses involving custom converters and a custom Expression Language resolver.

Our sample application also contains logic to handle pagination when there is a large number command link is displayed if thereof customers in the database. We will discuss this functionality in the next section.

Implementing pagination

The standard Jakarta Faces data table component simply displays all elements on a list on the page. This works fine when we have a small number of elements to display, but becomes cumbersome when displaying lots of elements. In many production environments, it is not uncommon to have to display hundreds of elements.

Our sample application implements custom pagination logic, if there are more than five customers to display, it only displays five customers at a time, then has **Previous** and/or **Next** links displayed as appropriate to navigate between all customers. *Figure 15.9* illustrates our custom pagination logic in action.

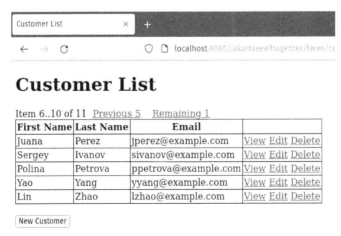

Figure 15.9 – Custom pagination

Our **Customer List** page renders a **Previous** link to navigate back to the previous link, or a **Next** or **Remaining** link to navigate to the next page. The **Next** link is rendered if there are at least 5 more customers to display, if there are less than 5, then the **Remaining** link is rendered.

All three links are conditionally rendered via the command link's rendered attribute, which takes a boolean expression to determine if the link should be rendered.

```
<h:commandLink action="#{customerController.prev}"
value="Previous #{customerController.pagingInfo.batchSize}"
    rendered="#{customerController.renderPrevLink}"/>
```

The **Previous** command link determines if it should be rendered by obtaining the value of the renderPrevLink property on our controller.

The next() and prev() methods update the value of the renderPrevLink property. The next() method is invoked when either the **Next** or **Remaining** link is clicked. The prev() method is invoked when the **Previous** command link is invoked. The updated renderPrevLink value is used to determine if the **Previous** command link should be rendered.

```
package com.ensode.jakartaeealltogether.faces.controller;
//imports omitted
@Named
@SessionScoped
public class CustomerController implements Serializable {
  @PostConstruct
  public void init() {
    pagingInfo = new PagingInfo();
  }
  private PagingInfo pagingInfo = null;
  private boolean renderPrevLink;
  @EJB
  private CustomerDao dao;
  //additional variable declarations omitted

  public PagingInfo getPagingInfo() {
    if (pagingInfo.getItemCount() == -1) {
      pagingInfo.setItemCount(dao.getCustomerCount());
    }
    return pagingInfo;
  }
  public boolean getRenderPrevLink() {
    return renderPrevLink;
  }
  public String next() {
    reset(false);
```

```
      getPagingInfo().nextPage();
      renderPrevLink = getPagingInfo().getFirstItem() >=
        getPagingInfo().getBatchSize();
      return "List";
    }
  public String prev() {
      reset(false);
      getPagingInfo().previousPage();
      renderPrevLink = getPagingInfo().getFirstItem() >=
        getPagingInfo().getBatchSize();
      return "List";
    }
    //additional methods omitted
  }
```

The **Next** command link is displayed if there are at least five more customers to display.

```
<h:commandLink action="#{customerController.next}"
value="Next #{customerController.pagingInfo.batchSize}"
rendered="#{customerController.pagingInfo.lastItem +
customerController.pagingInfo.batchSize le customerController.
pagingInfo.itemCount}"
```

In this case, the logic of the `rendered` attribute is embedded on the page, as opposed to relying on the controller as is the case for the **Previous** command link.

The **Remaining** command link is displayed if there are less than five customers to display on the next page.

```
<h:commandLink action="#{customerController.next}" value="Remaining
#{customerController.pagingInfo.itemCount - customerController.
pagingInfo.lastItem}"
                        rendered="#{customerController.pagingInfo.
lastItem lt
  customerController.pagingInfo.itemCount and
  customerController.pagingInfo.lastItem +
  customerController.pagingInfo.batchSize gt
  customerController.pagingInfo.itemCount}"/>
```

This command link also embeds the logic of its rendered attribute as an expression on the page.

The pagination logic relies on a `PagingInfo` utility class, this class has methods to obtain the first and last elements to display, as logic to determine which elements to display on every page of our data table.

```
package com.ensode.jakartaeealltogether.faces.util;
public class PagingInfo {
  private int batchSize = 5;
```

```java
private int firstItem = 0;
private int itemCount = -1;
//trivial setters and getters omitted
public int getFirstItem() {
  if (itemCount == -1) {
    throw new IllegalStateException(
      "itemCount must be set before invoking " +
      "getFirstItem");
  }
  if (firstItem >= itemCount) {
    if (itemCount == 0) {
      firstItem = 0;
    } else {
      int zeroBasedItemCount = itemCount - 1;
      double pageDouble = zeroBasedItemCount / batchSize;
      int page = (int) Math.floor(pageDouble);
      firstItem = page * batchSize;
    }
  }
  return firstItem;
}
public int getLastItem() {
  getFirstItem();
  int lastItem = firstItem + batchSize > itemCount ?
    itemCount : firstItem + batchSize;
  return lastItem;
}
public void nextPage() {
  getFirstItem();
  if (firstItem + batchSize < itemCount) {
    firstItem += batchSize;
  }
}

public void previousPage() {
  getFirstItem();
  firstItem -= batchSize;
  if (firstItem < 0) {
    firstItem = 0;
  }
}
}
```

As seen in previous code examples, our controller relies on the `PaginationInfo` utility class to implement pagination.

Summary

In this chapter, we illustrated how to integrate several Jakarta EE technologies via a sample application. We covered the following topics:

- How to create customer data by integrating Jakarta Faces, CDI, Jakarta Enterprise Beans and Jakarta Persistence

- How to view customer data by integrating Jakarta Faces, CDI, Jakarta Enterprise Beans and Jakarta Persistence

- How to update customer data by integrating Jakarta Faces, CDI, Jakarta Enterprise Beans and Jakarta Persistence

- How to delete customer data by integrating Jakarta Faces, CDI, Jakarta Enterprise Beans and Jakarta Persistence

- How to implement custom pagination logic when displaying tabular data with the Jakarta Faces data table component

Jakarta EE APIs are designed to work together, and, as seen in this chapter, they can be seamlessly integrated to build robust applications.

Index

`www.packtpub.com`

Subscribe to our online digital library for full access to over 7,000 books and videos, as well as industry leading tools to help you plan your personal development and advance your career. For more information, please visit our website.

Why subscribe?

- Spend less time learning and more time coding with practical eBooks and Videos from over 4,000 industry professionals

- Improve your learning with Skill Plans built especially for you

- Get a free eBook or video every month

- Fully searchable for easy access to vital information

- Copy and paste, print, and bookmark content

Did you know that Packt offers eBook versions of every book published, with PDF and ePub files available? You can upgrade to the eBook version at `packtpub.com` and as a print book customer, you are entitled to a discount on the eBook copy. Get in touch with us at `customercare@packtpub.com` for more details.

At `www.packtpub.com`, you can also read a collection of free technical articles, sign up for a range of free newsletters, and receive exclusive discounts and offers on Packt books and eBooks.

Other Books You May Enjoy

If you enjoyed this book, you may be interested in these other books by Packt:

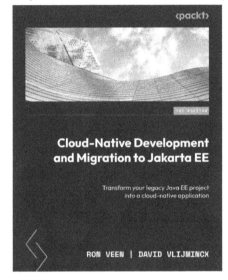

Cloud-Native Development and Migration to Jakarta EE

Ron Veen, David Vlijmincx

ISBN: 978-1-83763-962-5

- Explore the latest advancements in Jakarta EE and gain a thorough understanding of its core features and capabilities
- Understand the principles and practices of designing and building cloud-native applications
- Gain a detailed understanding of containers and Docker
- Uncover how to embrace containers in your IT landscape
- Move from your own hardware to managed hardware in the cloud
- Discover how Kubernetes enhances scalability, resilience, and portability

Developer Career Masterplan

Heather VanCura, Bruno Souza, Ed Burns

ISBN: 978-1-80181-870-4

- Explore skills needed to grow your career
- Participate in community and mentorship programs
- Build your technical knowledge for growth
- Discover how to network and use social media
- Understand the impact of public speaking
- Identify the critical conversations to advance your career
- Participate in non-technical activities to enhance your career

Packt is searching for authors like you

If you're interested in becoming an author for Packt, please visit `authors.packtpub.com` and apply today. We have worked with thousands of developers and tech professionals, just like you, to help them share their insight with the global tech community. You can make a general application, apply for a specific hot topic that we are recruiting an author for, or submit your own idea.

Share Your Thoughts

Now you've finished *Jakarta EE Application Development*, we'd love to hear your thoughts! Scan the QR code below to go straight to the Amazon review page for this book and share your feedback or leave a review on the site that you purchased it from.

`https://packt.link/r/1835085261`

Your review is important to us and the tech community and will help us make sure we're delivering excellent quality content.

Download a free PDF copy of this book

Thanks for purchasing this book!

Do you like to read on the go but are unable to carry your print books everywhere?

Is your eBook purchase not compatible with the device of your choice?

Don't worry, now with every Packt book you get a DRM-free PDF version of that book at no cost.

Read anywhere, any place, on any device. Search, copy, and paste code from your favorite technical books directly into your application.

The perks don't stop there, you can get exclusive access to discounts, newsletters, and great free content in your inbox daily

Follow these simple steps to get the benefits:

1. Scan the QR code or visit the link below

https://packt.link/free-ebook/978-1-83508-526-4

2. Submit your proof of purchase
3. That's it! We'll send your free PDF and other benefits to your email directly

www.ingramcontent.com/pod-product-compliance
Lightning Source LLC
Chambersburg PA
CBHW080625060326
40690CB00021B/4818